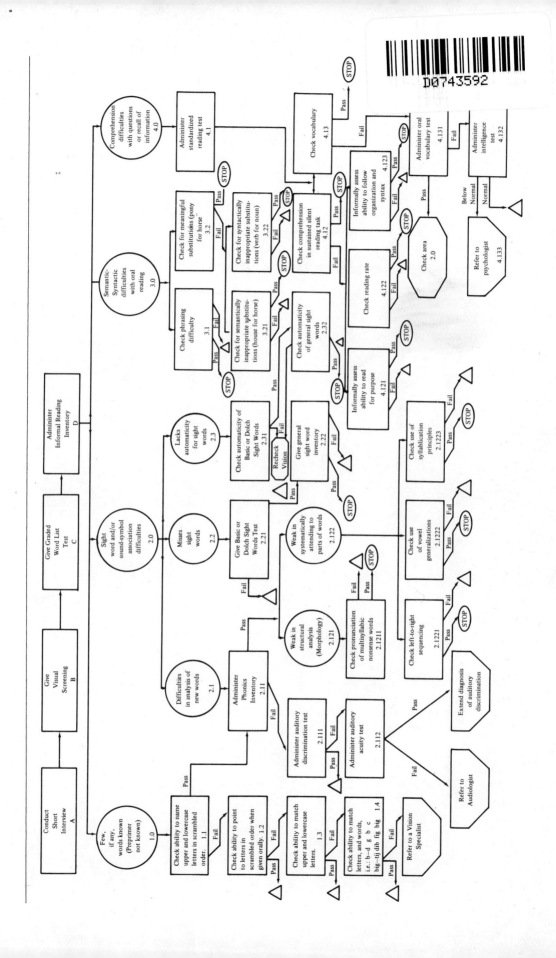

READING DIAGNOSIS AND REMEDIATION
IN CLASSROOM AND CLINIC

Reading Diagnosis and Remediation
in Classroom and Clinic

A guide to becoming an effective
diagnostic-remedial teacher of
reading and language skills

LOIS A. BADER
Michigan State University

MACMILLAN PUBLISHING CO., INC.
New York
COLLIER MACMILLAN PUBLISHERS
London

Macmillan Publishing Co., Inc.
866 Third Avenue, New York, New York 10022

Collier Macmillan Canada, Ltd.

Library of Congress Cataloging in Publication Data

Bader, Lois A
  Reading diagnosis and remediation in classroom and
clinic.

  Bibliography: p.
  Includes index.
  1. Reading—Remedial teaching. 2. Reading—Ability
testing. I. Title.
LB1050.5.B25   428'.4'207   79-10042
ISBN 0-02-305100-0

Printing: 1 2 3 4 5 6 7 8   Year: 0 1 2 3 4 5 6

PREFACE

This book is intended to be used by prospective or inservice teachers and specialists who have had at least one course in reading instruction. Although there are some fine texts available in the field, there has seemed to be a need for one that focuses on (1) the development of keen observational skills, (2) the dynamics of teacher-student interaction, and (3) diagnostic teaching. Because these areas are important to both classroom teachers and specialists, it is hoped that both groups will find these emphases helpful.

Another feature of this text is a guide to the scope and sequences of diagnosis and remediation. Many students in diagnosis courses seem to have a tendency to overtest in some areas and neglect others, or they fail to probe for underlying problems. Most seem to need considerable help in using trial teaching to confirm their choice of procedures. Field tests seem to indicate that teachers and diagnosticians using the aids presented in this text tend to be more efficient and accurate in their diagnoses.

In addition, the reader will find an emphasis on diagnosis and remediation of comprehension difficulties. Students who can recognize words but have trouble with comprehension have frequently been passed over for special help, yet theirs is a serious need. Few introductory reading texts have considered this area in depth, and it is given extensive treatment here.

Most of all, it is hoped that by helping teachers and specialists refine their diagnostic and remedial techniques, this book and its particular features will benefit the children and adults who will look to these teachers for help.

Acknowledgments: I would like to thank Clifford Bush from Kean College; Eldon E. Ekwall, University of Texas; and James Walker, Northern Illinois University, for their helpful suggestions. My appreciation is extended to my graduate students for their assistance in field studies in diagnosis and remediation. I am especially grateful for the valuable assistance of Jacquelyn Tennis in manuscript preparation. And, finally, I would like to thank my family for their confidence and support.

L.A.B

CONTENTS

                                                                     ix

CHAPTER 1

Becoming an Effective Diagnostic-Remedial Reading Teacher

Teachers who wish to become skilled in reading diagnosis and remediation are provided some insights into the requirements of the role.

Anyone experiencing severe difficulties in reading or other language-related areas arouses feelings of concern in relatives, teachers, and friends. Because of the importance given to reading in our society, most nonreaders have problems in vocational, academic, and other life roles; and many experience feelings of inadequacy. When the difficulties of disabled readers are not properly assessed or when remediation is ineffective, the feelings of failure may be intensified. Those who wish to learn how to help disabled readers must acquire as much information as possible about the reading process and diagnostic-remedial procedures in order to be efficient in their work. Further, efforts should be continued to develop programs that minimize or prevent failure.

The vast store of knowledge required of a good diagnostician may be acquired in two steps: one, by learning as much as possible about what *others* have learned, by drawing on previously developed techniques, materials, and information about all known aspects of the reading process as well as ideas and theories about what is not yet known. After absorbing as much literature, laboratory training, and experience as is accessible, serious professionals must use this store of knowledge as background material for their own ongoing "research"—the day-to-day, trial-and-error implementation (but educated trial and error) of what has been learned.

1

The focus of this book is on the mental effort, or thinking processes, a classroom teacher or reading specialist must encounter during observation and trial teaching. An emphasis is also placed on attaining a high degree of flexibility in thinking about and using the vast store of information available. It is assumed that readers of this book have acquired some familiarity with teaching techniques but may lack confidence in their ability to transfer what has been learned to the instructional situation or may not have had sufficient opportunity to apply their learning.

Observers of unusually capable classroom teachers and reading specialists have often made comments such as, "I don't know how she does it! She just seems to know instictively what the student's problems are and what needs to be done." The specialist smiles and accepts the compliment and replies, "Well,

FIGURE 1.1.   Learning about the field of reading.

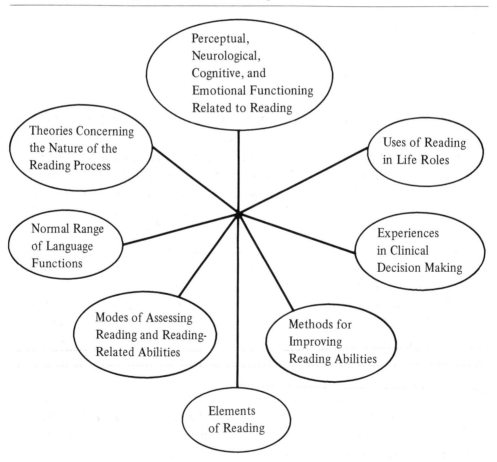

it just comes with experience," or "Oh, I just found some things that work for me."

The phrases "just seems to know," "know instinctively," "it just comes," and "found some things" reflect the present status of knowledge transmission in reading diagnosis and remediation. *Verbalizing* what one does and why and how is an extremely difficult task that, like *thinking,* has many unknown aspects. However, realizing the limitations, one can still reasonably conclude that there are many facets of diagnostic and remedial processes that *can* be shared. Therefore, this text is written on the assumption that diagnostic-remedial procedures can be made less subjective; that more information from the knowledge store of proficient teachers can be transmitted to those entering the field; and that teachers can increase their expertise by a combination of reading, application, feedback, and practice.

The most crucial question for one learning about diagnosis and reading remediation is, "What do I need to know?" There are, as indicated above, two parts to the answer. First is background knowledge and second is knowledge specific to the role. Several aspects of background knowledge are outlined in the following sections, after which is a discussion of that which is germane to the intent of this book—an outline of specific information to be obtained by the teacher/diagnostician. Figure 1.1 provides an overview of areas with which one learning about the field of reading should become familiar.

PART I:
BACKGROUND KNOWLEDGE
HELPFUL TO DIAGNOSTIC/
REMEDIAL TEACHERS

Factors That May Influence
Reading Achievement

Ideally, professionals in the field of educational diagnosis and remediation should possess a great deal of information related to their field, as well as a large fund of information specific to their field. Many factors can influence communication skills and some that *may* influence reading achievement are found in Figure 1.2. Generally, these factors are interrelated.

For example, emotional stress may contribute to a student's lack of

FIGURE 1.2.   Factors that may influence reading achievement.

SENSORY	*INTELLECTUAL*	*EMOTIONAL*
Visual	Speech	Motivation
Acuity and	Language	Interest
Perception	Conceptual Development	Personality
Auditory	Symbolization Abilities	Security
Neurological		
(Maturation and		
Integration)		

GENERAL HEALTH	*EDUCATIONAL*	*CULTURAL*
Nutrition	Opportunity	Family
Endocrine	Suitability	Peers
Disturbances		Community
Allergies		
Other		

attentiveness, which may, in turn, result in his failure to learn.[1] However, rarely can one make a generalization that fits most students. Some students may *escape* physical or emotional stress by concentrating harder on their reading. Also, reactions differ in cases of similar disabilities. Some students with certain kinds of visual problems give up quickly, whereas others with the same kind and degree of disability will struggle to make near point discriminations despite physical discomfort.

Frequently, as students mature they may become more able to acquire abilities that were quite difficult for them at another time. But because of feelings of inadequacy caused by previous failure, their learning may be impaired, or they may have difficulty because their parents or teachers feel they cannot learn.

Reference to the influence of the factors noted in Figure 1.2 are made throughout the text. More extensive discussions can be found in the list of professional readings.

---

[1] Simply to avoid confusion and awkwardness, I have used "he" to refer to individual students, and "she" to refer to teachers. The discussions in this book are of course applicable to every student and teacher, male or female.

The Normal Range of Language Functioning for Children and Adults

If teachers are to make a determination that a student's language is immature or deficient or different in comparison with others, they need to know what is encompassed within a normal range of development and under what conditions those factors outside of what is considered typical may interfere with learning.

There are two ways to obtain such knowledge. One is by direct experiences with large numbers of children of all ages and with adults from a variety of backgrounds. The other way is by readings and direct study of language development. These, of course, are not mutually exclusive. The problem is that too often those designated as "remedial" teachers or specialists have had neither experience with students nor preparation in language development. This may result in their attempting to "remediate" a behavior that is within the normal range of linguistic or psycholinguistic functioning. Or it could result in their ignoring behavior that should signal further assessment.

The Nature of the Reading Process

To some extent this subtitle is presumptuous because the exact nature of the reading process(es) is unknown. To the extent that reading can be described as thinking and that much remains to be learned about thinking processes, especially with respect to language, we can only theorize about reading processes. Nevertheless, the position is taken here that an attempt needs to be made by teachers to study various reading theories and then to clarify their understandings through discussion. In this way they may be more apt to avoid having a narrow view that would limit diagnosis and remediation.

The Elements of Reading

The elements of reading include letters, letter order, words, word order, punctuation, sentences, sentence order, paragraphs, and other larger organizational patterns. These can also be described as graphemic, syntactic, and semantic factors. Though one's view of the reading process would influence one's notion of *how* these elements are related, many authorities agree that they seem to be related.

The area of largest disagreement among reading authorities is instructional: how can most students learn to be proficient readers? Many contend that attention needs to be given to all areas of communication—thinking, listening, speaking, writing, and reading—because these promote growth interactively. Some say, with regard to the graphemic area, for example, that students should study single letter-sound associations; others argue for the syllable as a unit of instruction; some, for whole words; some, for phrases or sentences; some, for a blend of these. Though no one really knows what is the best instructional approach for all or even most students, we do know that inadequate processing of important reading elements can be dysfunctional for some students.

Typical Methods Employed in Elementary and Secondary Classroom Reading Instruction

The more common approaches to reading instruction include graded basal programs, language experience approaches, phonic drills, literature analysis, and an eclectic blend of these. Teachers attempting diagnosis and remediation need to be familiar with the most common reading approaches and organizational plans so that they can better understand their students' background of experiences in order to be able to work with other teachers to adjust approaches and organizational plans for fitting student needs and abilities.

Varied Kinds of Reading for Different Life Roles

Some children and adults are not adept at adjusting their reading to the demands of various tasks. It has been said that they read everything the same way: cereal boxes, comic books, textbooks. Yet some materials such as light adventure novels can be skimmed rapidly whereas others such as legal contracts need to be read slowly and carefully. Chapters in textbooks usually require an overview to discover major topics and determine the writer's pattern of organization, followed by a slower reading.

In order to help their students become proficient in reading materials typically encountered in their daily lives, teachers have to know what their students want to read and need to read in academic, vocational, business, societal, and personal areas. Next they need to analyze the reading tasks to learn what skills are required in each area, and, finally, they should help their students define their purposes for reading and practice, adjusting their reading modes to their purpose. In order to effect transfer, they should apply this practice to the materials used in the life role areas, at least in the final stages of instruction.

Note on Part I.   The preceding six areas of background knowledge pertinent to teachers working with diagnosis and remediation are not given intensive attention in this book. An entry level of sophistication is assumed, one that could be obtained by an introductory course in reading or by wide reading in the field.

PART II
KNOWLEDGE SPECIFIC TO
DIAGNOSIS AND REMEDIATION

Using This Book

How this book will be used will depend on (1) the knowledge possessed by its readers, (2) the needs of the populations they serve or wish to serve, and (3) the setting in which they are working—classroom, clinic, resource room, learning center, or laboratory.

The content of the chapters is consonant with the ten areas of specific knowledge required by those who work as diagnostic-remedial teachers or specialists as described in the sections that follow. The titles of teacher, specialist, diagnostician, and the like have been used interchangeably in this work because the author takes the view that, with regard to competency, some well-informed, experienced classroom teachers possess the same skills as those with a title such as specialist. The difference often lies more in the direction of job responsibilities and time for individual work and planning than in capability. The intent of this book is to serve both classroom teachers and specialists or clinicians who are interested in reading diagnosis and remediation on elementary, secondary, and adult levels.

Procedures for Eliciting, Observing,
Interpreting, and Recording Cues

One way to obtain information related to student performance is to ask questions or prompt the student to talk about areas pertinent to the diagnosis. This can be a helpful, time-saving procedure. As this information can also be inaccurate, it will need to be confirmed with additional evidence; but this is true of most information obtained in diagnosis.

Another method of collecting information is to observe students closely as they work. Their attending behaviors, posture, comments, sequencing, checking, and self-correcting behaviors are examples of areas that should be observed. Observations of behavior can be made informally or can be made in a structured manner by setting up a specific task or situation and recording student performance with a check list or inventory.

In order to evaluate students' functioning, teachers need to know (1) what behaviors they should observe carefully and (2) how these behaviors are related to learning difficulties. This memory store of diagnosticians has been described as "the questions they have in their heads." The more knowledge one has of behavioral cues and their possible significance, the more likely it will be that the diagnosis is accurate and complete. Furthermore, because diagnosis really should be continuous throughout instruction, teachers who are constantly alert to their students' behaviors can more easily adjust instruction than can those who "diagnose" with a test battery.

Other important sources of information about student abilities are, of course, obtainable from teacher-made or published tests that require oral, written or nonverbal responses. Student test performances can be interpreted (1) in relation to the task presented by each test or subtest, (2) in comparison with others (norm groups) who have taken the test, (3) in the construction of a profile of the student's abilities over a range of different tasks that may reveal a pattern of strengths and weaknesses, and (4) in relation to other observations and samples of the student's efforts.

Secondary sources of information include school records, medical reports, psychological reports, and family histories. Secondary sources should be used cautiously because of possibilities of error.

Sequences of Cue Collection

The order of cue collection can affect the length of time it takes to make the initial diagnosis. Efficiency here is essential. First, the student may not tolerate lengthy periods of testing; secondly, the teacher may not have the time to devote several hours to individual diagnosis; and third, a valuable aspect of diagnosis, *trial teaching*, takes place as part of the instruction and should not be delayed by excessive testing.

to make better a tolerate

Trial Teaching as Confirmation of Diagnostic and Instructional Techniques

Whatever caused or contributed to the student's difficulties in the past may never be discovered. If these factors are known and if they still exist, they should be corrected or ameliorated if possible. But it is more important to find out how the student *can* learn than to search for reasons why he cannot or has not learned.

Trial teaching, as the term implies, involves selecting one or more instructional procedures that would appear to be appropriate for the student, based on initial diagnosis, and implementing them under controlled conditions to determine their effectiveness with regard to such factors as rate of learning and retention. The student's response to instruction can serve to confirm the tentative analysis of his abilities. In addition, if the remediation will not be carried out by the diagnostician, trial teaching becomes an even more essential part of the diagnosis, for the tutor or teacher will need to be given specific recommendations for instruction. In order to select and implement trial teaching procedures, the diagnostician should have a high degree of proficiency with a variety of remedial approaches.

Remedial Techniques for Specific Areas of Reading and Reading-Related Difficulties

Although the reading process appears to be integrative in nature, some students have difficulties with specific skill areas and respond well to highly structured techniques. Teachers need to be familiar with a wide range of procedures because the effectiveness of any one technique varies with different students. Teachers also need to be made aware of difficulties that can be caused by dwelling too long on skills. A useful guide is the following: begin in context; isolate to teach; return to context.

Context skill context

For purposes of organization and clarity, writers often list reading skills under discrete headings such as word recognition, vocabulary, and comprehension. These, of course, are not separate from each other. Diagnosis and remediation should be conducted with an awareness of the interactive nature of the reading process.

Remedial Techniques for Students with Severe Difficulties

For those students who have not responded to standard developmental and corrective instruction, teachers need to be proficient in using special techniques that have been found to be effective for students with severe difficulties. As these special procedures usually require one-on-one instruction several times a week over a long period of time, they are used for selected cases. Often these are incidents of neurological impairment, but not in all cases. Teachers wishing to learn these techniques should prepare by carefully reading the manuals or texts in which the procedures were *originally* described and by practicing under supervision until they are proficient.

The Dynamics of Student-Teacher Interaction

So much can occur verbally and nonverbally between a student and his teacher in the diagnostic-remedial process that the interactions defy a full description. Generally, teachers need to be as sensitive as possible to the way students seem to be perceiving themselves and their teachers. They need to recognize signs of restlessness and boredom so that they can shift instruction or stop for a rest, to know whether the student is putting forth his best effort, to recognize student strategies for avoiding instruction, and to sense when a student is afraid to risk making a mistake. Teachers need to be aware of the signals they may themselves be sending unconsciously, for students will constantly read them. "Does my teacher think I can succeed? Does she think I am stupid? Does she respect me? Does she like me?"

In addition to the ever-present affective dimension, there is an ongoing cognitive aspect to diagnosis and remediation, which may take the form of hypothesizing and confirming-disconfirming behavior on the part of the teacher. For example, "Mark has a mild articulation problem, which may be associated with a hearing loss. I think I'll look at his spelling to see if he is fairly accurate in representing sounds. Yes, *awae* for *away*, *tellefon* for *telephone* and *redjester* for *register*. For the present, I don't think he needs an audiometric evaluation. Actually, his auditory processing seems to be his strength. All the sounds are represented in proper sequence . . ."

The dynamics of student-teacher interaction in diagnosis and remediation are often overlooked, but these processes can be enhanced when an effort is made by an experienced teacher to bring unconscious or unspoken thoughts to a conscious level for examination.

Difficulties Most Likely to Occur in Corrective and Remedial Cases

A knowledge of (1) difficulties that are most likely to occur at various stages of learning to read, (2) the most common factors associated with reading difficulties, along with (3) a memory for single-problem and multiple-problem cases, can contribute greatly to the efficiency of diagnosticians. For example, a situation involving a seven-year-old child who can only recognize six or seven words at the end of the first grade should result in a different diagnostic memory search from that in a case of a fourteen-year-old reading on the third grade level.

Though this kind of mental processing can be helpful to experienced teachers, they need to be aware that having a set formula for finding certain kinds of problems can interfere with their being open to the possibility that less common factors may be present in the situation.

Materials Analysis and Selection

Though it is true that talented teachers can be successful with a minimal investment in materials, creating and/or finding materials suitable to the interests and needs of a large number of students can take a great deal of time that could be better spent on instruction. Therefore, most teachers try to have a variety of stories, articles, and exercises on hand that have been obtained from publishers of instructional materials. Acquiring knowledge of materials and their appropriate uses requires a certain amount of sophistication on the part of teachers because there is a vast quantity of software and hardware on the market, and these vary widely in quality.

Test Analysis, Selection, and Construction

In the area of test selection, too, the teacher is confronted with a tremendous array of survey and diagnostic tests available. Group-administered survey tests that have been carefully normed can offer a basis for comparing group performances, and they can serve as screening devices to identify students who would appear to need an individual evaluation. Their usefulness as diagnostic instruments, however, is limited.

Individually administered diagnostic tests are more useful in evaluating specific areas of student strengths and weaknesses, but probably none of these is without limitations. Diagnosticians who intend to use published tests should consult professional test reviews such as those found in the *Buros' Mental Measurement Yearbooks.* Common errors in administering these tests are (1) failing to follow directions in the manuals on proper administration and interpretation, (2) assuming, incorrectly, that the subtests measure what they claim to measure, (3) using culturally biased tests, (4) failing to observe closely the behaviors of the students as they take the tests, and (5) depending solely on test scores rather than comparing them with student performances on other tasks.

Eventually, many diagnosticians build their own test battery, which consists of a combination of published tests and those they have constructed themselves. Teacher-constructed tests can be especially useful for placement of students in particular materials and for planning instruction utilizing them. However, teachers should realize that many of the cautions that apply to published materials apply as well to their own efforts, and they should be careful in their use.

CHAPTER 2

Assessment Procedures: Interviews, Observations, and Tests

A definition of the disabled learner and the primary methods of gathering cues—observation, interview questions, and testing—are presented with the perspective of helping the diagnostician evaluate the student's functioning in areas that may be influencing his reading performance.

DEFINING THE DISABLED LEARNER IN READING AND RELATED AREAS

The disabled learner in reading and related areas is one who is performing well below his expected level. It is important to define the population most in need of individual help because resources are often limited and should, therefore, be allotted on the basis of priorities. The following examples are given to illustrate *performing below expected level*.

1. Slow learning and retarded children and adults are sometimes referred for remedial help when they have been progressing well at their own rate. As long as this is true, there is no need for them to be given additional, special help. However, when this is not the case, they should be given a careful evaluation, including trial teaching, to identify their best mode of learning, and a supervised program of special instruction.

2. Children and adults with average abilities are usually evaluated by a comparison with others in their age-grade range. Being six months to

a year behind their peers may be a serious matter for primary school children, but on the upper elementary levels a difference of a year or so may be less significant, as would be true of a difference of two years or less in secondary and adult levels. Test score variation, interest, or similar factors result in less precision in estimating performance in the upper levels. As a *rough* guide, upper elementary age students performing two or more levels below age-grade placement and secondary and adult students performing four or more levels below should be referred for an individual assessment. Those performing slightly below level might be considered in the *corrective* rather than the *remedial* category and may be given assistance in a classroom setting.

A common practice has been to ignore students with severe problems in writing, spelling, and study skills simply because their scores on reading tests have been adequate. As these abilities, too, are necessary for realization of potential in academic, vocational, and personal life roles, those with severe difficulties in these areas should be given special attention.

3. Children and adults with above average abilities may also require individual assistance when they are found to be performing well below their expected level. Unless they have serious physical or emotional problems, these students usually respond quickly to instruction and do not require a great deal of individual attention. However, they, too, deserve whatever assistance they require to realize fully their potential.

4. On all levels, adequate assessment and remediation in comprehension are often ignored. Most remedial teachers seem to be focusing on abilities in word recognition with attention to comprehension limited to literal processing. Referrals for special help are often not made when students are proficient in pronouncing words and recalling the literal content of what they have read, even though they have serious difficulties with other aspects of comprehension.

Procedures for evaluation and instruction in comprehension have been given limited attention in textbooks on diagnosis and remediation. This text attempts to provide assistance in these areas and considers students to need several aspects of comprehension. Those with severe problems in any of the aspects should be given special assistance regardless of their proficiency in word recognition.

DESCRIPTION OF CUE COLLECTION
IN DIAGNOSIS

The first task of the teacher when working with a student is to establish rapport and to learn whether he may be a disabled reader by estimating the level on which the student is functioning in comparison with his age/grade placement. This may be done by a word list test, by a graded paragraph test, or, for those students fearful of tests, by the reading of a few words in a newspaper or on a 3-inch by 5-inch card and by comparing the student's performance with that of average students.

Secondly, the teacher obtains clues through conversation with the student and through observation regarding possible language, physical, or emotional problems. If they are detected, the teacher gives further tests or makes an appropriate referral.

Thirdly, the teacher may read aloud with the student and engage in informal discussion. Thus, the teacher determines as specifically as possible the sound-symbol associations of the student, his strategies for recognizing unknown words, and his knowledge of sight words. This can be done by first listening to oral reading and talking with the student to decide which criterion-referenced tests to give and then by administering the selected tests. The teacher also uses checklists for oral reading in context and in isolation to make a list of unknown letter-sound associations, an estimate of sight word level, and an estimate of ability to use context.

Recording Information

Any pertinent information, referred to in this and subsequent chapters as "cues," should be recorded either during the interview session, immediately afterwards, or whenever the instructor feels an adequate observation has been made.

The *Student Record Forms* found at the end of Chapters 3, 4, and 7 are helpful in recording cues collected through interviewing, testing, and/or observation. The *Term Record,* part of the *Student Record Form,* provides a record of the student's daily progress in the materials and notes dates of satisfactory performance in the various categories. The *Term Record* may be found in Chapter 4, Figure 4.8. By maintaining accurate records, the diagnostician may immediately perceive changes affecting the student's functioning, whether in the elements of reading or in reading-related factors.

Reading-related factors, discussed in Chapter 3, include visual, auditory, and verbal abilities; sensory-based learning difficulties; and affective influences. They are essential areas to be considered when working with remediation of reading difficulties, especially as they may affect the mechanics or elements of reading. The elements of reading referred to here and discussed in Chapters 4 and 7 include recognition of words, sound-symbol associations, reading comprehension, and so forth. Although word recognition and comprehension are treated separately in successive chapters for the sake of organization, it should be kept in mind that no cue can be considered in isolation. An alert diagnostician will be aware that there may be an interaction of areas at any time.

The *DCRL Checklist* (Descriptions of Characteristic Responses to Learning) is useful in recording observations of the student's affective characteristics. His or her material type preferences and previously used modes of instruction may be recorded in the "Affect" category of the *Student Record Form.* Evidence of problem characteristics may occur during the initial interview and testing sessions and later on during the testing-teaching situation. The DCRL Checklist may be found in Chapter 3, Figure 3.3.

Assessment Procedures

During the initial interview, student behaviors should be observed closely. For example:

Auditory Acuity

* Does the student appear to watch the face of the speaker?
* Does he or she turn his or her head to favor one ear?
* Does the student have articulation problems?

Visual Acuity

* Does the student show symptoms of eye fatigue and/or distress (blinking, squinting, rubbing eyes)?
* Does the student assume a posture so that he or she reads with only one eye?

Verbal Ability

- Is the student's speech fluent?
- Is there a problem with articulation?

It is appropriate to question the student directly about each of the factors previously mentioned when observed behavior suggests that a problem may exist. Any information volunteered by the student may be recorded in the appropriate section on the *Student Record Form.* Some sample questions are listed below.

Visual Acuity

Do you have glasses?
Do you get tired when you read?

Auditory Acuity

Have you ever had earaches or infections? (Tell me about it.)
Do you have trouble hearing sometimes? When?

Verbal Ability

Have you ever had difficulty with your speech? (Tell me about it.)

Affect

How do you feel about getting special help?
Can you manage to practice on your own?
Can you attend on a regular schedule?

Writing

Can others read your writing easily?
Is your writing as fast as you would like it to be?

Spelling

Do you think you need help in spelling?
Can you tell by looking at a word if it is spelled correctly?

Care must be taken not to grill the student; rather, one should ask selected questions in a conversational manner. By encouraging the student to describe his activities, the diagnostician can obtain information from which inferences can be made that determine which tests need to be given. When observation and/or direct questioning indicate the need, the diagnostician should administer appropriate tests.

The interview sessions and testing may reveal that a student has a problem requiring outside professional help. Such problems may be due to poor vision, poor hearing, health problems, family problems, or a number of other related factors. In this case, the diagnostician may consider referring the student to an appropriate outside agency. Even though everything may appear satisfactory during the initial interview and testing, the teacher should remain aware of the fact that problems in these areas may arise at any time during the testing-teaching sequence. In most instances, reading instruction can be provided while other problems are being treated by another professional. Care should be taken to communicate with others who are working with the student.

Questioning the student directly about what he feels are his present reading strengths and weaknesses may reveal much about the student's ability level before any actual testing of reading behavior begins. Some sample questions are:

Sight Words

Do you have difficulty recognizing little words? (The student is not
    expected to know the term "sight" words.)
Do you know little words right away without looking hard at them?
    (The language used should be geared to the maturity of the student.)

Sound-Symbol Association,
Structural Analysis,
Problem-Solving Strategies

Can you "sound out" words?
Can you break words apart?
What do you do when you come to a word you don't know?

Comprehension

Do you have trouble knowing what words mean?
Can you understand what you read aloud?

Can you understand what you read silently?

After you discuss such questions with the student, it is appropriate to give a word list test and a contextual reading assessment. Information should be recorded on the *Student Record Form,* as discussed earlier.

If cues collected seem to indicate a problem with sound-symbol association, structural analysis, and/or problem-solving strategies (checklists may be found in Chapter 4, which would be helpful in making an assessment), a criterion-referenced individual reading assessment test may be administered. Such tests are listed in Chapter 4.

Throughout the testing and teaching sessions that follow the initial interview and cue collection session, sensory-based difficulties or deficits in the area of writing or spelling may become apparent. Some sample observations the teacher may make in these categories are as follows:

Sensory-Based Difficulties

Does the student accurately perceive information?
Can the student make appropriate connections between new information and previously learned experiences?

Spelling

Do the student's errors indicate he does not hear or attend to some of the phonetic elements?
Do the student's errors indicate he is unaware of the most common spelling generalizations?

Writing

Is rate adequate?
Is letter formation adequate?
Is spacing adequate?

Any questionable areas in the preceding categories may be further tested (test suggestions are listed under each category in Chapters 3 and 4). Pertinent information may be recorded on the *Student Record Form.*

Once as much information as possible has been accumulated, the teacher and student can together plan a remedial program that matches the particular needs of the student. Care should be taken to obtain, record, and respond to the student's instructional priorities. Student priority checklists are provided at the ends of Chapters 4 and 7 (see Figures 4.7 and 7.2).

In Chapters 3, 4, and 7, we will examine specific cues to be collected during the observation and testing of the student.

CHAPTER 3

Assessment of
Reading-Related Abilities

Means of gathering assessment cues related to physical and affective factors are described.

Specific cues to a student's functioning in reading-related areas are outlined in the following sections. Under each category are presented interview questions, observations to be made during interviews and while working with the student, and tests that may supplement these procedures. These cues can be recorded in the Student Record Form, Figure 3.5, at the end of this chapter.

VISUAL ABILITIES

Interview

1. Do you have glasses? Are you satisfied with them? Do you wear them? When did you discover you needed them?
2. Do your eyes bother you when you do close work? Can you see writing on a chalkboard?
3. Do you get tired quickly when you read?
4. Do you have headaches? When?

5.   Have you ever had your eyes examined by a doctor, an optometrist, or an ophthalmologist?
6.   What do you like to do in your free time? (Do the activities indicate an avoidance of tasks requiring visual discrimination?)
7.   Which do you remember the best: names, faces, voices? Which do you have the most difficulty in remembering?
8.   Can you read maps very well? (If not, what problems do you have?)

Observations

Does the reader

1.   Show symptoms of eye fatigue and/or distress, that is, blinking, squinting, rubbing eyes.
2.   Assume a posture that results in only one eye's being used in reading?
3.   Point or use other devices to keep his place as he reads?
4.   Make frequent copying errors at near-point or far-point tasks?
5.   Hold reading material very close or at a distance when reading?
6.   Appear to have some type of eye infection indicated by "redness or eyes watering readily"?
7.   Easily lose his place when reading?
8.   Appear to be sensitive to light?

Informal Tests

1.   Visual Discrimination. A visual matching task can be constructed to learn more about students' discrimination abilities. In the informal test shown in Figure 3.1, the student is instructed to circle all items that match the underlined item. The teacher should note whether the number of errors and time taken to accomplish the task were excessive compared with peers, as well as the mode of working. For example:

     head close to page
     matching letter-by-letter
     constant rechecking
     using fingers to hold place
       carelessness

FIGURE 3.1   Visual discrimination task

EXAMPLE: <u>B</u>   A C B O P X B L M N O B C

<u>a</u>   g f j c e a l m n e o l b q a b a c x

<u>ralg</u> ralg role rall raly rolg raly ralg rolg rapg
<u>flag</u> flay fbly flag plag flug fbov blag plag flag

<u>Eastern High</u>   Andorn High Eastern High Eostern High
                Eastern Heyl Eistern High Eastern Hiyl
                Eastern High Eustern High

<u>round the bend</u>   ring the bend   round the bowl round the bend
                round the bind round thi bend round tha bend
                round the bend rouse the bend round tbe bend

<u>BEST</u> BENT BEST BENT BECT BEST BEIT BESF BIST BINH

2. Near-point Copying. The student is given a short passage on his instructional reading level to copy at his desk or table.
3. Far-point Copying. The student copies a short passage on his instructional reading level from a distance of about sixteen feet.

    Student efforts on both near-point and far-point tasks are compared for accuracy, rate, and mode of copying (letter-by-letter, word-by-word, phrases, or sentences).
4. Spelling Analysis
    Look for the following behaviors:
    a. Reversals (*was-saw; upset-setup*).
    b. Errors on common nonphonetic words: *wen* for *when* or *rit* for *write*, but not on phonetic words: *bat, ship.*
    c. Persistent confusion of homonyms, that is, *to, too,* and *two.*
    d. Omits letters not heard.
    e. Adds letters.

Formal Tests

1. *Keystone Visual Survey.* Screens visual functions at near-point and far-point.

2. *Spache Binocular Reading Test.* Tests use of both eyes during the act of reading.

    (Both the Keystone Survey and Spache tests can be obtained from Keystone View Division, Mast Development Company.)

3. *Ortho-Rater.* Visual screening. Bausch and Lomb Optical Company.
4. *Professional Vision Tester.* Visual screening. Titmus Optical Company.

Examiner's Conclusions

____ 1. No apparent visual acuity difficulties.

____ 2. Severe visual acuity problem; should be referred to vision specialist.

____ 3. Can read with glasses, but must be reminded to wear them.

____ 4. Acuity problem only at far-point. Needs proper seating in classroom.

____ 5. Mild discrimination problems that may be due to faulty initial learning. Student should respond to instruction that emphasizes letter or word presentation of dissimilar forms. Do not focus on similar forms (ex.: *b* and *d*) on the same day; do not work with similar letters or words until one form is "overlearned."

____ 6. Severe discrimination problems that may suggest testing for neurological difficulties.

____ 7. Severe visual discrimination problems that suggest a deemphasis of visual instruction and the use of auditory-visual and/or auditory-visual-motor instruction in reading and spelling.

____ 8. Severe visual motor problems that suggest the use of a tracing-fading, matching, copying, production-from-memory sequence of instruction.

AUDITORY ABILITIES

Interview

1. Have you ever had earaches or infections? (Tell me about it.)
2. Do you have trouble hearing sometimes? When?

3. Do you learn better when someone *shows* you what to do or when someone *tells* you what to do? (Tell me about it.)
4. Have you ever had your hearing tested? When? (Tell me about it.)
5. What do you like to do in your spare time? (Do the activities indicate an avoidance of tasks requiring auditory discrimination of speech sounds?)

Observations

1. Does the student watch the face of the speaker closely?
2. Does the student not hear when the speaker turns his head?
3. Does the student have difficulty hearing when there is background noise?
4. Does the student appear to be inattentive?
5. Does the student turn his head to favor one ear?
6. Does the student have articulation problems?
7. Does the student use a nonstandard dialect? (If so, auditory discrimination rather than acuity may be a problem.)

Informal Tests

1. *Auditory Discrimination.* An auditory task can be constructed to learn whether students can hear fine differences in speech sounds. In the informal test shown in Figure 3.2, the student is asked to tell whether sets of words are the same or different. This test is administered so that the student cannot watch the lips of the examiner. Before administering the test, the teacher should determine that the student understands the concepts *same* and *different.* The results of the test are examined to learn (1) whether errors were excessive in comparison with peers; (2) whether more errors occurred with vowels, consonants, or their combinations; and (3) whether more errors occurred in word beginnings, middles or endings.
2. *Phonemic Segmenting.* The dissimilar words in Figure 3.2 can be used to learn whether the student can isolate a sound within a word. For example, the examiner might ask: Do you hear /s/ in *said* or *head*?

FIGURE 3.2   Auditory discrimination

(Check incorrect responses.)

1. ____ (d)	said, head	11. ____ (s)	ditch, ditch
2. ____ (d)	fig, pig	12. ____ (d)	clock, click
3. ____ (s)	show, show	13. ____ (s)	car, car
4. ____ (d)	bat, bath	14. ____ (d)	then, thin
5. ____ (s)	ledge, ledge	15. ____ (d)	ship, sip
6. ____ (d)	bull, pull	16. ____ (d)	jumped, jump
7. ____ (s)	man, man	17. ____ (d)	vest, test
8. ____ (d)	lock, luck	18. ____ (d)	runs, run
9. ____ (d)	pin, pen	19. ____ (s)	push, push
10. ____ (s)	ring, ring	20. ____ (d)	went, want

3.   *Spelling Analysis.* Analyze the student's spelling to note whether the following errors have occurred:
   a.   Omission of word endings.
   b.   Nonphonetic substitutions of vowels or consonants.
   c.   Omission of sounds.
   d.   Incorrect sequencing of sounds.

Formal Tests

1.   Discrimination
   a.   *The Auditory Discrimination Test* (Wepman), Language Research Associates.
   b.   *Goldman-Fristoe-Woodcock Test of Auditory Discrimination,* American Guidance Service.
   c.   *Lindamood Auditory Comprehension Test,* Teaching Resources.
2.   Acuity
   a.   Beltone, Model 9D, Electronics Corporation.

b.   Maico, Model MA-19. Maico Electronics Corporation.

c.   Zenith, Model ZA-100T, Zenith Hearing Aids Corporation.

Examiner's Conclusions

_____ 1.   No apparent auditory difficulties.

_____ 2.   Severe auditory acuity problem; should be referred to audiologist.

_____ 3.   Audiometer indicates loss in high range; may have difficulty with word endings and with sounds of *s, l, t,* and their combinations.

_____ 4.   Audiometer indicates loss in low range; may have difficulty with sounds of vowels and with sounds of *h, b, g, m,* and their combinations (low range loss is less detrimental to decoding skill acquisition than high range loss).

_____ 5.   Discrimination problem may be caused by dialect or acquisition of English as a second language. Some auditory discrimination practice is suggested.

_____ 6.   Discrimination, sequencing, memory span, or synthesis problems are mild and do not require special handling.

_____ 7.   Preceding problems are severe and require instructional techniques that favor visual emphasis.

VERBAL ABILITIES

Interview

1.   Have you ever had difficulty with your speech? (Tell me about it.)
2.   Are there any situations now that sometimes cause you to have problems with your speech?
3.   Do you have trouble understanding other people? (Tell me about it.)
4.   Do people have trouble understanding you? (Tell me about it.)

Observations

1.   Is the student's command of English adequate?
2.   Is there a problem with articulation?

3. Is speech fluent?
4. Is speech content appropriate?
5. Is volume appropriate?
6. Is speaking vocabulary adequate?
7. Is length of spoken sentences appropriate to the age of the speaker?
8. Is grammar of oral language appropriate to the age of the speaker?
9. Does the student have adequate conversational comprehension?
10. Is limited oral expression caused by emotional considerations: shyness, fear, hostility?

Informal Tests

Because formal assessment of language can be inhibiting, an analysis of spontaneous language can be more revealing for some students. A sample of fifty or more consecutive sentences should be recorded, transcribed, and analyzed. This might be obtained by asking the student to "tell about" an object, a picture, or an incident or by recording spontaneous speech in a work or play setting. The sample is then analyzed for (1) mean length of utterances, (2) grammatical maturity, (3) vocabulary, (4) articulation, (5) fluency, and (6) content. These results are compared with similar elements in the speech of those within the same age range as the speaker. A similar procedure can be followed for obtaining and analyzing written language.

Formal Tests

1. *Goldman-Fristoe Test of Articulation.* Articulation of sounds.
2. *Peabody Picture Vocabulary Test.* Receptive vocabulary.
3. Other. Some diagnosticians use selected subtests from the *Detroit Tests of Learning Aptitude* and the *Illinois Test of Psycholinguistic Abilities in conjunction with* informal observations.

Examiner's Conclusions

____ 1. Verbal abilities appear to be adequate.
____ 2. Verbal abilities seem to indicate (below average, average, above average) potential.

_____ 3. Verbal abilities inadequate in the following areas:

_____

_____ 4. Should be referred for speech therapy.

SENSORY-BASED LEARNING DIFFICULTIES

Interview

As this is a sensitive area, direct questions about birth injuries, strokes, or other cerebral trauma should be avoided, unless the student is old enough *and* comfortable enough to discuss such things. The student might be encouraged to describe how he best learns and remembers and what seems to inhibit his learning and retention. For example: Do you learn better by watching something being done or by listening to instructions on how to do something? Tell me about it. Do you learn better by getting information step-by-step or by being given an overview and figuring out the steps yourself. Tell me about it.

Observations

1. *Intersensory difficulty.* Observe student for difficulty *across* channels. For example, a student may be able to spell *truck orally: t-r-u-c-k;* but he might *write* truck as *truxd.*
2. *Receptive difficulty.* The student may not accurately perceive information although he may not have an acuity problem. (See preceding auditory and visual discrimination checklists).
3. *Associative difficulty.* The student may not be able to make an appropriate connection between new information and previous experiences. He may have difficulty in classifying or generalizing.
4. *Production difficulty.* The student may have difficulty in *retrieving* auditory and/or visual information, or he may have trouble in *expressing* his thoughts through oral or written speech. For example, a student may be able to point to a letter or word that is pronounced for him but may not be able to say it. Another example: The student may be able to *recognize* a paraphrased statement of what he has read (association) but may not be able to *express* (production) his

thoughts in either spoken or written language. A final example: The student may frequently have difficulty in thinking of a word he wants to say. He may say, "What you write with" because he can't bring the word *pencil* to mind (auditory retrieval).

5.   Other observations may include

    a.   Short attention span.

    b.   Perseveration.

    c.   Lack of retention.

    d.   Irritability caused by strain of functioning with handicap.

    e.   Loss of memory.

    f.   Marked differences between verbal and nonverbal functioning.

Formal Tests

1.   See listings under auditory discrimination, visual discrimination, and verbal abilities.

2.   *Detroit Tests of Learning Abilities,* Bobbs-Merrill.

3.   *Illinois Test of Psycholinguistic Abilities,* University of Illinois Press.

4.   Slingerland, *Screening Tests for Identifying Children with Specific Language Disability,* Educators' Publishing Service.

5.   *Wechsler Intelligence Scales* (*WISC-R,* children; *WAIS,* adult), Psychological Corporation.

    Note. Before referral, diagnostic teaching should be used to determine whether the student responds to instruction. Selected criterion-referenced tests may be preferred to norm-referenced tests. The goal of diagnostic teaching is to discover which form of instruction appears to be the most effective for each learning task.

Examiner's Conclusions

_____ 1.   No apparent learning disability.

_____ 2.   Appears to have a learning disability in the area(s) of _____

              _____

_____ 3.   Appears to have a learning disability *and* does not respond to instruction. Should be referred for further diagnosis.

       4.   Appears to have a learning disability but does not respond to instruction under the following conditions:

              _____

              _____

AFFECT

Interview

1. How do you feel about getting special help?
2. Can you manage to practice on your own?
3. Can you attend on a regular schedule?
4. What reading methods were used with you in the past? Do you feel they helped you?
5. What are your preferences in materials, work setting, tutoring approaches?
6. Do you have any ideas on how you can best be helped?
7. How long do you think it will take for you to read as well as you need to read?
8. Is there anything you want to be able to read?

Observations

1. Can the student attend closely to critical elements of reading tasks?
2. Can the student attend for long periods of time?
3. Does the student appear to intend to remember?
4. Is the student often absent or late or need to leave early?
5. Does the student frequently try to distract the teacher with discussions unrelated to the instructional tasks?
6. What are the student's major interests?
7. What can the student do well?
8. Does the student practice on his own regularly?
9. Does the student appear to be emotionally distressed?

Informal Tests and Checklists

1. *The DCRL Checklist* (Figure 3.3) provides the teacher with descriptions of personality factors that may interact with learning. The teacher will need to be aware of the conditions under which these behaviors occur so that instruction can be planned that will most likely elicit positive behaviors. Check only those descriptions that seem to be typical.

FIGURE 3.3.   Descriptions of characteristic responses to learning (DCRL) checklist

The following are personality factors that may interact with learning. Check factors that apply to student. Date and initial each remark that applies to student.

☐	impulsive—responds quickly without thinking	☐	reflective
☐	resistant—reluctant to change	☐	open
☐	dependent—relies on others instead of figuring out the next step	☐	independent
☐	inflexible—finds difficulty in shifting to alternative strategies	☐	flexible
☐	unable to concentrate—cannot focus on the task at hand	☐	able to concentrate
☐	lacks confidence—unable to risk making a mistake	☐	confident
☐	lacks ability to generalize—has difficulty deducing the principle or seeing the point	☐	makes acceptable generalizations
☐	unable to transfer learning—has difficulty in applying knowledge in different settings	☐	applies knowledge in different settings
☐	fails to identify critical differences—has difficulty focusing on critical elements	☐	identifies critical differences
☐	lacks persistence—unable to stay on task for reasonable length of time	☐	persistent
☐	unwilling to practice—impatient with review and repetition	☐	willing to practice
☐	cannot accept failure—failure results in strong emotional interference with further efforts	☐	learns from failure

FIGURE 3.4.   Unfinished sentences

___

1. Sometimes

1. Sometimes I like to _____ .

2. Last summer I _____ .

3. I hope I'll never_____ .

4. When I read, I_____ .

5. My friend likes to _____ .

6. When I'm at home I _____ .

7. Going to school is _____ .

8. Someday I want to_____ .

9. The person I like best is _____ .

10. I wish someone would _____ .

11. Learning to read is_____ .

12. My eyes are _____ .

13. I wish my teacher would_____ .

14. My favorite television show is _____ .

15. I have fun when_____ .

16. I would like to be able to read _____ .

17. If I had three wishes, I would wish for _____ .

18. After school I like to _____ .

    2.   *Unfinished Sentences.* (Figure 3.4) are best administered by having the examiner read aloud and the student respond verbally. If the subject is at ease, the teacher may quickly write his responses; otherwise, responses may be written after the student departs. Responses can be used to elicit further discussion. Example: "What did you mean when you said, 'We go up north'"? Unusual responses may require follow-up. A student who said, "My eyes are very excellent" actually had poor vision.

Examiner's Conclusions

____ 1.   Appears optimistic.

____ 2.   Appears pessimistic; will require frequent proof of progress and much encouragement.

____ 3.   Previous mode of instruction was _____.
It (was, was not) effective.

____ 4.   Student prefers to work with _____ materials.

____ 5.   Student is able to practice regularly on his own.

____ 6.   Student becomes bored easily, needs frequent shift in materials and methods.

____ 7.   Student needs highly structured practice session.

____ 8.   Student does best with self-selected materials and self-pacing.

____ 9.   Student appears to need counseling for personal problems.

Figure 3.5   Student record form—related reading factors: all levels

Obs.*	Sat.*

I. VISUAL ACUITY

A.   No apparent visual acuity difficulties. +[†]

B.   Severe visual acuity problem; should be referred to vision specialist (see directory). –

C.   Can read with glasses, but must be reminded to wear them. –

D.   Acuity problem only at far-point. o

E.   Mild discrimination problems that may be due to faulty initial learning. –

F.   Severe discrimination problems that may suggest testing for neurological difficulties. –

G.   Severe visual discrimination problems that suggest a deemphasis of visual instruction and the use of auditory-visual and/or auditory-visual-motor instruction in reading and spelling. –

H.   Severe visual motor problems that suggest the use of
____ a tracing-fading o
____ matching o
____ copying o
____ production-from-memory sequence of instruction. o

*Key: Observed, date. satisfactory, date.

†Code: Depending on circumstances, behavior   +   may be helpful
                                              –   may be detrimental
                                              o   may provide information to plan instruction.

FIGURE 3.5.   Continued

Obs.*	Sat.*	
		II. AUDITORY ACUITY

II. AUDITORY ACUITY

A.   No apparent auditory difficulties. +

B.   Severe auditory acuity problem; should be referred to audiologist (see directory). −

C.   Audiometer indicates loss in high range; may have difficulty with word endings and with sounds of *s, l, t,* and their combinations. −

D.   Audiometer indicates loss in low range; may have difficulty with sounds of vowels and with sounds of *h, b, g, m,* and their combinations (low range loss less detrimental to coding skill acquisition than high range loss). −

E.   Discrimination problem may be caused by dialect or acquisition of English as a second language. Some auditory discrimination practice is suggested. −

F.   Discrimination, sequencing, memory, span, or synthesis analysis problems are mild and do not require special handling. o

G.   Preceding problems are severe and require instructional techniques that favor visual emphasis. −

H.   Appears to have physical handicap other than vision and hearing. −

I.   Handicap does appear to interfere with learning: (specify)_____

_____

III. VERBAL ABILITY

A.   Verbal abilities appear to be adequate. +

B.   Verbal abilities seem to indicate (average, above average) potential. +

C.   Verbal abilities inadequate in the following areas: _____

_____ −

D.   Should be referred for speech therapy. −

IV. SENSORY-BASED DIFFICULTIES

A.   No apparent learning disability. +

B.   Appears to have a learning disability *and* does not respond to instructions. Should be referred for further diagnosis. −

C.   Appears to have a learning disability but does respond to instructions under the following conditions: _____

_____ o

FIGURE 3.5.   Continued

Obs.*	Sat.*	
		V. AFFECT
		A. Appears optimistic. +
		B. Appears pessimistic; will require frequent proof of progress and much encouragement. –
		C. Previous mode of instruction used was _____ . It (was, was not) effective. o
		D. Prefers to work with _____ material. o
		E. Is able to practice regularly on his or her own. +
		F. Will need to be scheduled for frequent practice sessions in the lab (with, without) a tutor present. o
		G. Learning style appears to be _____ . Should be encouraged to be more _____ . o
		H. Becomes bored easily; needs frequent shift in materials and methods. –
		I. Needs highly structured practice sessions. o
		J. Does best with self-selected materials and self-pacing. o
		K. Appears to need counseling for personal problems. –
		L. Learning style affecting performance. See DCRL Checklist. o
		M. Major interests are_____ . +
		VI. WRITING
		A. Handwriting is adequate. +
		B. Handwriting may indicate a sensory-based difficulty that needs to be considered in remediation. –
		C. Inadequate handwriting skills caused by lack of instruction or practice. –
		D. Poor handwriting seems to interfere with ability to visualize correct spelling of words. –
		E. Content seems to indicate difficulty caused by language problems. –
		VII. SPELLING
		A. Appears not to know the following phonetic elements: _____ _____ . –
		B. Appears to have difficulty in discriminating: (list specific vowels and consonants) _____ _____ . –
		C. Appears to have difficulty in discriminating inflectional endings and suffixes. –

FIGURE 3.5.   Continued

Obs.*	Sat.*	
		D. Is unaware of the following common spelling conventions:_____
		————————————————————————————————— -
		E. Appears to have poor visual memory and would appear to respond to:
		1. practice with word patterns o
		2. memory devices such as: "the question words—*who, which, when, where, why, what*—begin with *wh*" o
		F. Appears to have a problem with visual sequence. –
		VIII. OTHER PHYSICAL DIFFICULTIES
		A. Appears to have a physical problem that interferes with learning (specify) ———————————————
		B. Needs the following instructional conditions: _____
		—————————————————————————————————

CHAPTER 4

Assessment of Abilities on Beginning Reading Levels

This chapter outlines assessment cues related to student performance in word recognition, word analysis, comprehension, writing, and spelling for those students functioning approximately on grade levels one through three.

A format similar to that of Chapter 3, using interview questions, observations, and tests, followed by Student Record Forms (Figures 4.6–8), continues in this chapter.

SIGHT WORDS

Interview

1. Can you tell me some words you do know when you see them?
2. How did you learn them?
3. Do you have difficulty in recognizing little words such as *from* and *the*?
4. Can you recognize little words right away without looking hard at them? (automaticity)
5. What words do you want to learn first?

Observations

1.   Sight Words in Context (Graded Paragraphs)
     a.   Is the student able to pronounce common service words in context as he reads aloud from graded paragraphs or instructional materials?
     b.   Does the student appear to have sufficient automaticity for sight words as he reads aloud in context?
     c.   What is the student's estimated sight word level in context?
2.   Sight Words in Isolation
     a.   Can the student recognize common words in his environment such as *Coca-Cola, K-Mart*?
     b.   What is the student's sight word level?
     c.   Does the student have automaticity for common service words?
     d.   Is the student's sight word level significantly above or below his instructional level?
3.   Meanings of Sight Words
     a.   Does the student have difficulty with the meaning of conjunctions, prepositions, and/or articles because of having English as a second language?
     b.   Does the student appear to have difficulty with the meaning of sight words because of limited conceptual background? (example, meaning of prepositions: *of* the country; *about* the time)

Informal Tests

1.   *Context.* Have the student read aloud from graded material on the preprimer through upper grade levels until he reaches frustration. Use preceding checklists to analyze performance on service words.
2.   *Isolation.*
     a.   Prepare lists of service words found in preprimer through third grade level materials, as in Figure 4.1, and have the student read aloud until he reaches frustration. Analyze performance with preceding checklist. As an estimate of level, the highest level list on which the student made no more than two errors may be used as his instructional level.
     b.   Prepare lists of words commonly found in student's environ-

FIGURE 4.1.   Service words

PP	P	1.0
____ 1. the	____ 1. come	____ 1. this
____ 2. a	____ 2. he	____ 2. like
____ 3. is	____ 3. get	____ 3. went
____ 4. and	____ 4. for	____ 4. three
____ 5. to	____ 5. you	____ 5. away
____ 6. go	____ 6. with	____ 6. out
____ 7. I	____ 7. will	____ 7. she
____ 8. am	____ 8. here	____ 8. from
____ 9. it	____ 9. want	____ 9. under
____ 10. can	____ 10. of	____ 10. your

2.0	3.0
____ 1. there	____ 1. near
____ 2. marry	____ 2. which
____ 3. they	____ 3. everything
____ 4. stopped	____ 4. morning
____ 5. when	____ 5. always
____ 6. how	____ 6. once
____ 7. again	____ 7. goes
____ 8. before	____ 8. together
____ 9. then	____ 9. because
____ 10. didn't	____ 10. round

ment and analyze performance. These may vary geographically. Some examples are

Stop   men
Coca Cola   women

Pepsi Cola	boys
K-Mart	girls
Texaco	one way
DANGER	KEEP OUT

Formal Tests

1. Dolch, *Basic Sight Word Test,* Garrard Press.
2. *San Diego Quick Assessment Test* (La Pray and Ross, "The Graded Word List: Quick Gauge of Reading Ability," *Journal of Reading* (January 1969).
3. Mills, *Learning Methods Test,* The Mills Education Center.

Examiner's Conclusions

____ 1. Service word list level appears to be: PP, P, 1, 2, or 3.
____ 2. Has difficulty with automaticity.
____ 3. Needs help with meanings of sight words.
____ 4. Sight word recognition (is, is not) aided by context.
____ 5. Results of trial teaching indicate sight words are best learned by_____ .

SOUND-SYMBOL ASSOCIATION, STRUCTURAL ANALYSIS, PROBLEM-SOLVING STRATEGIES

Interview

1. Do you know letters of the alphabet? Can you name them? Put them in order? Do you know their sounds?
2. Do you know the sounds that letters make in words? Did anyone ever try to teach you letter sounds? Tell me about it.
3. Do you know the sounds of two letters together, such as *ph* or *tr*?
4. Can you "sound out" words?
5. Can you "sound out" words quickly?
6. What do you do when you come to a word you do not know?

7. Do you have difficulty with long words?
8. Can you break words apart?
9. Can you make a good guess when you don't know a word?
10. How do you check your guess?

Observation

1. Oral reading in *context.* After listening to the student read an appropriate oral selection (graded paragraphs or other material) and recording his responses, the teacher should complete the following checklist. Context reading behavior is marked as *c* in yes or no column, as appropriate.

   a. *Sound-Symbol Association*
      Did the reader
      (1) Make single consonant errors?
      (2) Make consonant combination errors?
      (3) Make single vowel errors?
      (4) Make vowel combination errors?
      (5) Make errors on silent letter phonograms?
      (6) Make errors on common phonograms?

   b. *Structural Analysis*
      Did the reader
      (1) Make errors on inflectional endings?
      (2) Make errors on prefixes?
      (3) Make errors on suffixes?
      (4) Make errors on multisyllabic words?
      (5) Make errors on compound words?

   c. *Syntactic-Semantic Applications*
      Did the reader
      (1) Make inappropriate surface structure word substitutions? (a verb for an adjective)
      (2) Make inappropriate deep structure substitutions? (words that do not fit meaning)
      (3) Make dialect substitutions?
      (4) Reread to obtain meaning?
      (5) Use appropriate phrasing?
      (6) Respond appropriately to punctuation?
      (7) Make more errors in long than short sentences?
      (8) Make errors in complex sentences using abstract referents such as *which, that, who*?

(9) Answer questions about the content accurately?

(10) Tell about the content accurately?

    d.   *Processing Strategies*

Did the reader

(1) Have a systematic approach to the identification of unfamiliar words?

(2) Use a spelling approach (say letter names)?

(3) Use configuration (substitute a word that looked similar)?

(4) Use an initial consonant-context approach (substitute a word that begins the same and fits meaning)?

(5) Use a phonetic approach (sound letters)?

(6) Blend sounds (blend without phoneticizing; *ca-t* instead of *cuh-ah-tuh*)?

(7) Use context (substitute meaningful word)?

(8) Regress to aid word recognition (reread to confirm accuracy of word choice)?

(9) Make errors in ____ beginning, ____ middle, or ____ end of words?

(10) Lack automaticity (instant recognition)?

(11) Attempt to analyze the entire word?

(12) Read at an appropriate rate?

    e.   *Affect*

Was the reader

(1) Under emotional stress?

(2) Flexible in his attempts to recognize words?

(3) Persistent?

(4) Willing to attempt unfamiliar words?

(5) Willing to attempt difficult passages?

(6) Under physical stress?

2.   Oral Reading in *Isolation*

After the recording of the student's responses to a graded word list, an analysis of his behavior should be made according to the preceding checklist. Behavior is marked *I* if observed in isolation.

Informal Tests

In addition to analysis of the student's oral reading performance in graded paragraphs according to the preceding checklists, the following inventory might be used to obtain information.

Individual Reading Analysis

Test 1. *Letter Names*

Directions: Say, "Name these letters in line one—two . . ."

Record all letters not known.

Record all incorrect letters called in error. (See Figure 4.2)

Look for confusion of letters; *m/n, u/n, p/b,* and *d/q.*

B	C	D	S	A	I	F	E	M	L	P	T	R
Z	J	W	X	G	U	H	Q	K	N	Y	V	O
m	y	n	l	r	o	t	p	z	v	k	i	a
j	u	g	w	b	c	s	h	d	f	x	q	e

Test 2. *Consonant Sounds*

Directions: With LIST A give these directions: "Point to the letter that begins the word I say: *man, soap, run, long, no, fast, zip.*"

With LIST B give these directions: "Point to the letter that begins the word I say: *piano, dog, win, cat, yellow, tap, kite, joke, house, go, big.*"

With LIST C give these directions: "Point to the letters that begin the word I say: *chop, that, where, ship, phone.*"

Record all sounds not known. Record all sounds made in error above the unrecognized stimulus letter.

Note. The letters *c* and *g* have hard and soft sounds. Record the student's choice, and retest later to see if both associations have been made.

LIST A:	r	n	l	m	z	s	f				
LIST B:	y	t	k	p	j	h	b	t	g	w	d	c
LIST C:	sh	ch	th	wh	ph						

Test 3. *Consonant Blends*

Directions: With LIST A say, "point to the letters in the first line that begin the word I say: *cloud, fly, blue, glue, plate, slow.*"

With LIST B say, "point to the letters in the second line that begin the word I say: *crown, from, grow, pretty, brown, tree, dress.*"

With LIST C say, "point to the letters in the third line that begin the word I say: *sweet, small, snow, screen, splash, street.*"

Record all sounds not known. Write all sounds made in error.

LIST A:	bl	fl	gl	pl	sl	cl	
LIST B:	br	cr	dr	fr	gr	pr	tr
LIST C:	scr	sn	sm	spl	str	sw	

Test 4. *Initial Consonant Blending*

Directions: The first word in each list is a common phonogram. Say, "Read the first word." (If the student doesn't know it, tell him the word.) Then say, "Read the second word in the list" (Pause) "Now read the last word in the list."

Look for ability to substitute seven out of ten consonants.

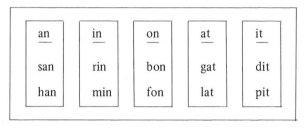

an	in	on	at	it
san	rin	bon	gat	dit
han	min	fon	lat	pit

Test 5. *Short Vowel Sounds*

Directions: Say, "I am going to say some words. Listen and point to the letter that makes the middle sound in the word I say:

mop—I mop the floor—mop
fed—I fed my dog—fed
bag—I have a bag of groceries—bag
tip—The waiter gets a tip—tip
mud—I walked in a mud puddle—mud
sit—Sit on the chair—sit
met—We met a friend—met
tap—Tap your pencil—tap
tub—Wash in a bath tub—tub
cob—Corn on the cob—cob

a	e	i	o	u

Students will have two opportunities to identify each short medial vowel sound.

Test 6. *Long Vowel Sounds*

Directions: Say, "Try to read these words as well as you can, even if you never saw them before."

Observe student's use of all long vowel sounds. (Remember some vowel generalizations do not hold more than 75 percent of the time and should not be taught as rules.)

bo	*de*	*fi*	*sa*	*mu*	*dune*
pone	*jeet*	*vie*	*soke*	*bote*	*weal*
nave	*trite*	*fate*	*maim*	*lune*	*kibe*

Test 7. *Reversals* (omit, if tendency is not suspected)

Directions: Say, "Read these words as fast as you can!"

A student who retains the early tendency of some children to reverse words, *was* for *saw, on* for *no,* and so on, will usually slip if he reads the test words rapidly.

pal	no	saw	raw	ten	tar
won	pot	was	on	lap	tops

Test 8. *Common Vowel Digraphs*

Directions: Say, "Here are some words you probably don't know. Try to read them as well as you can."

Note carefully any vowel digraphs missed.

jook	wail	clout	foy
toil	play	haul	jowl

Test 9. *Blending Sounds in Syllables*

Directions: Say, "Here are some nonsense words. They really are not words at all, but I'd like to see if you can read them."

If a student knows the consonant and vowel sounds, as well as the two common long-vowel patterns, and can blend sounds, he should be able to read the nonsense words listed here. The nonsense syllables are used to prevent the student's recalling words he knows by sight.

rud	cope	bive	del	rute	pame	kult
jobe	mag	lome	keam	nit	faib	dote
lim	keel	slue	jote	dat	bot	hin

Test 10. *Compound Words*
Directions: Say, "Read these words as well as you can."

Failure to pronounce these test words with confidence indicates the need for corrective teaching of compounds.

workhorse	nightbank	carwash
paperjumper	basketmeet	houseboat

Test 11. *Common Prefixes*
Directions: Say, "Here are some more nonsense words. Read them as well as you can."

Carefully listen to the pronunciation of the prefix units that begin each nonsense word. A failure to recognize nearly all of the prefixes indicates the student is weak in the ability to visualize word parts.

subman	inwell	prohid	recar
ungo	prehit	enrun	conmet
distap	besell	exwin	depan

Test 12. *Common Suffixes*
Directions: Say, "Read these words as well as you can."

Carefully note the specific suffixes with which the student experiences difficulty. He should be able to see the suffixes as visual units.

bookness	tubous
carment	sixing
roomly	bandive

hilltion	burnant
waterest	pondance
drumless	juger
bandful	fourable

Text 13. *Phonograms: Silent Letters*
Directions: Say, "Read these words as well as you can."
Look for un-known patterns.

fight	through	beautiful
laugh	rough	straight
could	bought	round
eight	ocean	fudge

Text 14. *Syllabication*
Directions: Say, "Divide these words into parts by marking the parts (draw lines between the syllables).

Observe the student as he divides the words into parts and attempts to read them. Uncertainty and confusion will indicate that he is not accustomed to seeing multisyllabic words by parts.

accented	important
confirmation	yesterday
wrinkle	cucumber
microscope	spidering
revolver	fumble

Test 15. *Contextual Clues*
Directions: Say, "This story has some words missing. Try to read the story by guessing the missing words."

If the student does not know most of the words, he is weak in his ability to use context clues as an aid to word identification.

> It was raining as I crossed _____
>
> street. I _____ not see the car _____
>
> the corner. The _____ came _____ fast.
>
> I had to _____ to the side _____ the
>
> street. I was _____ , but I _____ safe.

Figure 4.3 is an individual progress record used by teachers working in the classroom or with groups of remedial students. The record management technique exemplified by this form enables the teacher to form quickly instructional groups by skills or by grade levels, whichever is appropriate to her purpose. The form is placed on cue sort cards (or teachers may fashion their own similar devices) with holes next to the edge of the card. As the skill is achieved, the corresponding hole is punched. Inserting a needle into the hole reveals which students have achieved which skills, and students with the same difficulties may be placed in the same group.

Formal Tests

See Chapter 9 for a list of published tests.

Examiner's Conclusions

____ 1. Appears to lack following sound-symbol associations:

_____

_____

____ 2. Needs help in using context as an aid to word identification.
____ 3. Needs help in the following structural analysis skills:

_____

_____

____ 4. Needs help in systematically applying knowledge of word analysis.
____ 5. Needs help in automaticity.
____ 6. Needs much emotional support to risk making an error.
____ 7. Needs help in eliminating ineffective strategies and learning new strategies, that is, _____ .

FIGURE 4.2.   Testing record for I.R.A.

Testing Record Individual Reading Analysis

Name _____   *Date* _____

Teacher _____

1. Letter Names:

   B   C   D   S   A   I   F   E   M   L   P   T   R
   Z   J   W   X   G   U   H   Q   K   N   Y   V   O
   m   y   n   l   r   o   t   p   z   v   k   i   a
   j   u   g   w   b   c   s   h   d   f   x   q   e

2. Consonant Sounds:
   List A: r   n   l   m   z   s   f
   List B: y   t   k   p   j   h   b   t   g   w   d   c
   List C: sh   ch   th   wh   ph

3. Consonant Blends:
   List A: bl   fl   gl   pl   sl   cl
   List B: br   cr   dr   fr   gr   pr   tr
   List C: scr sn   sm   spl str sw

4. Initial Consonant Blending:
   <u>an</u>   <u>in</u>   <u>on</u>   <u>at</u>   <u>it</u>
   san   rin   bon   gat   dit
   han   min   fon   lat   pit

5. Short Vowel Sounds:
   e   i   o   u   a

6. Long Vowel Sounds:
   bo   de   fi   sa   mu   dune
   pone   jeet   vie   soke   bote   weal
   nave   trite   fate   maim   lune   kibe

7. Reversals:
   pal   no   saw   raw   ten   tar
   won   pot   was   on   lap   tops

8. Common Vowel Digraphs:
   jook   wail   clout   foy
   toil   play   haul   jowl

9. Blending Sounds in Syllables:
   rud   cope   bive   del   rute   pame   kult

FIGURE 4.2.   Continued

jobe	mag	lome	keam	nit	faib	dote
lim	keel	slue	jote	dat	bot	hin

10. Compound Words:

workhorse	nightbank	carwash
paperjumper	basketmeet	houseboat

11. Common Prefixes:

sub	in	pro	re
un	pre	en	con
dis	be	ex	de

12. Common Suffices:

ness	est	ing	er
ment	less	ive	able
ly	ful	ant	
tion	ous	ance	

13. Phonograms/Silent Letters:

fight	through	beautiful
laugh	rough	straight
could	bought	round
eight	ocean	fudge

14. Syllabication:

accented	important
confirmation	yesterday
wrinkle	cucumber
microscope	spidering
revolver	fumble

15. Contextual Clues:

It was raining as I crossed _____ street. I _____ not see the car

_____ the corner. The _____ came fast. I had to _____

to the side _____ the street. I was _____ , but I _____

safe.

FIGURE 4.3.   Progress record for I.R.A.

Name _____

Teacher _____

*Skill Needs**

0   1. Letter Names
0   2. Consonant Sounds
0   3. Consonant Blends
0   4. Initial Consonant Blending
0   5. Short Vowel Sounds
0   6. Long Vowel Sounds
0   7. Reversals
0   8. Common Vowel Digraphs
0   9. Blending Sounds in Syllables
0   10. Compound Words
0   11. Common Prefixes
0   12. Common Suffices
0   13. Phonograms/Silent Letters
0   14. Syllabication
0   15. Contextual

Instructional
Reading Level*

PP   0
P   0
1^1 0
1^2 0
2^1 0
2^2 0
3^1 0
3^2 0
4   0
5   0
6   0

Observations

0 _____
0 _____
0 _____
0 _____
0 _____

*Sight Words**

PP   0
P   0
1   0
2   0
3   0

Standardized Test Results

0 _____
0 _____
0 _____
0 _____

Comprehension Abilities

_____ 0
_____ 0
_____ 0
_____ 0
_____ 0

Interests

0 _____
0 _____
0 _____
0 _____

_____ 0
_____ 0
_____ 0
_____ 0
_____ 0

*(Punch or check those achieved.)

___ 8. Needs help in letter or word discrimination.
___ 9. Needs help in left-to-right letter or syllable sequencing.
___ 10. Needs help in attending to critical features of words.
___ 11. Needs help in refining new learnings.
___ 12. Needs help in retaining new associations.
___ 13. Needs help in transferring new learning.
___ 14. Needs help in predicting the writer's use of a word.

READING COMPREHENSION

Interview

1. Can you understand what you read when you read aloud?
2. Can you understand what you read when you read silently?
3. Do you have better understanding after reading aloud or after reading to yourself? Why do you think that is so?
4. Do you remember better after reading aloud or reading to yourself?
5. Do you have any problem understanding material when it is read to you? Please explain.
6. Do you remember what is read to you?
7. Do you have trouble knowing what words mean?
8. Are long sentences difficult for you to follow?
9. Are commas helpful in understanding long sentences? Please explain.
10. Can you often guess what a writer is going to say?

Observations

Under conditions of oral reading:

1. Does the student substitute words appropriate to the surface structure of the selection? (Example: a verb for a verb or a preposition for a preposition.)
2. Does the student substitute words appropriate to the deep structure of the selection? (Example: not "I got on my house (for *horse*) and rode away," but "I got on my pony (or *stallion* or *mare*) and rode away."

3. Does the student use appropriate phrasing?
4. Does the student respond appropriately to punctuation marks?
5. Does the student's use of pitch, stress, inflection, and pause indicate appropriate language processing?

Under conditions of oral and silent reading:

6. Is the student's rate appropriate?

Under conditions of oral reading, silent reading, and listening:

7. Can the student tell in his own words what was said in the passages?
8. Can the student respond accurately to questions about the content of the passages? (Be sure questions are passage-dependent and cannot be answered without reading the passage.)
9. Can the student recognize the content of the passage in paraphrase?
10. Can the student improve his response after rereading of the passage?
11. Does the student make dialect substitutions, indicating he understands the content?
12. Does the student obtain meaning from long sentences?
13. Does the student obtain meaning from complex sentences?
14. Does the student obtain meaning from dependent clause constructions using *which, that, who*?

Informal Tests

1. Administer teacher constructed graded paragraph tests or cloze tests as described in Chapter 10.
2. Administer cloze listening test as in Figure 4.4.

Formal Tests

See Chapter 9 for a list of published tests.

Examiner's Conclusions

____ 1. Problems with slow or inaccurate word recognition appear to be interfering with comprehension.
____ 2. Student is overly concerned with accurate word perception to the detriment of comprehension.

FIGURE 4.4.   Semantic and syntactic cloze tests

Directions: Listen as I read these sentences aloud and tell me what word I left out.

SEMANTIC CUES

1.   She has one sister and one _____ .

2.   I drowned my plants with too much _____ .

3.   When I hurt my leg, I went to the emergency room at the _____ .

4.   The soup was so _____ I burned my tongue.

5.   I waited at the crosswalk for the light to _____ .

6.   Please wipe your feet on the _____ .

SYNTACTIC CUES

1.   Your new dress is _____ . (adj.)

2.   I like hotdogs, _____ I like hamburgers better. (conj.)

3.   She waited for her _____ . (n.)

4.   I can't _____ very fast. (v.)

5.   Talk _____ so he can't hear you. (adv.)

6.   Pour the coffee _____ the cup. (prep.)

____ 3.   Student's slow rate appears to be interfering with comprehension.
____ 4.   Student is not attending to meaning.
____ 5.   Comparison of listening comprehension to silent and oral comprehension indicates student may have _____ potential for growth in reading comprehension.

WRITING (HANDWRITING AND EXPRESSION)

Interview

1.   Do you use *handwriting* or *printing*? (Student may not use the terms *cursive* or *manuscript*.)

2. Can others read your writing easily?
3. Is your writing as fast as you would like it to be?
4. Are you satisfied with how well you can write your ideas?

Observations

Under copying, dictating, and student-production conditions:

1. Is rate adequate?
2. Is letter formation adequate?
3. Is word order accurate?
4. Is spacing adequate?

Under dictating conditions:

5. Is spelling accurate?
6. Can student reproduce words in phrases?

Under student-production conditions:

7. Is expression adequate?
8. Are mechanics adequate?
9. Is organization adequate?
10. Are length, variety, and complexity of sentences appropriate to student's age and ability?

Informal Tests

Obtain samples of student writing across grade levels, and select passages that appear to indicate typical performance for each grade. Use these as a basis of comparison for judging students' growth in writing.

Examiner's Conclusions

_____ 1. Student's manuscript handwriting is adequate.
_____ 2. Student's cursive handwriting is adequate.
_____ 3. Student's handwriting may indicate a sensory-based difficulty that needs to be considered in remediation.

___ 4.   Student has inadequate handwriting skills caused by lack of instruction or practice.
___ 5.   Student's poor handwriting seems to interfere with student's ability to visualize correct spelling of words.
___ 6.   Content of student's writing seems to indicate difficulty caused by language problems, sensory-based difficulties, or lack of instruction and practice.

SPELLING

Interview

1.   Do you think you need help in spelling?
2.   When someone asks you how to spell a word, do you write it before you tell them the letters, or do you just say the letters?
3.   Can you tell by looking at a word if it is spelled correctly?
4.   When you ask someone how to spell a word, do you prefer his writing it for you or just telling you?
5.   What kinds of materials do you like to use to practice spelling?
6.   Can you remember spelling rules? Tell me some.
7.   Do you try to spell a word by the way it sounds or by the way it looks?

Observations

Collect samples of spelling errors through informal writing or the administration of a list of spelling words.

1.   Do student's errors indicate he does not know some phonic elements? (nonappropriate phonetic substitution)
2.   Do the student's errors indicate he does not hear some of the phonetic elements? (omission of a letter or letters to represent a sound or syllable; or substitution of a letter or letters with a similar sound)
3.   Do the student's errors indicate he is unaware of the most common spelling rules?
4.   Do the student's errors indicate a poor visual memory? (errors on

common nonphonetic words, but not on phonetic words; confusion of homonyms)

5. Do the student's errors indicate a problem with visual or auditory sequencing? (reversals such as *was-saw; upset-setup*)
6. Does the student have poor handwriting?

Informal Tests

Dictate a list of words such as those in Figure 4.5 that reflect auditory abilities, visual abilities, and knowledge of spelling conventions. Analyze student performance.

FIGURE 4.5.   Diagnostic spelling test

Directions: Pronounce the word; use the word in a sentence; repeat the word.

LIST ONE: Words with Silent Letters, Requiring Visual Memory

1. store   We went to the store.
2. often   We went there often.
3. high   How high can you jump?
4. laugh   She made me laugh.
5. write   Will you write me a letter?
6. hour   We were there an hour.
7. wait   We didn't like to wait.
8. loan   Please loan me your pencil.
9. would   Would you go with me?
10. light   Please turn on the light.

LIST TWO: Words Spelled Phonetically, Requiring Ability to Hear and Write Sounds

1. wish   Make a wish.
2. bat   I have a ball and a bat.
3. this   This is my pencil.
4. fed   I fed my dog.
5. open   Please open the door.
6. last   This is my last piece of paper.

FIGURE 4.5.   Continued

7. find   I can't find it.
8. chip   There is a chip out of this cup.
9. bus   We rode on the bus.
10. test   I took a test.

          LIST THREE: Words Illustrating Common Spelling Rules or Conventions

1. stopped   She stopped the car.
2. glasses   Do you wear glasses?
3. coming   He is coming home.
4. flies   My friend flies a plane.
5. cookies   We had cookies and milk.
6. cutting   We will be cutting wood.
7. hoped   I hoped you would come.
8. using   Are you using your ruler?
9. finally   We finally went home.
10. beginning   We were beginning to get tired.

Examiner's Conclusions

____ 1.   Spelling appropriate for reading level.

____ 2.   Appears not to know the following phonetic elements:

_____

____ 3.   Appears to have difficulty in discriminating: (list the specific vowels and consonants)

_____

_____

____ 4.   Appears to have difficulty in discriminating inflectional endings and suffixes.

____ 5.   Student is unaware of the following common spelling conventions:

_____

____ 6.   Appears to have poor visual memory.

FIGURE 4.6.   Student record form levels 1–3

Name: _____

Teacher: _____

Date: _____

Obs.*	Sat.*	
		I. SIGHT WORDS
		A. Word list level is this: PP, P, 1, 2, 3. o†
		B. Has difficulty with automaticity. –
		C. Needs help with meanings of sight words. –
		D. Has the following configuration confusions: –
		E. Sight word recognition (is, is not) aided by context. o
		F. Results of Mills Test indicate sight words are best learned by o

I.   SIGHT WORDS
    A.   Word list level is this: PP, P, 1, 2, 3.   o†
    B.   Has difficulty with automaticity.   –
    C.   Needs help with meanings of sight words.   –
    D.   Has the following configuration confusions: –

    E.   Sight word recognition (is, is not) aided by context.   o
    F.   Results of Mills Test indicate sight words are best learned by   o

II.   SOUND-SYMBOL ASSOCIATION, STRUCTURAL ANALYSIS, PROBLEM SOLVING
    A.   Sound-Symbol Association   –
        1.   Needs help learning the alphabet.   –
        2.   Needs help in visual discrimination of words and in left-to-right sequencing.   –
        3.   Needs help in attending to critical features:
           ____ of letters   –
           ____ descendents and ascendents   –
           ____ reversals   –
        4.   Appears to lack the following sound-symbol associations: –
           ____ single consonant
           errors (circle):   *r, n, l, m, z, s, f, y, t, k, p, j, h, b, t, v, w, d, k, z, c, g,* soft *c, g*   –
           ____ consonant combination
           errors (circle):   *sh, ch, th, wh, ph, bl, fl, gl, pl, sl, cl, br, cr, dr, fr, gr, pr, tr, st, scr,*

*Key: Observed, date. Satisfactory, date.
†Code: Depending on circumstances, behavior + may be helpful
                                      – may be detrimental
                                      o may provide information to plan instruction

FIGURE 4.6.   Continued

Obs.*	Sat.*	

sn, sm, spl, str, sw, sp, dr, sc, shr, sk, sch, tw, thr, wr –

____ single vowel
errors (circle):   short sounds of *a, e, i, o, u*
long sounds of *a, e, i, o, u* –

____ vowel combination
errors (circle):   *oo, ou, ai, oy, oi, ay, au, ea, oe, oa, ee* –

____ *r* controlled
vowels (circle);   *or, ir, ur, aw, ar, er* –

____ silent letter
phonograms
(circle):   listen, comb, knee, light, could, write, fudge, laugh, bought, ocean, straight, through, rough –

____ common phonograms
(circle):

at	*an*	*it*	*ap*
in	*on*	*et*	*ay*
all	*en*	*ad*	*un*
ate	*ell*	___	___ –

B.   Structural Analysis Skills
   1.   Needs help in the following structural analysis skills:
      ____ inflectional endings
      (circle):   *s, es, ing, ed* –
      ____ common prefixes
      (circle):   *sub, dis, pre, pro, ex, con, un, in, be, en, re, de* –
      ____ common suffixes
      (circle):   *ness, ly, est, ful, ing, ant, er, ment, tion, less, ous, ive, able* –
      ____ errors on multisyllabic words –
      ____ errors on compound words –
   2.   Needs help using configuration clues. –
C.   Problem Solving
   1.   Needs help in eliminating ineffective strategies and learning the following new strategies:
      ____ a systematic approach to the identification of unfamiliar words. +
      ____ a spelling approach –
      ____ an initial consonant-context approach + .

FIGURE 4.6.   Continued

Obs.*	Sat.*

      ____ a phonetic approach +

      ____ blend sounds +

      ____ use context +

      ____ regress to aid word recognition +

      ____ make errors in ____ beginning ____ middle or ____
      end of words –

      ____ attempt to analyze the entire word +

      ____ read at an appropriate rate +

      ____ use knowledge of common phonograms and sound
      symbol association to recognize words not seen
      before +

      ____ letter by letter sounding (ex.: "cuh/ah/tuh" for
      cat) –

    2. Needs help in eliminating the following syntactic-semantic
     applications and learning the following new applications:

      ____ inappropriate surface structure word substitutions –

      ____ inappropriate deep structure substitutions –

      ____ dialect substitutions o

      ____ regress to obtain meaning +

      ____ use appropriate phrasing +

      ____ respond appropriately to punctuation +

      ____ more errors in long than short sentences –

      ____ errors in anaphora constructions –

  D. Needs help in predicting writer's use of a word. +

  E. Needs help in associating new learnings with old. +

  F. Needs help in retaining new associations. +

  G. Needs help in systematically applying his or her knowledge. +

  H. Needs help in transferring new learning. +

 III. COMPREHENSION

  A. Problems with show or inaccurate word recognition appear to
   be interfering with comprehension. –

  B. Overly concerned with accurate word perception to the detriment of comprehension. –

  C. Slow rate appears to be interfering with comprehension. –

  D. Problems responding appropriately to punctuation marks. –

  E. Is not attending to meaning. –

  F. Comparison of listening comprehension to silent and oral comprehension indicates student may have _____ potential for growth in reading comprehension. o

FIGURE 4.7.   Student priorities levels 1–3 mature students

Directions: On first reading with student, place a check for each area of student concern. Explain each item as necessary. Select columns and items for responses that seem pertinent. Then, reread with student, indicating first, second, third, and fourth choices of student.

I. I need specific help with   (or) I. I need specific help with

    A. ____ the letters of the alphabet

    A. ____ short words

    B. ____ the sounds for the letters of the alphabet

    B. ____ long words

    C. ____ meanings of words

    C. ____ sounds of each letter

    D. ____ remembering what I hear

    D. ____ sounds of letters together

    E. ____ understanding what I hear

    E. ____ reading faster

    F. ____ writing my name

    F. ____ meanings of words

    G. ____ reading street signs

    G. ____ understanding what I read

    H. ____ using the telephone book

    H. ____ remembering what I read

    I. ____ reading directions

    I. ____ remembering what I hear

    J. ____ reading words on food packages

    J. ____ spelling

    K. ____ reading menus

    K. ____ handwriting

    L. ____ reading the *TV Guide*

    L. ____ how to study

II. I want to study words connected with

    A. The courses I am taking in _____

    _____

    B. My job as a (manual, directories, directions) _____

    _____

    C. My practical needs such as (forms, maps, schedules) _____

    _____

    D. My hobby _____

    _____

FIGURE 4.7.   Continued

III. I like to read about _____

_____

_____

FIGURE 4.8.   Term record

Name: _____

Term: _____

Initial Materials Placement: _____

Hours	2	4	6	8	10	12	14	16	18	20
Tutor										
Date										
Rdg. Level										

Hours	22	24	26	28	30	32	34	36	38	40
Tutor										
Date										
Rdg. Level										

Comments (Please Date):

Final Materials Placement: _____
Final Evaluation Narrative:

CHAPTER 5

Integrating Diagnosis and Remediation on Beginning Reading Levels

A review of diagnostic and remedial methods is placed in perspective with a discussion of language process functioning, typical learning approaches, the effects of auditory and visual processing, and the role of affect in learning.

Information obtained from interviews, observations, and tests (cue collection) must be integrated with the students' language process functioning; their responses to instructional formats and sequences; their auditory and visual processing; and their feelings, attitudes, and habits.

LANGUAGE PROCESS FUNCTIONING

To examine the psycholinguistic functioning of the student, the diagnostician should review information under Chapter 3 categories such as Verbal Abilities, Comprehension, Problem-Solving Strategies, Sensory-Based Difficulties, and Affect. The students' behaviors can then be analyzed according to their language concepts and modes of behavior. Most of us take important concepts of language for granted and may be unaware that they may be lacking in older, severely disabled students or young children. The following are the kinds of language concepts beginning readers should learn and disabled readers may have missed.

Experience precedes speaking and writing.

67

What is written becomes reading.

A word is a meaning unit.

Words have boundaries (*cupacoffee* is not one word).

Any speech sound can be recorded with letters of the alphabet.

Words that sound alike may have different spellings and meanings.

Word order provides expectancy cues to meaning.

Speech sounds can be segmented by syllables and single letter sounds.

Letter order in written words is related to phoneme sequence in spoken words.

Redundancy of language and language patterns facilitates language production.

Punctuation provides cues to meaning.

Determiners (example: *the, an, a, this, my*) predict nouns in sentences.

Word, phrase, sentence, paragraph, and book meaning cannot be separated.

Experience determines what we can understand.

These are a few of the understandings that underlie one's ability to become a proficient processor of written language. The diagnostician needs to learn what concepts of language students have acquired and which they will need to learn. This is not to say, however, that students need to be able to verbalize the concepts.

Next the students' modes of language processing need to be studied. Some students have the concepts they need, but they may not apply their knowledge. Feelings, attitudes, and habits interact with language concepts; and whereas some of these interactions are helpful to students, others are not.

The behaviors in Table 5.1 are typical of the beginning reader

TABLE 5.1   LANGUAGE PROCESSING BEHAVIORS

Enhances Printed Language Processing	*Inhibits Printed Language Processing*
Predicts appropriate words from sentence word order	Reluctant to guess
Predicts appropriate words from underlying meaning	Makes wild guesses
Uses initial consonant and context to guess	Attends to only part of a word
Looks for familiar word parts	Makes substitutions by similar configuration

TABLE 5.1   Continued

Enhances Printed Language Processing	Inhibits Printed Language Processing
Confirms guess by quickly matching sounds in left-to-right fashion through entire word	Uses a spelling approach to identify words
Confirms guess by appropriateness to context	Does not attend to meaning
Approximates pronunciation by attempting alternative sounds of letters	Uses letter-by-letter sounding: *cah-a-tuh*
Approximates pronunciation by shifting accent	Does not attempt to self-correct
Reads prepositions as parts of phrases	Reads in a slow, word-by-word fashion
Growing toward increasing automaticity in word recognition	Has difficulty in attending
	Seems not to intend to remember; no rehearsal activity observable

INSTRUCTIONAL APPROACHES
AND SEQUENCES

The next major consideration is the learning approach best suited to the student. Will he learn better with a deductive, an inductive, an intensive semantic, or an operant approach? Suppose the student lacked the association of the silent letter phonogram *ight* and its pronunciation. Before selecting or preparing materials, the teacher needs to decide which learning approach might be most effective for the student in question. Here are some possible applications of these approaches.

Inductive Approach.   The student is to *discover* that *i-g-h-t-* is pronounded /īt/.

Example (1):
Teacher: The opposite of day is _____?_____ .
Student: Night.
Teacher: What sound do you hear at the beginning of
  night?

Student:	*Nn.*
Teacher:	[Writes *n* on the board.] What is the rest of the word?
Student:	/īt/.
Teacher:	[Adds *ight* to *n* (may use a different color chalk)] This word is *night*. What word would we have if I change *n* to *f*?
Student:	Fight.
Teacher:	[Continues with other substitutions.]

Example (2):

The student is given analogies to solve, as: *late* is to *rate* as *light* is to _____ (*take, bite*).

Deductive Approach.   The student is told that *ight* is pronounced /īt/ and is asked to *apply* his knowledge to other words.

Teacher:	[Writes *fight* on the board.] This word is *fight*. The letters *g* and *h* are silent. [Adds slashes over *g, h* in word *fight*.] Here is a list of words that end in *i-g-h-t* [points to list]. You are to write the appropriate word for each blank in the sentences on the page I will give you. Find the word you need on the chart.

Intensive Semantic Approach.   The student will recall the forms of words with the phonogram *ight* through close attending and meaningful *associations*.

Teacher:	[Shows card with word *light*.] This word is *light*. How many letters does it have?
Student:	Five.
Teacher:	How many of the letters are tall?
Student:	Three.
Teacher:	How many letters go below the line?
Student:	One.
Teacher:	What does light mean?
Student:	A lamp.
Teacher:	What else?
Student:	Red light-green light.
Teacher:	Imagine the most beautiful light you have ever

seen. Close your eyes and try to see it. [pause]
Tell me about what you imagined.

[Later student is asked to find pictures from a magazine that refer to "light," cut them out, and paste them on a collage that contains the word.]

Operant Approach.   The student will *respond* to the phonogram *ight* with its correct pronunciation through shaping and reward.

The student is given a paper with a programmed exercise presented frame by frame, as:

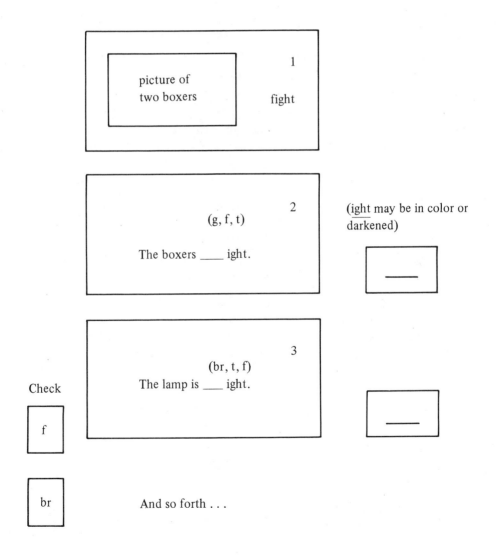

These are a few examples of instructional sequences based on theories of learning. For students with severe problems, it would be desirable for the instructor to engage in trial teaching to find the optimum instructional approach resulting in the largest gains and the most positive feelings. Teachers should select a concept or process to be learned, plan two or more alternative instructional sequences, and observe the outcome. Students may be involved, if possible, in the decision as to the best method.

AUDITORY-VISUAL PROCESSING

To determine strengths and weaknesses in auditory and visual areas, the diagnostician should first consult the Student Record and then review the interview, observation, and test results indicated as significant by the conclusions on the Student Record. The next step is to complete the auditory-visual modality checklists (Figure 5.1) for those items that seem to apply to the student. The teacher may wish to ask the student to respond to the checklist *if* the student would not find the procedure threatening. The instructor can explain that some people seem to learn better one way than another and that the checklist is a way to get some hints on the best way a particular person learns.

If there appears to be a significant difference between the lists, instruction should begin with the stronger modality. If problems appear to be severe in both lists, the student may do better with kinesthetic-tactile approaches to learning. If both lists are similar and there are not many problems in either list, the student's other characteristics, such as a need for structure, might dictate the approach; or the instructor could use a combination approach of listening, seeing, and doing.

Although some authorities feel that such an approach is logical, much research needs to be done before we can be confident of modality diagnosis and remediation. Factors such as syntactic-semantic abilities and previous experience make modality diagnosis difficult, and there is a need to be open to the possibility of error in diagnosis and selection of method. In addition, a student's strong modality may change over time. The safest course is to determine which modality is best for the task at hand. This procedure may not be practical, in terms of time, for all learners, but it is suggested for those with severe problems.

FIGURE 5.1   Modality checklist

Difficulty in Auditory Modality	*Difficulty in Visual Modality*
____ Speech difficulties.	____ Needs to use finger or pencil to keep place while reading.
____ Problems in following oral directions.	____ Very poor handwriting.
____ Strong preference for leisure or school activities that require little or no listening to language.	____ Difficulty in copying from board or from a paper.
____ Previous failure in phonic approaches.	____ Leaves out or reverses words or letters when writing or copying.
____ Few or no sound-symbol associations, but some sight words.	____ Often confuses words that look alike (*dine, pine; dill, pill*).
____ Remembers better when shown what to do rather than told.	____ Difficulty in reading maps.
____ Prefers silent filmstrips to tapes.	____ Difficulty in remembering directions when walking or riding.
____ Spelling errors for phonetic association.	____ Often fails to notice changes in environment (objects or changes in physical appearances).
____ Trouble recalling everyday words in conversation.	____ Understands better when reads aloud than silently.
____ Difficulty in remembering assignments, phone messages without making notes.	____ Spells better aloud than in writing.
____ Inability to hear similarities in initial or final sounds of words (*big, pig; fib, fit*).	____ More nonphonetic errors in spelling than phonetic errors.
____ Inability to hear syllables within words.	____ Difficulty in describing visual characteristics of familiar people or places.
____ Difficulty in blending sounds.	____ Very slow rate of perception in visual matching of letters and words.
____ Can read better silently than orally.	____ Much difficulty in retaining sight words.
____ *Many* Spoonerisms (you hissed my mystery class, for you missed my history class).	____ Previous failure in look-say reading instructions.
	____ Better memory for what was said than for what was seen.
	____ Prefers tapes to filmstrips.
	____ Difficulty in copying figures and signs in mathematics.

MATCHING LEARNING APPROACHES
TO AUDITORY AND VISUAL
STRENGTHS

Teachers should be aware of the cautions under auditory-visual processing as they attempt to match instruction to auditory-visual-tactile-kinesthetic abilities. As with other aspects of selection of remedial procedures, they will need to observe carefully and make adjustments if their initial judgment was in error. Labeling students as "auditory learners" or "visual learners" should be avoided. Over time the student may change; he may learn some things better with an auditory emphasis, other things with a visual emphasis, and still others with a combination of methods.

Suggestions for learners who appear to be *strong in visual functioning and weak in auditory functioning:*

1. Encourage the student to look at an unfamiliar word and think of another word or a part of another word it looks like.
2. Encourage the student to create mental images to associate with words and letters in initial learning.
3. Use material that presents letters embedded in a picture. Example: ⓕ *face.* Or material that presents picture keys for words and letters. Example: ☕ *cup.* Or help the student make his own keys.
4. Use flash cards; make sight word charts.
5. Create language experience stories.
6. Choose materials that employ "whole-word," "repeated pattern" presentations.
7. Use picture and word-matching activities.
8. Employ devices such as the language master.
9. For spelling, have the student look at the word (later he might use a hand tachistoscope), close his eyes and picture it (or use the afterimage of the tachistoscopic presentation), and then "copy" the letters from the mental picture, check his work, and use the word in a sentence.
10. If copying from the board or page is a problem, have the student look at the whole word or sentence, visualize it, and then write it.

Suggestions for students who appear to be *strong in auditory functioning and weak in visual functioning:*

1. Begin with dissimilar letters and words such as *m, t* (not *d, b*) and *mop, he* (not *saw, was*).

2. Begin with high-meaning words with ascendant and descendant features as [hot] and [tiger] rather than words such as [come] and [were].

3. Teach sounds of letters first and names later. Do not teach both at once. The alphabet song is helpful for letter name-form association, if the student is not embarrassed to use it. Have him learn to listen to it *in his head.*

4. Use an alphabetic or phonovisual approach. Begin with isolated sounds (be careful *not* to say consonants followed by a vowel sound, such as *c-uh, p-uh*); then blend the sounds in high meaning words. Next teach word families (*pan, ran, fan*) with initial consonant and then consonant blend substitution. In beginning stages employ words highly consistent in sound-letter correspondence. Encourage writing of stories with basic vocabulary. Provide necessary new words as needed.

5. For students with visual acuity problems, make a referral to the appropriate professional; obtain suggestions from him for instructional procedures; avoid small fuzzy print, purple dittoes; consider special materials such as books in large print and materials for the partially sighted.

6. If students do not hear spoken words as separate ("Dyutyet?" for "Did you eat yet?") use materials with wide spaces, or draw lines between each word. Later draw lines between phrases and clauses.

7. If words are reversed, use color to highlight the first letter or confusing words, fading color in subsequent presentations, or have the student point to the beginning of each word as he reads. Later let him use a card to follow each line.

8. For writing, have the student use horizontally lined paper with margin guidelines and skip lines as he writes. Use a tracing-fading technique as necessary. Example:

    trace with pencil:

    follow dotted lines:

    fade lines:

9. For students with problems in copying, have the student say the word or sentence silently to himself before he begins to write.

10. Students strong in auditorization and weak in visualization should not be discouraged from lip moving and whispering while such support is needed. They might be encouraged to "say the words in their heads." Speed can be developed at a later time.

11. For spelling nonphonetic words: teach high-frequency generalizations (rules) or mnemonic devices or memory clues, such as the following: The question words *who, which, where, when, why, what* all start with *wh;* the verbs do not (*was, were*). Use manuscript writing to present spelling words because it is clearer than cursive.

AFFECT, LEARNING STYLE

The final consideration—and perhaps the most important—is the feelings, habits, interests, and attitudes of the students. Strong positive or negative feelings about the content of materials or the instructional activities can override other seemingly logical reasons why the plan of instruction should succeed or fail. The section in Chapter 3 dealing with *affect* should be reviewed before selecting materials or procedures for remediation.

Decisions need to be made with respect to such aspects as

1. Success or failure of previous approaches.
2. Amount of structure needed.
3. Rate of learning.
4. Amount of practice required.
5. Content of fiction or nonfiction.
6. Suitability to maturity and interests.
7. Need for variety.
8. Opportunity to transfer learning to new contexts.
9. Perception of the learner as to value of activity.
10. Frequency of opportunities for success.
11. Intrinsically interesting materials and activities.
12. Immediate feedback opportunities.
13. Opportunity for self-checking.
14. Demonstration of growth in reading.
15. Opportunities to interact successfully with others.
16. Emphasis on active learner participation.

17.   Selection of teacher or tutor who *believes* the student can succeed and transmits that belief to the student.

Summary

Diagnosticians have a complex task in selecting remedial methods and materials. They need to review

1.   Student phonological, syntactic, and semantic knowledge.
2.   Student application of the preceding understandings in processing language in reading, writing, speaking, and listening.
3.   Student response to various instructional procedures.
4.   Student abilities in auditory, visual, and other sensory areas.
5.   Student feelings, attitudes, habits, and goals.

The diagnostician should be able to justify his instruction by statements based on his observations of the student's knowledge, application of understandings, sensory abilities, feelings, and response to instructional procedures.

SOME REMEDIAL METHODS[1]

The following methods are reviewed here because they have been reported to be successful with certain types of learners. Instructors should be familiar with these methods and learn to adapt them to the particular needs and interests of their students.

Impress

In the impress method (neurological impress) teachers select materials interesting to the students on their instructional reading level. During stage one the teacher and student read aloud with the teacher's voice slightly louder and slightly ahead of the student's voice. The teacher uses her hand as a pacer with

[1] Although the term *remedial* is used here, the reader should be aware that many of these and other methods described in this book have been successful in developmental reading as well. The term *remedial* is often employed when methods require one-to-one instruction, selected for an individual.

the student taking over as soon as he feels ready to do so. During stage two the voices should be in unison with the same volume. During stage three the student's voice should lead in pace, and the teacher's voice should be soft. Throughout this experience there should be no correcting, no direct instruction, and no questioning or testing. The sessions should be frequent, but brief. Duration of use of methods and time to move from one stage to another will depend on the growth and interest of the student. This approach has been used successfully with students who have not been successful with phonic approaches. It is described more fully in Chapter 6.

Language Experience

In the initial stages of the language experience approach (LEA), the learner draws on experience to dictate his thoughts, making his own reading material. The sequence is as follows: experiencing, listening, speaking, reading, writing. The teacher provides an experience or draws on a previous experience of the learner. After discussing the topic with the learner, the teacher asks him to dictate a story, description, poem, instructions, or whatever the situation indicates. The teacher writes exactly as the student speaks, adding only punctuation marks. Next the teacher reads the material to the student and asks if the student is satisfied with what has been written. If the student wishes to make changes, they are made; otherwise, the material stands. Next the student reads the material. Through these and similar activities the student experiences communication.

Guided Reading

In guided reading (directed reading activities) the teacher selects material within the student's understanding with respect to concepts, vocabulary, and language patterns. In the readiness stage, the teacher engages the student in conversation on the topic. If any concepts or vocabulary are unknown, explanations are made. In the second stage, the teacher directs the student's psychological set by giving him a purpose for reading (read to identify, describe, evaluate . . .). The purpose should be stated clearly and briefly. The student next reads silently to find the information or answer a question. Finally, the student responds to the directive and discusses his comments. The student may reread for another purpose, his own or the teacher's, as a result of the discussion. The teacher stimulates thinking by asking such questions as, What do you think the writer will say? Why? Were you right? Why? Why not? Can you prove it?

VAKT

The visual-auditory-kinesthetic-tactile approach is often referred to as VAKT. The learner chooses a word he wishes to learn. The word is written for him in large manuscript or cursive letters. The teacher models the pronunciation and tracing of the word for the student by tracing her finger smoothly over the letters while pronouncing the word slowly, by syllables. Distortion of pronunciation should be avoided. The student then traces and pronounces the word by syllables, imitating his teacher. This is repeated until the student feels he can successfully write the word himself. The stimulus word is then covered. No copying is permitted. If the student forgets before finishing writing the word, he is not permitted to look at the stimulus word. The student returns to tracing until he once more feels ready to try again. Words are constantly reviewed. When a sufficient number of words is learned, the student is helped to write phrases, sentences, and paragraphs with the teacher supplying additional words as needed. Language experience approach (LEA) methods are used in later stages. The Fernald approach to VAKT is described in Chapter 6.

Oral Reading

There are several variations of oral reading:

1. The teacher alternates with one or more readers every other sentence or paragraph.
2. Choral reading with highly rhythmic or smooth patterns, with light and dark voices, with humorous or dramatic selections is used with groups.
3. Plays produced for poor readers or plays rewritten by the teacher for easier reading are read in small groups.
4. Taped stories, plays, or nonfiction selections are used with the reader following the text. Some are only partially taped, and the reader finishes the story on his own.

Cloze Approaches

Materials are prepared by omitting words randomly or selectively. The student is to guess a word that might be suitable for the missing one. There are several variations. When adjectives and adverbs are omitted, students who work independently to insert descriptors read these selections to each other and compare the changes in meaning. Nouns and pronouns might be removed after determiners, such as *a, the, an, some,* and stories compared. Varying amounts of structure can be provided:

1.   You must _____ when the light is red.
2.   You must _ _ _ _ when the light is red.
3.   You must s _ _ _   when the light is red.
4.   You must st _ p when the light is red.
5.   You must _____ when the light is red.

      (shall, stop)

This method can be used to help the student attend to meaning, make predictions as he reads, use context as an aid to word recognition, and attend to fine differences within words.

ANALYZING COMMERCIAL MATERIALS[2]

Just as instructors need to analyze carefully the ability of the student, so will they need to examine carefully the characteristics of materials and select those that best fit the students' needs. Teachers may sharpen their perceptions of the task by first reviewing Chapters 3 and 4 and earlier parts of this chapter and by asking themselves questions about the material such as the following:

1.   What concepts of language processing underlie the activities?
2.   What elements of phonological, syntactic, and semantic knowledge are present?
3.   Do the activities emphasize listening, speaking, reading, and/or writing?

[2] A list of materials is presented for the convenience of the reader at the end of this chapter in Figure 5.3.

4. Are heavy demands made on visual or auditory abilities?
5. What is the pace of the presentation (gradual introduction of concepts, opportunities for practice)?
6. What is the underlying learning theory or theories exemplified by the activities?
7. Is the format appealing?
8. Is the content suited to the maturity and interest of the students?
9. Are the activities suited to individual responses or group interaction?
10. What opportunities are present for the student to attain automaticity and fluency?

INITIAL PLANS FOR REMEDIATION

With all the things to learn and to consider about the student and with all there is to learn about remedial methods and materials, many new instructors feel somewhat confused. However, the diagnostic-remedial process is not separate; it is intermixed. Therefore, instructors should expect to learn more about their students and adjust their instruction as they work with each student, for each is different.

To begin, teachers should find materials and activities on the students' levels of functioning. If a student brings in something he very much wants to read and the material is quite difficult, the material may be read to him, working with a few words or a short excerpt from the material. After locating materials on the student's level, the teacher may show two or three sets of the material to the student and let him make the selection. Later, teacher and student can discuss the material and change it, if necessary. Whenever possible, the teacher should work with the student's strengths.

An effective plan for the teacher is to be prepared every day with something to teach, something for fun, and something for practice. Some teachers keep on hand a snack to share, if the student is hungry, or will offer something to drink. They should take occasional breaks. Although teachers must be sensitive to problems, they must avoid being led into daily rap sessions.

From time to time the instructor might review this and earlier sections of this book in order to evaluate growth and adjust instructional procedures. She should continually ask herself:

1. What does the student need to learn?
2. What is the best way for the student to learn?

3.   How does the student feel about what he is doing?
4.   What evidence do I have for my answers to the preceding questions?

In order to keep track of the complex interaction of conditions of in-struction with processes and skills to be acquired, instructors might make charts similar to Figure 5.2. Only those parts need to be completed that per-tain to each student. As the instructors fill in the charts, they should reflect on encounters they have had with their students, the cues mentioned in Chapters 2, 3, and 4, and suggestions in this chapter. Instructors should have a rationale for each decision based on their observations.

Student Name _____

Instructor _____

FIGURE 5.2   Analysis of remedial approach

	Structure			Methods/Materials										Instructional Format				Sensory Emphasis			
	Low	Moderate	High	Workbook	Tape and Filmstrip	Tape	Programmed	Oral Rdg.	Guided Rdg.	Trade Books	Impress	Controlled Vocabulary	LEA	I. Semantic	Operant	Inductive	Deductive	VAKT	A-V	Visual	Auditory
1. Sight Words a. Initial Stock b. Dolch																					
2. Sound-Symbol Association (specify)																					
3. Comprehension a. Vocabulary b. Literal c. Inferential																					
4. Fluency a. Automaticity b. Phrasing c. Flexibility																					
5. Writing a. Handwriting b. Expression																					
6. Spelling																					

FIGURE 5.3.   Instructional materials

I. MATERIALS FOR READING READINESS OR RELATED SKILLS

TITLE	INTEREST LEVEL	PUBLISHER
Creative Involvement Cards	Elementary	Benefic
Goldman-Lynch Sounds and Symbols Development Kit	Elementary and Jr. High	American Guidance Service
Distar Language I and II	Elementary	Science Research Associates
Language and Thinking Program	Elementary	Follett
Listening for Speech Sounds	Elementary	Harper & Row
Peabody Language Development	Prekindergarten and Elementary	American Guidance Service

II. BEGINNING READING LEVELS (1–3)

TITLE	INTEREST LEVEL	PUBLISHER
Aud-X Programs	Elementary, Secondary & Adult	Educational Development Laboratories
Conquests in Reading	Secondary and Adult	Webster
Dr. Spello	Secondary and Adult	Webster
Dolch Word Cards (and many other games and devices)	Elementary and Secondary	Garrard
Get Set Games	Elementary	Houghton Mifflin
Language Experiences in Reading Program	Elementary	Encyclopaedia Britannica
Lift-Off to Reading	Elementary	Science Research Associates
Macmillan Reading Spectrum	Elementary	Macmillan
Michigan Language Program	Elementary, Secondary, and Adult	Ann Arbor Press
Mott Basic Language Skills Program Beginning Reading	Secondary Adult	Allied Education Council
Peabody Rebus Reading Program	Elementary	American Guidance Service

FIGURE 5.3.   Continued

II. BEGINNING READING LEVELS (1–3)

TITLE	INTEREST LEVEL	PUBLISHER
Phonovisual Method	Elementary	Phonovisual Products
Programmed Reading Series (Buchanan & Sullivan)	Elementary Secondary Adult	McGraw-Hill
Remedial Reading Series Programmed (Sullivan)	Elementary Secondary Adult	Behavioral Research Laboratory
RX Reading Program	Elementary Secondary Adult	Psychotechnics
Scope	Secondary	Scholastic
Sprint	Secondary	Scholastic
Speech-to-Print Phonics	Elementary	Harcourt, Brace, Jovanovich
Webster Word Wheels	Elementary	Webster/McGraw-Hill
Words in Color	Elementary Secondary Adult	Xerox
Writing Manual for Teaching the Left Handed	Elementary	Educators Publishing
Writing Road to Reading	Elementary	William Morrow & Co.

III. EQUIPMENT

NAME	TYPE	SOURCE
Flash-X	Small, Mechanical Tachistoscope	Educational Developmental Laboratories
Language Master	Card/Tape-recorder Reader	Bell & Howell
Tach-X	Tachistoscope, Projector	Educational Developmental Laboratories
T-Matic 150	Tachistoscope, Projector	Psychotechnics

CHAPTER 6

Special Methods of Remediation in Reading and Spelling

The methods discussed in this chapter have often proved effective when other techniques have failed. They are presented in brief form here but should not be used without reading the original sources cited for each approach.

This chapter presents an overview of some special methods formulated for students experiencing great difficulties in reading. A careful reading of the summary of each approach should serve as an introduction to the techniques described. As many remedial teachers, including the writer, have found these methods to be successful for students who have failed with other techniques, students of diagnosis and remediation should become adept in using these procedures.

FERNALD METHOD

An effective approach that emphasizes tracing and language experience sequences is presented by Grace Fernald.[1] Visual, auditory, kinesthetic, and tactile (VAKT) senses are employed in the learning process. This is termed an analytical method in that whole words are studied from the beginning of in-

[1] Grace M. Fernald, *Remedial Techniques in Basic School Subjects* (New York: McGraw-Hill Book Company, 1943). Permission to describe the Fernald approach has been granted by the McGraw-Hill Book Company.

struction, in contrast to synthetic methods that begin with letter sounds and word parts. Sound-symbol associations are acquired inductively. Words are pronounced by syllables rather than letter-by-letter.

Those with total or extreme disability are guided through four stages, as follows:

Stage 1.   The student selects the word he wishes to learn. The word is written for the student by his teacher with a crayon in large script or manuscript. As the student watches and listens, the teacher pronounces the word as she writes it. The word is pronounced slowly, by syllables, without distortion. Next the teacher demonstrates tracing, with one or two fingers, and pronunciation by syllables. This is paced, so that the voice and finger begin each syllable concurrently. (V-A)

Now the student traces over the word, using the technique of his teacher. He is checked to be sure he keeps finger contact and pronounces the word without distortion. (V-K-T) The student is told to trace and pronounce the word as many times as he feels is necessary so that he will be able to write the word without looking at it. The student is *not* permitted to copy the word.

When the student indicates he is ready, he writes the word without the copy, pronouncing the word aloud or to himself while writing. If the student stops or makes an error, he returns to tracing until he feels ready once more.

After the student has written the word correctly, he writes the word in context, that is, a sentence or paragraph. This is typed for him within twenty-four hours, and he reads his "story" in print. There is no restriction on the words or subject the student chooses to write about. What is important is that the words and content, coming from his own experiences and oral language, are meaningful.

After his story is finished, the student files his words alphabetically. These words are reviewed periodically, and the student refers to them to check his work from time to time.

The teacher may chart the number of words learned, number of tracings required for each, and retention of the words over time.

Stage 2.   Stage 2 is the same as stage 1 except that tracing is no longer required to learn a word. The student looks at the word he has requested his teacher to write for him and says it over to himself while looking at it. When the student feels ready, he writes the word, without copying, saying each part as he writes.

The student continues to do a great deal of writing with his production quickly typed so that he can read it in print. The transition between stages 1 and 2 may be gradual, with some words learned by tracing and others learned by looking, saying, and writing.

A smaller file box is used in this stage, for words written by the teacher are in normal size rather than chalkboard size, as in stage 1.

Stage 3.   In stage 3 the student learns new words directly from the printed word without having the word written for him. He begins to read books, in addition to his own writing. Words he doesn't know are pronounced for him on request and underlined. The student studies the words by saying and writing them as in stage 2. These words are added to his file and reviewed periodically.

Stage 4.   In stage 4 the student begins to generalize to new words from the words he knows. He is encouraged to read as much fiction and/or nonfiction as he wishes on subjects of his own choosing.

To help him read more easily, the student is encouraged to look over material to find words he doesn't know. The student is helped with the pronunciation and/or meaning of these before reading. Retention of new words is aided by the student's repeating the word as he looks at it and writing the word on scrap paper. If a word is missed in oral reading that is a common word the student should know, it is recorded for later study. The only "sounding out" of words that is permitted is in prereading in certain cases, but sounding is not allowed in the course of sustained reading.

At the conclusion of his work the student should be able to recognize new words easily, have an adequate reading vocabulary, and be able to perceive word groups so that he reads smoothly and fluently with comprehension.

Spelling.   The general procedures for teaching spelling that can be adapted for groups or individuals are these:

1.   The teacher writes the word on the chalkboard or paper.
2.   The teacher pronounces the word distinctly, without distortion, and the students pronounce the word clearly and distinctly, repeating as necessary.
3.   Students study the word by visualizing it with their eyes closed or saying it softly or tracing it, depending on which is the best method for each individual.
4.   When they indicate they are ready, the word is erased, and students write it from memory.

5. The work is checked, and the word is written a second time.
6. The word is used in written expression.
7. Use of the dictionary is taught and encouraged to avoid practicing an incorrect spelling.
8. Misspelled words in the student's papers are crossed out so they are obliterated with a crayon or marking pen; the correct spelling is written above the error. These words are studied by the student, and his original passage is dictated to him when he indicates he is ready. A file box or alphabetized notebook can be used to keep track of words he is learning so they can be rechecked or used as a reference.

GILLINGHAM-STILLMAN METHOD

A highly structured approach to phonetic associations that uses visual, auditory, and kinesthetic elements (VAK) is presented by Gillingham and Stillman,[2] who were strongly influenced by the work of Samuel T. Orton, M.D.

Their program has been described as *synthetic* in that they begin with sounds and build them into words rather than beginning with words and analyzing their sounds as in the *analytic* approach.

The visual forms and sounds that are most regular are introduced first. Care is taken, also, that potentially confusing elements such as *b* and *d* are not introduced together. This system emphasizes language regularities.

The sequence of VAK associations has been as carefully planned as the content. The associations are presented as follows:

I.   A.   The name of the letter is associated with its printed symbol. The teacher shows a letter and says its name. (V-A) The pupil looks at the letter and repeats its name. (A-K) (Here kinesthetic refers to the student's feel of his speech organs as he produces a sound.)

B.   The sound of the letter is next associated with its printed symbol, as in the preceding item. (V-A and A-K)

---

[2] Anna Gillingham and Bessie W. Stillman, *Remedial Training for Children with Specific Disability in Reading, Spelling and Penmanship*, 7th ed. (Cambridge, Mass.: Educators Publishing Service, Inc., 1974). Permission to describe the Gillingham-Stillman approach has been granted by the Educators Publishing Service, Inc.

II.   The sound of the letter is associated with its name. (A-A) The teacher says the letter's sound (not visible) and asks for the name of the letter that has the sound she produced.

III. A.   The form of the letter is associated with its written production. (V-K and K-V) The teacher makes the letter as the student observes; then the student traces, copies, writes from memory, and writes with eyes averted.

   B.   The written production of the letter is associated with its sound. (A-K) The teacher makes the sound of the letter and asks the student to write the letter that has the sound she has produced.

Letters are learned with key words. For example, the correct student response to exposure of the *a* card is, "Apple\ă\." After ten letter names and sounds are known by all associations, visual, auditory, and kinesthetic, blending begins. For example, drill cards with *t, a,* and *p* are put before the student, who is asked to give their sounds rapidly in succession until he perceives he is saying a word. The student is encouraged to say the first two sounds together, *ta–p.*

After blending has started, the student is helped to analyze spoken words in order to spell them. He listens to a word pronounced, for example, *pat,* and finds the letter among his drill cards for the beginning, then the middle, and finally the ending sounds. The spelling sequence requires that the student (1) pronounce the word *pat,* (2) name the letters *p–a–t,* (3) write, naming each letter as he writes it, *p–a–t,* and (4) read the word he has written, *pat.*

When the student has learned to read several words made from the ten letters in the first group, he begins to read short stories composed with words he knows. He is asked to read sentence by sentence after silently preparing himself for each sentence so that his reading "sounds like talking." The same stories can be used for dictation exercises where care is taken with proper letter formation and spacing to develop the student's penmanship. Thus, the student progesses in reading, spelling, and handwriting through each set of letters.

Rules for pronunciation are provided, and the student is drilled in their application. Instructions in dictionary use are given for pronunciation of irregular words.

To use this method, teachers will require the manual *Remedial Training for Children with Specific Disability in Reading, Spelling and Penmanship* by Anna Gillingham and Bessie W. Stillman, as well as the drill cards published by Educators Publishing Service. It may be helpful to seek instruction from the Orton Society to perfect teaching techniques for this approach.

HEGGE-KIRK-KIRK METHOD

The Hegge, Kirk, and Kirk approach is described in *Remedial Reading Drills.*[3] This method, too, may be described as a synthetic approach because instruction begins with drill on isolated letter sounds. However, in later instruction words are pronounced for the student who analyzes the sounds in order to write the words he hears. Disabled readers of normal and subnormal intelligence have been successful with the drills.

This method, in brief, requires the student to sound each word letter-by-letter; blend the sounds together; say the word, then write the word, pronouncing each sound as he writes. (Letter names are not emphasized.) The following parts are included in the book:

Introducing the Method.   The student is given a preview of the method, and an effort is made to help him realize that he can be successful. He is shown the letters *s, a, c, t,* and *p.* If the student doesn't know their sounds, he is given instruction. (The hard sound of *c* is taught.) For example, *a* is written on the board, and he is told that /ă–ă–ă/ is the sound a crying baby makes. Then the *a* is erased, and the student writes the letter and says the sound as he writes. This is repeated as necessary. The other letters are taught in a similar fashion with appropriate vivid associations. When the sounds of all five letters have been mastered, the student is presented with the word *cat* and asked to say the sounds, then blend them to say /căt/. Blending is accomplished by having the student say the sounds at his own rate, then faster and faster until the blend is made. (Other suggestions for blending are offered.) Next *cat, pat, tap, cap, at, sap,* and *sat* are presented on paper or on the chalkboard, and the student is helped to say these words. The student is told that he can learn other words in this fashion and that he can start with short words and then go on to longer words.

Part I.   After the student knows the sounds of most single consonants and the ă sound and can blend sounds, he begins the first drill, which consists of lists of three-letter words containing ă. Examples: *lap, wag, ran, dad, ham, fan,* and so forth.

---

[3] Thorleif G. Hegge, Samuel A. Kirk, and Winifred D. Kirk, *Remedial Reading Drills* (Ann Arbor, Mich.: George Wahr Publishing Company, 1965). Permission to describe the Hegge, Kirk, and Kirk approach has been granted by the George Wahr Publishing Company.

Drill two consists of words containing ŏ, as *hot, pop, fog, sod, rob, hop.* Drill three is a review of *a* and *o* words in a mixed presentation.

Drills in the first part include the short vowels, long vowels, consonant combinations, vowel combinations, and some common phonograms. The student voices the words sound by sound (as they are presented visually), blends the sounds, pronounces the words, and writes the words from dictation.

Examples of the visual presentation in the first half of a drill:

d	ee	d	f	ee	d	‖	r	ate	p	ine
b	ee	r	d	ee	r	‖	c	ape	t	ape

At the end of a drill:

deem	reel	‖	made	wine
leek	heel	‖	poke	rope

Part II.   Drills in the second part contain many combinations of sounds, such as *ink, ang, ound, ill,* and *est.*

Part III.   Drills contain advanced sounds such as *aw, ew, ly, ge (j), ce, ci (s), ought, sion,* and *tion.*

Part IV.   Drills contain exceptions to previously taught configurations; combinations such as *kn, gn, ph, wr, ould, ous, eigh, ois,* and *ex*; compound words; some generalizations such as those regarding final *e*, changing *y* to *ies, ied,* and other plurals and exercises for letter confusions. In the later drills the student moves from sounding in small units. Example: *p-i-n* into larger units, *p-in.*

Sentence Reading.   Sentence reading may begin with words the student has learned in his drills and a few words presented as whole words. For example: *The cat had the rat. Pat the fat cat.*

Story Reading.   Generally, the student does not begin to read from books until he has completed Part I, or at least the first twenty drills. Books with many phonetically regular words, mature in content, without picture stories, are selected for beginning reading. Words that cannot be sounded according to the drills the student has mastered are pronounced for him by the teacher. The teacher keeps a record of common words she repeatedly supplies for the student and provides special drills to enable the student to master these, such as having him write them or practice them with flash cards.

HECKLEMAN IMPRESS METHOD

The neurological impress technique, a system of unison reading, differs from other remedial approaches in that emphasis is on hearing and pronouncing words in context rather than attending to letter-sound correspondences to words in isolation. R.G. Heckleman has described the approach in detail. The following outline provides an overview of his method:[4]

1. Select material a little below the student's instructional reading level to start, but rapidly increase the level of difficulty as sessions progress.

2. Briefly explain to the student that he is not to be concerned with application of specific reading skills but should try to move his eyes across the lines at the same time the words are being spoken by the student and teacher, together.

3. Seat the student slightly in front of the teacher so that the teacher's voice is close to the student's ear.

4. In the first stage of unison reading, the teacher's hand is used for pacing, and the teacher's voice is slightly louder and slightly ahead of the student's voice. If the student and teacher have difficulty in adjusting to each other's rate, the initial lines or paragraphs may be repeated several times. Teachers using this technique may ask someone to observe them to be sure they are synchronizing voice, finger movements, and words.

5. At times the teacher may drop in volume and rate so that the student leads. If desired, the student takes over the finger movement. Pacing, however, is important, and the student should be moved along to increasingly faster rates. No questioning, testing, instructing, or drilling is used with this technique.

6. Heckleman has suggested that the daily sessions should be about fifteen minutes in length and instructional time should total about eight

[4] R.G. Heckleman, "Using the Neurological Impress Remedial Reading Technique," *Academic Therapy Quarterly,* Vol. I, No. 4, San Rafael, California. Permission to describe the Heckleman approach has been granted by Academic Therapy Publishers, Inc.

to twelve hours. This, of course, is a guide, and adjustment may be made to allow for student differences.

7.   If the student does not respond to the NIM. technique within four hours of instruction, Heckleman suggests using other methods or the "echoing" technique. In this procedure the teacher has the student repeat phrases, then sentences. For example:

He wanted to play football.

The teacher says, "To play football," and the student repeats. Then the teacher says, "He wanted to play football," and the student repeats the entire sentence, imitating the teacher's inflection. After several oral repetitions the teacher and student read the sentence aloud together. The "echoing" procedure may be helpful for some students with auditory discrimination or oral expression difficulties.

BECOMING PROFICIENT WITH SPECIAL METHODS

To become proficient with the previously described methods, the teacher will need to (1) read the original source describing the method, *carefully* and (2) practice each method under observation.

All too often teachers report that a particular approach has failed when, after questioning, the situation that is revealed is a failure on the part of the teacher to apply the technique properly. Not reading carefully is a behavior that can afflict reading teachers as well as others. Even advanced graduate students in reading have used shortcuts such as attempting to apply a technique from a handout or a brief summary or a quick superficial reading of an original source.

A technique the writer has found helpful in workshops and courses designed to help teachers acquire skill in special remedial techniques is the shifting triad simulation. Each participant prepares a lesson using a special method. Another participant serves as the student, and a third is the observer. The observer is held responsible for noting teacher strengths and teacher violations of techniques, as well as slowness or clumsiness that might inhibit learning. After a lesson presentation and debriefing, the participants in the triad shift roles. This procedure is repeated as needed until everyone is proficient with at least four approaches. It is hoped that this will lessen the likelihood of producing a teacher who uses only one technique for all students.

The final step is for the total group to analyze each approach with regard to factors such as its demands on the learner, abilities of the learner, evaluation of effects, and possible need for method adaptation.

MATCHING APPROACHES
TO STUDENTS

A question frequently asked by teachers is, How can one decide which technique would be most efficacious for a particular student? At the present time there is no reliable way of matching a technique to a set of student behaviors. The best procedure would seem to involve a careful analysis of the *total* student—his feelings, attitudes, instructional history, auditory, and visual abilities, cognitive functioning, duration of attending under various conditions, and so forth—then to select *tentatively* an approach that would seem to be suitable and test it for a reasonable length of time.

There are some criteria for method selection that would seem to be logical. For instance, if a student seems to have great difficulty in hearing fine differences of sounds within words, then a method that stresses such an approach should probably be avoided. An exception to this would be a situation in which the source of the student's inability was simply that he had not been taught. This can be discovered by some trial teaching to learn whether the student can *learn* to discriminate fine sound differences without undue effort. If not, one might consider avoiding single-letter sounding methods in favor of a syllabication technique, that is, sounding words by parts. In cases where even the syllabication procedure would not be desirable because of student difficulty in hearing syllable breaks, the teacher might consider a whole word approach. An opposite example: if a student is strong in auditory skills but seems to be weak in visual memory, one might reason that he would do best with a technique that avoids drill or flashing sight words but rather focuses on sound-symbol association. If the student does have sound-symbol associations but is overanalytical, an approach that emphasizes context and fluency should be considered.

Overriding these ideas, of course, is the attitude of the student toward a particular approach. If the student sees it as babyish or making him appear stupid or as simply tedious drill with no payoff in his progress, he will be unlikely to put forth much effort. It is important to discuss procedures and progress with the student and enlist his cooperation in giving an approach a fair trial.

CHAPTER 7

Assessment of Abilities in Comprehension

This chapter provides cues for the diagnosis of disabled readers who have acquired most or all of the word-recognition abilities but remain deficient in reading comprehension commensurate with their age/grade expectancy level.

Three major difficulties faced by the diagnostician seeking to understand a student's comprehension abilities are (1) the number of factors that influence comprehension, (2) the interrelatedness of the factors, and (3) the range of abstractness of the factors.

Although much remains to be learned about the nature of language comprehension, several aspects appear to be important:

association	learning names for objects and ideas
conception	abstracting elements to categorize objects and ideas
perception	attending to selected information
syntactic-semantic interpretation	inferring meaning from word order and word use
reasoning	using logic and critical thinking to verify and evaluate information
cognition	manipulating information on various levels of abstraction

The student's language and nonlanguage experiences will determine his abilities in the aforementioned areas. Also, physical and attitudinal conditions, such as those mentioned earlier, interact with various aspects of comprehension. Some experiences seem to be specific to content or subject areas, so that experiences may not necessarily transfer from one style of writing to another or from materials in one content area to another area. In addition, most aspects of comprehension seem to be influenced by the degree of abstractness and complexity of the information to be comprehended. Therefore, some mental operations may be performed by students on easier, simpler material, but not on more difficult material. All of these conditions—background experiences, physical abilities, and content of material—complicate an understanding of the comprehension of an individual at any time.

Finally, *rate* of processing information and *recall* of information are also related to comprehension. There seems to be some evidence that students who are presumed to be low in verbal ability can learn to comprehend on abstract levels, given more structure, repetition, and time to experience and manipulate concepts. Also, most students *can* learn to process ideas more rapidly and to select a rate appropriate to their purposes. Though recall of information seems to be related to meaningful associations with previously acquired knowledge, here, too, students can be helped to increase their abilities to recall information by learning to organize ideas, seek meaningful associations, review, and practice. A consideration of the comprehension abilities of a learning disabled student should include the rate of processing and recall of information.

In addition to the preceding categories, the diagnostician should realize that several categories presented in Chapters 3 and 4 will be pertinent to levels 4 and above. Therefore, any of the categories listed in levels 1–3 that seem to be essential to understanding the functioning of any given student should be checked on the 1–3 Record Form. That form should then be attached to the form for levels 4 and above, which may be found at the end of this chapter, Figures 7.1 and 7.2.

Just as differences in comprehension abilities will appear among readers on beginning levels, so will differences appear in the word-recognition abilities of readers on intermediate levels. For example, problems with automaticity, analysis of multisyllabic words, sound-symbol association for silent letter phonograms and blends continue to be hindrances to comprehension for some readers above the third grade level.

The same suggestions given for the use of interview and observation cues in Chapters 3 and 4 apply in this chapter. The following cues should be reviewed immediately before and after working with the student and while analyzing the student's tests, tapes, or papers. Conclusions are to be recorded on the student's record form(s).

CONCEPTUAL KNOWLEDGE

Interview

1. How many different things[1] can you think of when I say, "Blue"? "String"? "Time"?
2. If I gave you a list of countries and asked you to organize the list, how might you do it? How else? Can you think of more ways?
3. If I gave you a list of feelings and asked you to organize the list, how might you do it? How else? Can you think of more ways?
4. What hints are given by writers on how they have organized their material?
5. Do writers in different subject areas organize differently? If so, can you give me some examples?

Observations

1. Can the student classify common concrete objects (chairs, carrots, cars) in his environment on the basis of identical elements (furniture, vegetables, vehicles)?
2. Can the student classify things or ideas on the basis of common relationships: (a) *whole-part* (stems and roots are parts of plants); (b) *cause-effect* (economic factors may cause a war)?
3. Can the student classify objects or ideas on the basis of their functional role: (a) *uses* (used in building: saw, hammer); (b) *definition* (happiness is an emotion); (c) *principle* (evaporation lowers air temperature)?
4. Does the student possess concepts of (a) *class* (a grouping based on similar qualities); (b) *definition* (a statement of the meaning of a word or phrase); (c) *principle* (a rule or method or tenet)?
5. Can the student classify objects or ideas across *and* within categories?

---

[1] Look for quantity *and* type of associations. Example: shades of blue: blue sky; bird; crayon; deep blue sea; word that rhymes with two; a sad feeling, type of music, blues; type of financing, blue sky; washing product, blueing; pun, he cried blue-who; improper language, air turned blue; unknown, came from out of the blue; mixed with red makes purple; and so forth.

(List things that can be eaten that are green, *and* put the items on your list in order of your preference.)

6. Does the student possess a range of concrete and abstract concepts compared with others in his age/placement level that is above average, average, or below average.

Informal Tests

As conceptual knowledge is specific in nature, formal testing may be unsatisfactory in that there may be cultural bias or that the content may not relate to the needs of the diagnostic situation. Therefore, informal tests or discussion is recommended.

A helpful procedure in assessing the background of students is to construct a series of statements pertaining to entry level knowledge related to the material to be read. For example, if oceanography is the subject of interest, students might be given the following kinds of statements and asked to check those that are true.

Conceptual Preassessment
(Oceanography)

_____ 1. Most of the oceans are covered by sand.
_____ 2. Parts of the oceans are several miles in depth.
_____ 3. Mammals do not live in the oceans.

(And so forth)

Examiner's Conclusions

In comparison with others in his age/placement level, student appears

Strong	Average	Weak	
_____	_____	_____	in fluency of associations
_____	_____	_____	in variety of types of associations
_____	_____	_____	in range of concepts
_____	_____	_____	in ability to manipulate concrete concepts
_____	_____	_____	in knowledge of conceptual bases

_____	_____	_____	in ability to manipulate abstract concepts
_____	_____	_____	in ability to use two or more levels of organization
_____	_____	_____	in knowledge of concepts basic to

_____

_____

(list specific subject areas)

PERCEPTUAL ABILITIES IN INFOR-MATION EXTRACTION

Interview

1. Do you have trouble paying attention to what you are reading? Tell me about it.
2. Do you look over what you are going to read before you start reading straight through? Tell me about it.
3. Do you look for anything in particular as you read subject-area assignments? Tell me about it.
4. How do you decide what to study in a subject-area chapter?

Observations

1. Does the student appear to have normal awareness of his environment?
2. Is the student distracted easily as he reads?
3. Is the student familiar with a variety of purposes for attending to information? (using set or a purpose for reading or listening)
4. Can the student *survey* information to select consciously a set for attending?
5. Does information appear to be distorted by the student's set?
6. Is the student capable of shifting his set?
7. Can the student respond acceptably to various purposes for attending selected by his instructor when directed to do so?
8. For which purposes can the student acceptably respond: identify,

list, describe, compare, contrast, evaluate, criticize, summarize, other _____ ?

9. Can the student identify the topic of a sentence?

10. Can the student identify the topic sentence in a paragraph in initial, medial, and final positions?

11. Can the student infer the main idea of a paragraph when it is unstated?

12. Can the student identify types of paragraphs: introductory, explanatory, definitional, illustrative, transitional, summarizing, narrative, other _____ ?

13. Can the student identify main ideas in chapters or books as conceptualized by different disciplines?
    a. Main idea as a theme in literature.
    b. Main idea as a theory in social science.
    c. Main idea as a principle or law in science.
    d. Main idea as a concept in mathematics.
    e. Other _____ .

14. Can the student identify statements of proof for main ideas?

15. Can the student identify the words that give clues to organization: *however, but, on the other hand, first, next, finally, since, because, for, as a result?*

16. Can the student perceive the organizational patterns of spoken or written information: cause and effect, compare and contrast, sequence, listing; other _____ ?

17. Can the student identify words and phrases that are clues to central ideas? Examples: to summarize; nothing is more important than; in essence; my point is.

18. Can the student discriminate among a statement of principle or central idea, a reason for a principle or central idea, and an illustration of a principle or central idea?

19. Can the student perceive patterns involved in problem solving in different disciplines: science—putting information into classification systems; math—perceiving patterns of procedures; social science—organizing information into cause and effect patterns; other _____ ?

20. Can the student perceive the underlying purpose of the writer: inform, persuade, entertain, other _____ ?

21. Does the student know where to find statements of purpose and main idea in chapters and books? Can he skim to find the statements?

Informal Tests

In this area of comprehension, also, it is desirable to test students informally by using the open-book reading assessment procedure as described in Chapter 10 and/or by setting up test-teaching tasks for the students during instructional sessions. For example, "Underline the words the writer used to show he was contrasting two ways of building."

Examiner's Conclusions

____ 1.   Student appears to need less distracting environment in which to read.

____ 2.   Student needs to learn to survey material to set his own purposes for reading.

____ 3.   Student needs to learn to read for a variety of purposes.

____ 4.   Student needs to identify paragraph types.

____ 5.   Student needs to learn to identify central ideas as they are presented in _____ .
                                              (subject field)

____ 6.   Student needs to identify organizational patterns in

          _____ .
                                              (subject field)

____ 7.   Student needs to learn to infer author's purpose.

SYNTACTIC ABILITIES

Interview

1.   Do you lose track of what is being said in long sentences? Why?

2.   Do you have any ways of making long sentences easier to understand? What are they?

3.   Do commas help you when you read? Why?

Observations

1.   Does the student use the sentence patterns in his speech that are found in the reading material he is given?

2. Can the student comprehend the sentence patterns used in his reading material when the material is read to him?
3. Can the student comprehend basic, simple sentence types?
   a. John cooked the hamburger. (subject, transitive verb, object)
   b. John was cook. (subject, intransitive verb, predicate nominative)
   c. John gave me a hamburger. (subject, transitive verb, indirect object, object)
   d. John rested. (subject, intransitive verb)
4. Can the student comprehend simple expansions of the basic sentence types? (John cooked the hamburgers. My brother John cooked the hamburgers on the grill after the ball game.)
5. Does the student perceive phrases (to the store) and clauses (when we go home) as chunks or units within a sentence?
6. Does the student perceive the relationship between a phrase or a clause and the word or words it describes? (The man [walking with my brother, Bill,] is a painter.)
7. Can the student recover the deep structure (underlying meaning) of a sentence by recognizing the same idea in other words?
   Example: Which of these sentences mean the same thing?
   a. She won the race easily.
   b. She won the easy race.
   c. The race was one that she easily won.
8. Can the student respond appropriately to syntactic-semantic signals?
   a. *Articles as words that precede nouns.*
      This is *an* _____ . *A* _____ is good to have.
      The _____ is here. I climbed *the* _____ .
   b. *Concrete noun referents.*
      Mother told me Mike and *Linda* are coming. *She* is my best friend. (pronouns)

      My best friend is _____ .   (1) Mike
         (2) Linda
         (3) Mother

   c. *Abstract referents.*
      After I saw Linda, I fell and hurt my knee. *That* made me decide to stay out of the race. (anaphora)

That refers to

(1) seeing Linda
(2) falling
(3) hurting my knee

    d.   *Combined Position and Structure Clues.*

He did it _____ ly. He barked and _____ ed his tail.

    e.   *Coordinate and Subordinate Connectors.*

I was invited, _____ I didn't go.

I went shopping _____ my sister wanted me to go.

    f.   *Tense.*

I _____ here now. I have _____ there.

I _____ there yesterday.

I _____ be there tomorrow.

I shall _____ there by this time tomorrow

    g.   *Punctuation.*

:   a list is coming   ;   strong divider

.   end of thought   ,   weak divider

?   question   !   strong feeling

9. Can the student explain or justify his responses to the above signals as he does cloze or similar tasks?

10. Can the student comprehend the following sentence forms?

    a.   *Passive.* Presents were given to the children.

            (verb and helping verb)

    b.   *Complex sentence.* When the sled started to go too fast, Mary jumped off quickly.

    c.   *Left embedding.* Mike, a friend of my brother Bill, and I went to the ball game.

    d.   *Complementation.* He gave the children biscuits to feed the dog.

    e.   *Modification by*

        (1)   adjective and adverbs:

            The *tall* man walked *slowly.*

        (2)   phrases:

            The man *with a dog* walked slowly.

        (3)   clauses:

            The man *who was six feet tall* walked slowly.

    f.   *Coordination of*

        (1)   phrases:

            With a whip and *with a chair* he tamed the lion.

(2) dependent clauses:
Where we went and *what we saw* was told to no one.

(3) sentences:
We saw a large steamer and *later that day we saw a large sailboat.*

g. *Modification of*
(1) subject:
The man *walking his dog* moved slowly.

(2) verb:
The man was walking *along the highway.*

(3) object of preposition:
The man with a dog *barking and jumping* walked slowly.

(4) object of verb:
The man called the dog *who just scampered away.*

Informal Tests

These and other examples of teacher-constructed tests in this section should be constructed with words students can recognize on subject matter within their range of experience.

---

1. *Nonsense Words.*
   That was a __gorpy__ lunch. (adjective)
   a. Which real words could you use instead of *gorpy*? Why?
   (or)
   b. *Gorpy* could mean:
   ___ bread   ___ good   ___ after
   ___ free   ___ quick   ___

2. *Cloze Sentences.*
   He _____ down the street. (verb)
   a. What words can you put in the blank? Why?
   (or)
   b. Which words would fit in the blank?
   ___ looked ___ running ___ runs ___ car ___ ran

3. *Paraphrased Sentences*
   Which of the following sentences have the same meaning as the first one (complex sentence patterns)?

When John went to his grandmother's farm, he loved to help feed the animals that were friendly to people who came near them.

____ John was friendly to people.

____ John liked to feed the friendly animals.

____ John liked his grandmother's farm.

____ John liked to help his grandmother.

4. *WH Questions* (complex or ambiguous sentences).

The pool standing quiet in the hot afternoon seemed to the visitor a welcome sight. Her friend, however, did not agree. She had had an unhappy experience there the year before.

Who or what was a welcome sight? To whom? When? Who or what stood quietly?

Examiner's Conclusions

____ 1. Student needs practice in reading material written in his language patterns.

____ 2. Student needs help in reading by phrases.

____ 3. Student needs help in perceiving relationships of sentence parts.

____ 4. Student needs practice in interpreting expansions of basic sentence types.

____ 5. Student needs help in interpreting the following syntactic signals: (list)_____

____ 6. Student needs help in comprehension of the following sentence types: (list)_____

SEMANTIC KNOWLEDGE

Interview

1. Do you think you need to improve your everyday vocabulary? Why?

2. Do you think you need to improve your vocabulary in any particular area or subject?

3. Can you sometimes figure out what a word means by the way it is used in a sentence or paragraph?

4. What do you usually do when you come to a word you don't know?
5. What kinds of problems occur when people don't have the same understanding as to what a particular word means to the other person?

Observations

1. Does the student possess basic understandings about words, such as
    a. Words are not the event. They represent events and are abstract. They leave out characteristics and mean different things to different people.
    b. Bias can result in not attending to information with which one disagrees. This can result in not remembering information.
    c. Words can cause emotions. Those who use words may arouse emotions intentionally or unintentionally.
    d. Experience determines how one learns, uses, and interprets words.
    e. One can learn to improve his knowledge and use of words and his understanding of how words are used by others.
    f. One can be creative with words.
2. Can the student use contextual clues to meaning?
    a. Comparison and contrast. (Glass is transparent, but wood is *opaque.*)
    b. Synonym or restatement. (Acid thickens, or *coagulates,* the proteins of milk.)
    c. Circumstance. (The result of wind and water was a land ruined by *erosion.*)
    d. Definition. (When a person acts without thinking, he may be described as *impulsive.*)
    e. Typographical aids: bold-faced type, parentheses, footnotes, symbols.
3. Can the student use structural clues to meaning?
    a. Word endings: He _(verb)_ ed the door.
       He closed the door _(adverb)_ ly.
    b. Affixes: He pre _(viewed)_ the film.
    c. Roots: Please _(mimeo)_ graph this paper.
4. Does the student possess knowledge of affixes and roots basic to each field of study he is encountering?

Examples:

science—*hydro, scope, helio*

social science—*cracy, ante, poly*

5. Does the student possess a general vocabulary sufficient to comprehend material he is encountering?

Examples:

denote, employ, illustrate

6. Does the student possess a technical vocabulary sufficient to comprehend material he is encountering?

Examples:

ventricle, anarchy, sauté, flange

7. Does the student possess a vocabulary to describe language and thinking?

Examples:

interpret, evaluate, suggest

8. Can the student infer connotation from
    a. word use and word placement? (I want to make some *easy* money. I earned the money *easily.*)
    b. a long description or series of events that summarize character, setting, motivation, or purpose?
    c. figurative language and idiomatic expressions?
9. Can the student indicate his understanding of words by
    a. recognizing a word or phrase that renames the stimulus word?
    b. recognizing an appropriate definition?
    c. giving a synonym?
    d. giving a definition in his own words?
    e. using the word correctly in context?
    f. doing something physically that demonstrates understanding?
10. Can the student sustain the relationship between central ideas and supporting details in
    a. a paragraph?

  b. a short multiparagraph selection?

  c. a book?

  d. fiction? (List types.)

  e. nonfiction? (List types and subject areas.)

11. Does the student relate his reading to personal meaning

  a. to identify ideas that reflect his values?

  b. to clarify his thinking or guide his decisions?

  c. to compare his values to those of others?

12. Does the student value reading

  a. as a way of sharing experiences and insights?

  b. as a tool for obtaining information?

  c. as an art form?

Informal Tests

In this as in preceding areas of comprehension, the following kinds of tasks can be constructed:

1. Open-Book Tests

2. Cloze Tests

3. Synonym Tests

4. Short-Answer Questions

5. Discussion

Semantic knowledge can be tested on various levels with different channels. For example, the student may be asked to

  a. *recognize* the correct construction when he

    (1) sees it or (2) hears it.

(or)

  b. *produce* the correct response through

    (1) writing, (2) speaking, or (3) demonstrating.

The preceding checklist may be used as a general guide to constructing informal tests.

Examiner's Conclusions

  ____ 1. Student needs to increase general vocabulary.

  ____ 2. Student needs to increase specialized vocabulary in _____ .

  ____ 3. Student needs to use structural clues to meaning.

____ 4. Student needs to use contextual clues to meaning.

____ 5. Student needs to use connotation to infer meaning.

____ 6. Student needs to acquire some techniques to retain new vocabulary.

____ 7. Student needs to acquire concepts basic to understanding semantics.

REASONING ABILITIES

Interview

1. Do you have some ways of deciding what seems to be fact and what seems to be opinion? How do you decide?

2. How do you decide that a conclusion seems reasonable?

3. What are some methods advertisers use to encourage you to buy? Are they appealing to your feelings or to your reason? How do you know?

4. When you say someone is not being logical, what do you mean?

Observations

1. Does the student recognize the problem inherent in most "all" statements?

2. Is the student aware of the basic form of a sentence in formal logic: quantifier, noun, verb, predicate noun?

> *All* dogs are animals.
> *Some* women are lawyers.
> *No* lettuce is fruit.

3. Given a reversed "all" sentence, does the student recognize it is not true? (Example: All animals are dogs.) Can he tell why?

4. Given a reverse "some" sentence, does the student recognize it is true? (Example: Some lawyers are women.) Can he tell why?

5. Can the student recognize various expressions for "all"? (Examples: implied all; use of each; every; if–then.

   Movie stars love Zippy Soda.

6. Can the student make inferences from logical statements?

   Everyone at the party was a musician. Mary was at the party, so Mary was a musician.

7. Can the student recognize fallacious conditions of either-or arguments?

   "If you don't like beef, you must like chicken."
   "Not true, I'm a vegetarian."

8. Does the student demonstrate the effective use or interpretation of qualifiers to exclude forms within a class?

   Some (not all) of the girls in my class (not necessarily other classes) seem (not are) to be interested in playing tennis.

9. Can the student recognize a statement of generalization and describe its limitations?
10. Can the student recognize the necessity of premises or assumptions to be true in order to result in a true conclusion?
11. Can the student detect inconsistencies in the presentation of information?
12. Can the student recognize a statement that lacks proof?
13. Can the student recognize that distortion can occur by taking a statement out of context?
14. Does the student know that people may not choose to use logic?
15. Can the student recognize
    a.   logical thinking?

   He said he would come if he had time. He isn't here. He probably didn't have time.

    b.   creative thinking?

She didn't have time to take us to the circus, so we brought the circus to us. We did acrobatics, ate cotton candy, and showed the tricks acrobats can do.

c. empathetic thinking?

He is so very busy. He seems to want to please everyone. Trying to do that can be exhausting and frustrating. He must be tired. I feel sorry that he is in this situation.

Informal Tests

Using the preceding checklist, open-book assessment tests, discussion, analogies, and short answer tests can be constructed. The following are examples of inferential test items:

1. If I don't fly to Chicago, I will take the train.
   If I fly I won't stop in Middletown.
   I will stop in Middletown.
   Will I fly?
2. We all like ice cream, but only some of us like strawberry ice cream.
   All of us who like ice cream eat it slowly.
   Do some of us eat strawberry ice cream slowly?
3. Mary loves her two-year-old brother and takes good care of him. One day he broke her new watch. Mary screamed, "I hate you!" When her brother began to cry, she was sorry. Does Mary hate her brother?

Examiner's Conclusions

_____ 1. Student needs to understand basic concepts of logic.
_____ 2. Student needs to identify common violations of logical reasoning.
_____ 3. Student needs to understand limitations of logical reasoning.
_____ 4. Student needs to discriminate among logical, creative, and empathetic reasoning.
_____ 5. Student needs to understand ways that concepts can inhibit new learning.

COGNITIVE LEVELS OF COMPREHENSION

Interview

1. Do you need help in understanding what you read?
2. What kinds of material are easiest for you to understand? Why?
3. What kinds of material are difficult for you to understand? Why?
4. Can you read something and tell what it was about?
5. Can you read something and explain why the author wrote it the way he did?
6. Can you read something and tell how you felt about it?

Observations

Read- Listen-
  ing   ing

1. Can the student *recognize information* heard or read when presented in paraphrase?
   a. Can he do so with passage-dependent information to comprehend on a literal level? (Example: She wore a diamond ring, silk gown, and mink coat. She was (1) expensively, (2) inexpensively dressed.)
   b. Can he do so with passage-dependent information to comprehend on an inferential level? (Example: Harry slammed the drawer on his finger. At the same time he dropped a pan on his toe. "What next?" he muttered. Harry felt (1) sorry, (2) angry, (3) afraid, (4) amused.
2. Can the student *translate information* heard or read?
   a. Can he respond acceptably to "tell me in your own words"?
   b. Can he respond acceptably to "act out in pantomime what you heard or read"?
   c. Can he respond acceptably to "draw a picture, diagram, or chart to describe what you heard or read"?
3. Can the student *discover a relationship* between two or more ideas he has heard or read? (Example: How are two

Read- Listen-
ing ing

characters different? How are two laws alike? What caused an event to occur?)

4. Can the student *apply information* he has heard or read?
   a. Can he do so in concrete settings: make something, repair something?
   b. Can he do so in abstract settings: apply a rule to language or behavior?

5. Can the student *solve a problem* from information he has heard or read? If not, at what stage does he have difficulty?
   a. goal clarification
   b. identification of information needed
   c. hypothesis making
   d. collecting information
   e. selection of solution
   f. evaluation of results

6. Can the student *synthesize information* he has read or heard?
   a. Can he summarize?
   b. Can he outline?
   c. Can he generalize?
   d. Can he draw a conclusion?

7. Can the student *evaluate information* he has heard or read by standards of
   a. logic?
   b. creativity?
   c. empathy?
   d. clarity?

8. Can the student *creatively interpret* or make discoveries from material he has heard or read?

9. Can the student *explain his reactions* to material he has heard or read?
   a. verbally
   b. symbolically
   c. physically

Note. On what level of abstraction and complexity can the preceding cognitive processes be performed successfully? Compared with students in his age/placement range, is the student functioning low (*L*), average (*A*), or high (*H*) in each observation category. Each column should be marked with *L, A, H* designations.

Informal Tests

Open-book assessment tests and graded paragraph tests can be used along with informal discussion. Other tasks can be constructed to fit the preceding checklist. See Chapter 10.

Formal Tests

A list of published comprehension tests appears at the end of Chapter 9. By doing a task analysis of the test items, teachers can obtain some useful diagnostic information. For example, a student may do well on literal items but poorly on inferential items.

Examiner's Conclusions

____ 1. Student needs to improve literal comprehension of (a) fiction, (b) nonfiction, (c) special subject areas:

_____

____ 2. Student needs to improve inferential comprehension of (a) fiction, (b) nonfiction, (c) special subject areas:

_____

____ 3. Student needs to improve comprehension of paragraphs, short selections, books.

____ 4. Student needs to improve his manipulation of information to (a) translate, (b) apply, (c) solve problems, (d) analyze, (e) synthesize, (f) evaluate, (g) interpret creatively.

RATE OF PROCESSING

Interview

1. Do you read as fast as you think you should? Tell me about it.
2. Should some things be read faster than others? What do you mean?

3.   Have you tried to read faster? What happened? [or] Why not?

Observations

1.   Is the student's rate (with comprehension) generally appropriate to his age/placement level?
2.   Is the student's rate appropriate for his purposes?
3.   Can the student preview material to determine the rate and purpose for which he should read?
      a.   to skim
      b.   to scan
      c.   to survey
      d.   to study
      e.   to reflect
4.   Can the student vary and adjust his rate to his comprehension needs as he reads?
5.   Is the student using crutches he no longer needs?
      a.   finger pointing
      b.   lip moving
      c.   whispering
      d.   regressing

Informal Tests

1.   Ask the student to read a passage on his independent reading level so that he will be able to answer a few questions about it. Record time and compute words per minute. Example:

      3 minutes reading time; 570 words in the passage

      $$570 \div 3 = 190 \text{ words per minute}$$

      Next ask the student to answer at least five literal questions about the passage or to tell about the passage. Estimate rate with comprehension; for example, 190 wpm with 80 percent comprehension.
2.   Passages can also be prepared with the cumulative total of words at the end of each line so that when the examiner calls time, the reader circles the number at the end of the line he is reading. The number

circled is divided by the minutes of reading time, one, two, three, and so on. Comprehension is tested as earlier, with questions or retelling.

3. Flexibility of rate can be tested by asking the student to read various kinds of materials for different purposes: to find a name or date, to outline the plot, to recall details, to critically analyze, and so forth.

Formal Tests

See standardized comprehension and rate tests at the end of Chapter 9.

Examiner's Conclusions

____ 1. Student's rate is generally too fast for adequate comprehension.
____ 2. Student's rate is generally to slow for efficient reading.
____ 3. Student needs practice in selecting rate to serve purpose.
____ 4. Student needs practice in the following rate skills:

_____

____ 5. Student needs to overcome the following habits that interfere with rate:

_____

RECALL OF INFORMATION

Interview

1. Do you have difficulty in remembering what you read?
2. What kinds of things do you remember best?
3. What kinds of things do you have difficulty remembering?
4. When you need to remember something you have read, what do you do to help yourself remember?
5. Why do you think some people remember better than others?
6. Can you remember some days better than others? Why?

Observations

1. Does the student seem to listen or read with the intention of remembering?
2. Is the student inconsistent in his ability to remember?
3. Can the student use a study sequence such as SQ3R?
4. Can the student discriminate important from less important information to select what should be remembered?
5. Can the student organize information for efficient recall?
6. Can the student select a method for reviewing information that is suited to each subject area and type of material to be read?
7. Can the student make and use mnemonic devices? (Example: to remember the Great Lakes, pretend you have HOMES on each one. Each letter of HOMES is the first letter of a lake: Huron, Ontario, Michigan, Erie, Superior.)
8. Can the student visualize or auditorize information for effective recall?

Informal Tests

1. A study habit checklist can be prepared for older students to learn what methods they use to study.
2. In order to discriminate between problems of *understanding* what is read and difficulty with *recall,* first have the student answer questions or tell about a passage that he has read and returned to the examiner and then answer questions about a passage before him for reference.
3. As questions about a passage may prompt memory, a student may be asked to retell the content. His recall can be evaluated by the order, number, and detail of his memories.

Examiner's Conclusions

____ 1. Student needs to apply SQ3R types of sequences in: ____
(*subject areas or types of materials*).
____ 2. Student needs to learn how to select information to be remembered.

____ 3. Student needs to learn how to organize material for recall.
____ 4. Student needs to learn how to associate information to be recalled with previous learnings.
____ 5. Student needs practice in remembering.

FIGURE 7.1. Student record form—levels 4+

Name: _____

Teacher: _____

Date: _____

Obs.*   Sat.*

I. CONCEPTUAL KNOWLEDGE (sampling experiential background)

A. Appears STRONG AVE. WEAK in fluency of associations.
B. Appears STRONG AVE. WEAK in types of associations. (category labels and relationships)
C. Appears STRONG AVE. WEAK in quantity of concrete concepts.
D. Appears STRONG AVE. WEAK in quantity of abstract concepts.
E. Appears STRONG AVE. WEAK in ability to manipulate concepts.
F. Appears STRONG AVE. WEAK in ability to classify objects or ideas across and within categories.
G. Appears STRONG AVE. WEAK in knowledge of concepts basic to: _____ (list specific subject area).
H. Appears STRONG AVE. WEAK in concepts basic to world knowledge.
I. Needs to apply reasons.

II. PERCEPTUAL ABILITIES (attending to, selecting, and organizing information)

A. Needs less distracting environment in which to read.
B. Needs to survey material to set his own purpose for reading.
C. Needs to read for a variety of purposes.
D. Needs to identify paragraph types (explanatory, illustrative, and so forth)

*Key: Observed, date. Satisfactory, date.

FIGURE 7.1.   Continued

Obs.*   Sat.*

     E.   Needs to identify central ideas as they are presented in:
_____ (list specific subject area).

     F.   Needs to perceive organizational patterns in:
_____ (list specific subject area).

     G.   Needs to infer author's purpose.

     H.   Needs to identify word clues to organization (list, sequence, cause/effect, and comparison/contrast).

III. SYNTACTIC ABILITIES (using word order to get meaning)

     A.   Needs practice in reading material written in his language patterns.

     B.   Needs help in reading by phrases.

     C.   Needs help understanding basic sentence types.

     D.   Needs help in interpreting the following syntactic signals in *intra*sentence situations:

    ____ common nouns   ____ coordinate connectors

    ____ concrete noun-referents   ____ subordinate connectors

    ____ abstract referents   ____ tense

    ____ combined position and structure clues   ____ punctuation

     E.   Needs help in interpreting the following syntactic signals in *inter*sentence parts:

    ____ common nouns   ____ coordinate connectors

    ____ concrete noun-referents   ____ subordinate connectors

    ____ abstract referents   ____ tense

    ____ combined position and structure clues   ____ punctuation

     F.   Needs help in comprehension of the following sentence forms:

    ____ passive

    ____ left embedding

    ____ complementation

    ____ modification

    ____ coordination

     G.   Needs to apply concepts to new learnings.

IV. SEMANTIC KNOWLEDGE (understanding word meanings)

     A.   Needs to increase general vocabulary.

     B.   Needs to increase specialized vocabulary in:
_____ (list specific subject area)

FIGURE 7.1.　Continued

Obs.*	Sat.*

_____　　C.　Needs to use contextual clues to meaning.

_____　　D.　Needs to use the following structural clues to meaning:

_____　　　　____ word endings

_____　　　　____ roots　　　　　　　____ possessives

_____　　　　____ affixes　　　　　　____ contractions

_____　　E.　Needs to use connotation to infer meaning.

_____　　F.　Needs to acquire techniques to retain new vocabulary.

_____　　G.　Needs to acquire concepts basic to understanding everyday
　　　　　　　　　　problems in communicating ideas.

_____　　H.　Needs to apply concepts to new learnings.

V. REASONING ABILITIES (relating ideas logically)

_____　　A.　Needs to identify the following common violations of logical
　　　　　　　　　　reasoning (that is, "allness" statements, if-then arguments and
　　　　　　　　　　promises, discriminating fact from opinion, and so forth): _____

　　　　　　　　　　_____

_____　　B.　Needs to understand limitations of logical reasoning.

_____　　C.　Needs to discriminate among logical, creative, and empathic
　　　　　　　　　　reasoning.

_____　　D.　Needs to apply concepts to new learnings.

VI. COGNITIVE LEVELS OF COMPREHENSION (manipulating information)

_____　　A.　Needs to improve literal comprehension of

_____　　　　____ fiction

_____　　　　____ nonfiction

_____　　　　____ special subject areas:

　　　　　　　　　　_____ (list specific subject areas)

_____　　B.　Needs to improve inferential comprehension of

_____　　　　____ fiction

_____　　　　____ nonfiction

_____　　　　____ special subject areas:

　　　　　　　　　　_____ (list specific subject areas)

_____　　C.　Needs to improve comprehension of materials at varying lengths:

_____　　　　____ paragraphs

_____　　　　____ short selections

_____　　　　____ books

_____　　D.　Needs to improve ability to

_____　　　　____ translate information

FIGURE 7.1.   Continued

Obs.*   Sat.*

_____	____ analyze information
_____	____ synthesize information
_____	____ evaluate information
_____	____ creatively interpret information
_____	____ solve problems
_____	E. Needs to apply concepts to new learning.

VII. RATE OF PROCESSING (adjusting reading rate)

_____   A.   Rate is generally too fast for adequate comprehension.

_____   B.   Rate is generally too slow for efficient reading.

_____   C.   Needs practice in adjusting rate to serve purpose.

_____   D.   Needs practice in the following rate skills:

_____   ____ scanning

_____   ____ skimming

_____   ____ speeded reading

_____   ____ study reading

_____   ____ careful and reflective reading

_____   E.   Needs to overcome the following habits that interfere with rate:

_____   ____ finger pointing

_____   ____ lip moving

_____   ____ whispering

_____   ____ regressing

_____   F.   Needs help in applying concepts to new learnings.

VIII. RECALL OF INFORMATION (remembering information)

_____   A.   Needs to apply SQ3R types of sequences in:

_____ (list specific subject areas or
                                                                types of materials)

_____   B.   Needs to learn how to select and remember information to meet
              student's purpose.

FIGURE 7.2.   Student priorities—levels 4+: mature students

Directions: On first reading with student, place a check for each area of student concern. Explain each item as necessary. Select columns and items for response that seem pertinent. Then, reread with student indicating first, second, third, and fourth choices of student.

I.   I need specific help with

A. ____ long words

B. ____ short sentences

C. ____ long sentences

D. ____ punctuation

E. ____ reading faster

F. ____ meanings of words

G. ____ understanding what I read in

____ paragraphs

____ short selections (short stories, essays, and so on)

H. ____ remembering what I read

I. ____ remembering what I hear

J. ____ picking out what to remember when I read

K. ____ paying attention while I'm reading

L. ____ telling about what I've read

M. ____ criticizing what I've read

N. ____ spelling

O. ____ handwriting

P. ____ knowing what to say when I'm writing

Q. ____ knowing how to write correctly

R. ____ writing research papers

S. ____ taking tests

FIGURE 7.2.   Continued

II.   I want to study words connected with

    A.   The courses I am taking in _____

             _____

    B.   My job as a (manual, directories, directions) _____

             _____

    C.   My practical needs such as (forms, maps, schedules) _____

             _____

    D.   My hobby _____

             _____

III.   I like to read about _____

      _____

      _____

      I like to read:

      ____ Newspapers   Parts: _____

      ____ Magazines   Kinds: _____

      ____ Short stories   Types: _____

      ____ Fiction   Types: _____

      ____ Nonfiction   Topics: _____

      ____ Comics   Kinds: _____

      ____ Other

      I hope I can be helped to _____

      _____

IV.   I prefer to work

    ____ in a small group with a tutor

    ____ with another student

    ____ individually with a tutor

FIGURE 7.2. Continued

_____ with audiovisual material

_____ with programmed material

_____ with skill books

_____ other _____

I do not do well with _____

_____

_____ approaches or materials.

I do well with _____

_____

_____ approaches or materials.

CHAPTER 8

Developing
Comprehension
Abilities

This chapter contains suggestions for developing growth in comprehension for those reading on level four and above. The categories match those in Chapter 7 and are arranged in the same order. In addition, an illustration is provided that synthesizes assessment and instruction in comprehension.

In selecting areas of study, materials, and procedures, the teacher should work from a view of the total student rather than focus on *deficiencies*. For each student, reading levels are considered to include interrelated ways to (1) obtain fluency, (2) build insight into the structure and content of presentations, (3) provide challenge for growth, and (4) reflect environmental requirements.

CONCEPTUAL KNOWLEDGE

Conceptual Differences

Many students do not have difficulties with the reading *process* in that they can use graphic, semantic, and syntactic cues in context. But they may not comprehend because they lack knowledge of the concepts used by the writer. Differences among students in conceptual knowledge are mainly a result of differences in experiences. At this point it is important to note that a student may not have the concepts needed to understand material within a particular subject

127

area, but that does not mean he does not possess a large number of concepts related to his own experiences. The *student* is not deficient; he simply has not had experiences necessary to comprehend particular kinds of materials.

The Nature of Conceptual Knowledge

Because there are different categories of concepts and different ways of demonstrating conceptual knowledge, teachers should be familiar with the nature of conceptual knowledge before analyzing material and diagnosing their students' comprehension abilities.

Generally, a concept is defined as a summary of essential elements that characterize common features. *Honor* is a concept. It is a term suggesting worthiness and respected behavior. *Triangle* is a concept pertaining to having three points or parts.

Concepts vary in their abstractness. A triangle is something that can be seen as a geometric figure, but honor can only be experienced or described with the aid of language.

Concepts vary as to types. Some concepts can be presented as (1) classification statements. (Example: A vertebrate is an animal with a backbone and an internal skeleton.) Another statement can be described as (2) relational. (Example: As changes take place in people's needs and wants, in supplies of natural resources, and in production factors, the market registers changes in prices and in activity.) Another type of concept can be described as (3) theoretical. (Example: Light is an electromagnetic wave.)

Concepts vary as to their dependence on underlying subconcepts. The preceding statement describing a vertebrate depended on the reader's knowing these concepts: animal, backbone, internal, and skeleton.

In summary, concepts vary as to abstractness, type, and dependence on subconcepts. These differences should be considered when instructional decisions are made.

Assessing Knowledge of Concepts

Students might demonstrate knowledge of a concept by giving a rule, a definition, or a description; by identifying or creating examples and nonexamples; by using the concept to solve a problem or gain insight into another concept. To gauge the depth of their students' understanding, teachers need to evaluate the students' knowledge in more than one way. Students may glibly recite,

"A noun is the name of a person, place, or thing" but be unable to identify various types of nouns within a sentence. Or they may be able to identify single words that are nouns but not noun phrases. Because of difficulties in assessing the extent of students' conceptual knowledge, many teachers assume that students know much more than they do.

Who Should Remediate Conceptual Differences?

When students appear to be severely deficient in conceptual knowledge required for comprehension of material used in particular subject areas, a decision needs to be made as to who should help them acquire the necessary concepts. Ideally, subject matter specialists, classroom teachers, and resource teachers should contribute; but realistically the remedial teacher may have the primary responsibility. However, remedial teachers should seek assistance from others in order to help their students. People need to be identified who can take students on field trips or involve them in other firsthand experiences. Subject matter specialists should be consulted as to the identification of major concepts and the methods that will be used to assess conceptual knowledge.

Instructional Procedures

Depending on the abstractness, type, and complexity of the concepts and the conceptual knowledge possessed by the student, the following approaches might be used in various combinations:

1. Firsthand experience. Students are physically or verbally involved.
2. Analogy. Students learn the characteristics of the concept through experiences such as role-playing or parodies or simulations.
3. Examples and nonexamples. Students are helped to discriminate between closely related concepts.
4. Part to whole. Students are taught subconcepts before concepts.
5. Whole to part. Students experience the concept first, then discriminate the components.
6. Simple to complex. Students are given only the most relevant characteristics first and experience the total configuration of characteristics gradually.
7. Modeling. Students observe demonstrations of principles or processes.

8. Concrete to abstract. Students are first given objects they can handle, then moved to representations through diagrams, pictures, and symbols.
9. Inductive learning. Students are helped to acquire concepts through guided discovery. (This type of learning is considered more permanent and more likely to be transferred.)
10. Deductive learning. Students are given rules or definitions and helped to apply their knowledge to make discriminations.

Note: With all approaches students should be encouraged to verbalize their experiences and to organize their experiences in relation to their own interests and cognitive structures. Students should be given feedback to facilitate their learning.

Teachers might find it useful to acquire a library of pictures books, elementary texts, easy-to-read trade books, films, and tapes in order to take some students from simple, concrete conceptual experiences to complex, abstract contexts. However, other students might be helped by having more difficult material read to them and working directly with unknown concepts. Decisions of these kinds will depend on the concepts to be acquired and the knowledge of the student. For those who are very weak in conceptual knowledge of a particular field, the former might be desirable; for those who are more knowledgeable, the "overview" approach may be better. With either approach students should be helped to relate the new concept to concepts they already possess.

PERCEPTUAL ABILITIES

The discussion of perception in this section is not concerned with fine sensory discrimination but with attending, selecting, and organizing information to obtain meaning. As these abilities appear to be associated with the maturity of the student, the diagnostician should not confuse *immaturity* with *deficiency* in attending and organizing. From about seven to eleven children are learning to classify categories and subcategories; later, they learn to consider causal relationships between abstract ideas. A student's ability to comprehend a verbal presentation is related to his or her ability to perceive its organization. If the content is abstract and the organization complex, the younger students are likely to have difficulty. Attempting to rush the development of the intellectual abilities of normal young children is not a desirable use of time by the resource teacher.

For mature students with difficulties in perceptual aspects of comprehension, there are instructional procedures that can foster selective attention and enhance comprehension. The device of the poor reader is to read and reread, attempting to remember everything. The better reader attends to important elements and relates ideas to previous knowledge.

Instructional Procedures

Overviews.   Preparation for what is to be heard or read helps to set an expectancy that the learner can use to select and disregard information. Depending on the material, the learner, and the purpose for presenting the information, the following devices may be helpful.

1. *Survey.* The first step in the SQ3R[1] (Survey, Question, Read, Recite, Review) procedure suggests that the student skim through a non-fiction chapter, reading the title, subheadings, pictures, and chart captions to determine the content and the writer's organization. He is then supposed to state or write in his own words what the selection is about and how it is organized. The instructor may encourage the student to talk aloud as he makes the survey and describe what he is reminded of as he sees the subheadings and pictures. Some students like to be timed. Example: "You have one minute to look through this chapter in order to tell me everything you saw." This can be followed by such questions as, Why do you think the writer is making such a comparison? What do you expect he is going to say when he discusses ____? Can you think of anything the writer might have left out?

2. *Subheading Outline.* In this procedure the teacher copies the chapter title and subheadings with sufficient space for writing between headings. She then asks the student to write a list of ideas under each heading that the student might expect to find. When he is finished, he is instructed to look at the chapter summary to find important ideas he may have omitted and add them under each subheading. Finally, the student reads the chapter and compares his notes with the chapter content.

3. *Skimming.* The learner reads the entire first paragraph, the first line

[1] Formulated by Francis P. Robinson, *Effective Study* (New York: Harper & Row, 1961).

of every paragraph, and the entire concluding paragraph in fiction or in nonfiction without subheadings in order to summarize the content. In the early stages he may be asked to identify a summarizing statement. Later, the student should be asked to make the summary in his own words. Other skimming patterns may be used for advanced students such as random fixations in a lazy *L* pattern or glancing down the center of a page.

4. *Conceptual Overview.* The instructor might work with the student to make a chart of major concepts to be introduced in a course, a unit, or a chapter. As the chart is constructed, the concepts are introduced, and relationships among the concepts are explained. As work in the unit progresses, frequent references are made to the chart by the instructor, and the student is encouraged to point out and explain how aspects under discussion relate to the chart. Some instructional materials are available with charts, but the student needs to be actively involved in chart construction, organization, reorganization, and explanation for the chart to have maximum effectiveness. An example of a chart that may be constructed in this fashion is Figure 8.1.

5. *Topic Preparation.* When the student will be required to read material written at a high level of difficulty on a topic with which he is unfamiliar, he can improve his ability to read the material by viewing filmstrips or video tapes, looking at pictures or charts, listening to tapes, or reading material on the topic that is written at a low level of difficulty. If such material is not available, the resource teacher can rewrite the material. Through such topic preparation the student can become familiar with the range of concepts to be presented, ways of organizing, and terminology. The student should be encouraged to visualize what he expects to be discussed in the more complex material, based on his preparatory experiences.

6. *Double Notebooks.* The student can keep a notebook for text and lecture notes, organized by topic, that might look like this:

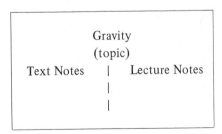

FIGURE 8.1.   Conceptual overview

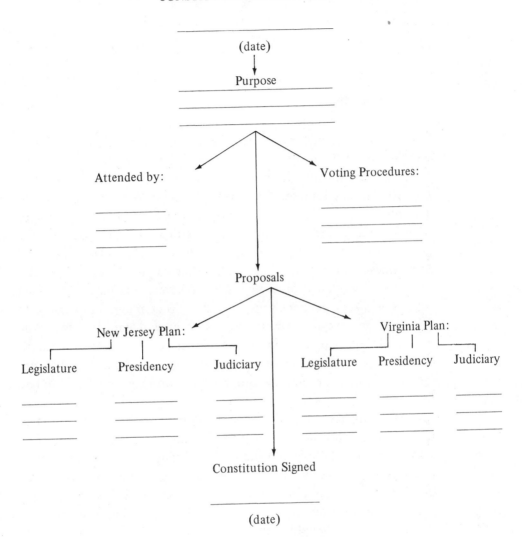

CONSTITUTIONAL CONVENTION

(date)

Purpose

Attended by:

Voting Procedures:

Proposals

New Jersey Plan:

Legislature   Presidency   Judiciary

Virginia Plan:

Legislature   Presidency   Judiciary

Constitution Signed

(date)

In this way, the text can provide preparation for the lecture, or the lecture can provide an overview for reading, depending on which is experienced first. As text notes and lecture notes on each topic are kept side by side, they are readily available for review.

7.   *Guided Reading Sequence.* In the guided reading sequence, or directed reading activity, the first step is to build readiness for reading by helping the student call to mind relative information he may

possess with regard to the topic to be read. At this time unfamiliar concepts are explained, and unfamiliar vocabulary is introduced. After some discussion, the student reads for a purpose, set by
himself or by a teacher, that is related to the overview received in
discussion.

Perceiving Organization

1. *Direct Experiences in Organizing.* For younger students and those
    with severe difficulties in perceiving organizational patterns, the
    experiences in organizing should first be with concrete objects, then
    with words that represent concrete objects, and finally with words
    that represent ideas. The first experiences should be with simple
    classifications and then with multiple classifications and subcategories.

    On the lowest levels students do sorting tasks: black beads and
    white ones; things that fly and things that do not fly. Stories are dis-
    cussed as a sequence of events: "What happened first? Then what
    happened? What happened at the end?" Students are encouraged to
    draw on their experiences to predict what will happen: "What do
    you think will happen next? Why?" Other ways of organizing can be
    demonstrated by having students make charts on likenesses or dif-
    ferences, causes or effects, order of importance, location, and so
    forth.

    On a higher level, students might be presented with a list of
    topics and asked how they might be organized. When presented with
    a list of famous people and the task of organizing, the student might
    respond by saying, "Men and women, good guys and bad guys, order
    of birth, country of birth, those with greatest influence on history,"
    and so forth. By helping to edit a collection of writings of others, the
    student can also be helped to see that decisions have been made as to
    the organization of printed material.

2. *Perceiving Organization Through Writing.* Frequently, students who
    have comprehension difficulties also have problems in writing. In-
    struction in one activity can be planned so that insights can be carried
    over to the other. While "story starters," diaries, and pictures can be
    used to stimulate a flow of ideas for many students, others seem to
    benefit by more structured experiences. For the student confronted
    with two major problems, what to say and how to organize, the in-
    structor can help by relieving the student of first one and then the

other problem. The student can be given a set of sentences, relating to a single topic, cut into strips. Example:

Some things need to be thrown away.

Boxes have to be found for packing.

Moving is a lot of work.

Breakable items have to be carefully wrapped.

Articles need to be sorted.

The student's task is to arrange the sentences and explain his reasons for his organization. After a series of experiences in organizing sentences within paragraphs and paragraphs within essays and stories, the student is then given *organizational outlines* and asked to provide the content. Example:

The day was a disaster. The first thing that happened when
   I awoke was . . .
Next, I
Then
Finally,

Another Example:

One of the best things about
On the other hand,
Generally, I would say

After the student has had some experience with organizing, developing content, and drawing a conclusion as separate activities, he may be helped to select his own topic, purpose, and organizational pattern. He should be helped to identify similar organizational structures in the writing of others. In his own writing and in the writing of others, the student should also be given experience in sorting ideas that are relevant and those that are not.

3. *Identifying Word Clues to Organization.* The student can be helped to make charts composed of words that indicate a particular pattern of organization. Examples:

Listing	Sequence	Cause/Effect	Comparison/Contrast
the following	first	since	however
in addition	second	because	yet
also	meanwhile	as a result	nevertheless
another	afterwards	therefore	although
moreover	while	consequently	still

Next the student can be asked to scan well-organized material to find words that are clues to organization. These might be circled. The teacher can prepare a key by using a plastic overlay with organization words circled that the student can use to check his own survey. After the organization words are found, they can be compared with the charts to identify the writer's pattern. Finally, the student can be asked *what* is being compared or listed. The questions should be designed to help him relate the writer's organization to his central idea and purpose.

4. *Identifying Paragraph and Chapter Clues to Organization.* Another aid to the process of selecting and disregarding information is the identification of paragraph types. Some examples:

introductory	transitional	interpretive
definitional	narrative	illustrative
explanatory	summary	

After helping the student identify the characteristics of the preceding types, the instructor can help him label paragraphs in various kinds of reading. Later, the student can be asked where he would look to find presentations of main ideas, definitions, explanations, illustrations, and so forth. Similar activities can be carried out with chapters within a book. The instructor can begin by reviewing the table of contents and preface to ask similar questions about where certain kinds of information can be found.

5. *Perceiving Paragraph Organization.* Because paragraphs have different purposes and structures, students should be aware that finding the topic sentence and supporting details is not necessarily a productive activity for all types of reading. However, this can be helpful for some students when the instructor has selected well-organized material. The student might begin by underlining introductory topic sentences, then those at the end of paragraphs, and lastly, those in a medial position. The details supporting the topic sentences can be numbered. Finally, the student can write topic sentences for those paragraphs without the main idea specifically stated. Students can draw diagrams of the paragraphs.

Examples:

Introductory:

Concluding:

Medial:

Inferred:

6. *Organizational Outlines.* The instructor can help the student follow the organization of a passage or a lecture by providing a highly structured outline with headings and subheadings to be filled in by the student. The teacher should gradually provide less structure until the student can outline material independently.

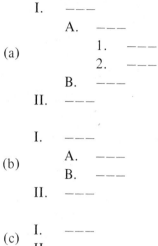

7. *Relating Organizational Patterns to Content Areas.* The student needs to be aware of typical patterns of organization used in various subject areas. A teacher can help by providing reading guides that require the student to direct his attention to elements within the pattern and to reflect or draw conclusions related to the pattern. For example, in social studies material organized in a cause-and-effect pattern, the student might be directed to list the four causes of an event and the three results (page numbers should be provided). Then the student might be asked to critique the causes and effects stated by the writer: "Were they really related? Were other more important factors omitted?" Or the student might be asked to reflect on the causality to explain why the causes had the effect they did. The student should consciously adjust his reading to the organizational pattern of the discipline. Some types of material such as instructions for experiments or explanations of technical processes require slow, careful reading with frequent references to charts or diagrams. The teacher might ask, "How is this material organized?" and "How should you read this material?"

Locating Central Ideas

1. *Teacher-Directed Set.* The teacher can introduce the student to various purposes for reading by using the guided reading sequence and reading guides, previously described. The purpose for reading should be briefly and clearly stated if the content is to be retained by the reader. Some examples of purposes are these:

Read to:	identify	contrast	describe
	list	compare	evaluate

   After reading for a specific purpose, the student should discuss his response. He may then reread the material to confirm his response or to read for another purpose.

2. *Self-Directed Set.* The student can select his own purposes for reading through procedures such as SQ3R. He might select from a list of purposes or turn subheadings into questions and read to answer them. The student will need to learn to evaluate his purposes and readjust them so that he can become skilled and flexible in purpose setting.

   Another approach is to have the student pause after each sentence (in short passages) or after each paragraph or section (in longer passages) and rephrase what he has just read. Next the student might ask himself these reflective questions: "What does this mean? Why did the writer say this? Do I agree with what was stated?" and so forth. This approach requires very close attention and considerable thought about the material on the part of the student.

3. *Author's Purpose.* The instructor should help the student be aware of *why* the material was written—to inform, entertain, explain, or persuade the reader. In some material a statement of purpose can be found in the preface or first or last chapters, but in other material the purpose must be inferred. The student should learn to distinguish between central ideas and author's purpose. The teacher might provide the student with a list of possible purposes and have the student select one and explain his reasons.

4. *Main Ideas.* The student should be aware of clues to important ideas such as these: nothing is more important than, in summary, therefore, in conclusion. He should learn to scan material for phrases that indicate a main idea statement. In some writing main ideas are followed by explanations or illustrations. The reader should learn to

look back over material that precedes such statements as "for example" and "as an illustration" to find a statement of central thought.

The reader should also have a set for finding central ideas stated in forms related to particular disciplines. Main ideas in science are often statements of laws or principles; in social science, statements of theory; and in literature, statements of theme, often implied. Reading guides and directed reading activities can be used to direct the student's attention to major ideas.

SYNTACTIC ABILITIES

Nature of Syntactic Processing Difficulties

A student may have difficulty in comprehending some written sentence patterns because they are not used in his spoken language. For such a student, material will need to be rewritten in the patterns he understands. Generally, if a student can comprehend a pattern he hears, he does not necessarily have to use the pattern in his spoken language in order to comprehend it as he reads. However, to help the student learn to read unfamiliar sentence patterns, the teacher should work with him to experience the patterns in integrated listening, speaking, and writing activities.

Some students may have difficulty in comprehending written sentence patterns because they do not perceive constituent parts as chunks or units within a sentence. Instead of reading by phrases, the students read word-by-word. When they look at a complex sentence, they may not be aware of cues that suggest a component. In the previous sentence, *when* in an initial position might have been a signal to the reader that a comma would appear and the words between the comma and *when* would express a thought. Within the clause *at* might have signaled a phrase that expressed a thought. The ability to perceive individual words as chunks helps readers extract and hold more information in short-term memory so that associations can be made and relationships manipulated. Most students without second language problems or receptive language difficulties seem to be able to comprehend basic sentence patterns, but some have problems with certain kinds of embeddings and structures. These students can be helped to become aware of syntactic-semantic signals, sentence parts, and intrasentence and intersentence relationships.

Instructional Procedures:

1. *Constituent Sentence Parts.* Several approaches have been successful in helping students to segment sentences visually:
    a. *Slash lines.* The student/is provided/ with some sentences/that are divided/ as this one/ is. The student can also learn to use oral clues to phrasing, such as pitch, emphasis, and pause, by listening to the teacher read with appropriate emphasis and inserting slash lines as he listens.
    b. *Highlighting.* Some commercial materials are available with phrases printed in contrasting color. The teacher can use a highlighter to achieve a similar effect or can use underlining or circling.
    c. *Phrase and Word Cards.* Students may be given sets of cards containing phrases and single words that can be used to construct sentences. These can be put in a game format.
    d. *Tachistoscopic Presentations.* Phrases may be flashed for the student, manually or in electrical or mechanical devices, at increasing rates to help the student increase his automaticity in recognizing short, common phrases.
    e. *Charts.* Various charts can be made of lists of modifying phrases for nouns and verbs. Students may create these or search for them in printed materials.
    f. *Moving and Deleting.* Long introductory phrases or clauses and embeddings between subject and verbs are often hard to process. These can be put on cards and shifted or lifted out so that the sentence kernel can become more apparent and the embeddings can be seen as units.

2. *Intrasentence Relationships.* Some approaches that might be used to help students understand relationships between words and phrases within sentences are these:
    a. *Expansions.* Basic sentence patterns can be expanded by adding adjectives, adverbs, phrases, and clauses. Students might suggest their own additions, or they might be provided with charts or cards. Control can be added by using cloze. Example:

    Dogs run.
    Fat dogs run _____ly.
    Dogs chasing cars run fast.
    Dogs run to catch a ball.

b. *Alterations.* Sentences might be altered by changing tense or by changing word position.

    (1) Dogs run today.
          Dogs ____ ____ tomorrow.
          Dogs ____ yesterday.

    (2) The dogs ran fast.
          The fast dogs ran.
          The dogs had a fast.

Again, students might create their own combinations, use cloze activities, or use charts and cards. It is important that students discuss their manipulations.

c. *Wh Questions.* Students can build and analyze sentences by asking *who, what, where, when, which, why* questions. Example:

    Every morning the girl next door walks quickly to the store to buy a newspaper.

Who?	The girl	Which?	Next door
What?	Walks quickly	When?	Every morning
Where?	To the store	Why?	To buy a newspaper

d. *Syntactic-Semantic Signals.* Cloze phrases or sentences can be constructed to help students become aware of clues that provide anticipation for certain types of words.

Examples:
    (1) The (noun) gave every (noun) a (noun).
    (2) Of the (noun)
          into every (noun)
          about a (noun)

Pronouns, conjunctions, punctuation, forms of *be,* inflectional endings, and affixes also signal relationships and should be included in instructional activities. In addition to cloze sentences, the teacher can use dictated writing, charts, word cards, and games.

3. *Intersentence Relationships.* When students are confused about what was said in a sentence, they often continue to read feeling that they

will obtain clarifying information from the larger context. Often this is true, and students should be encouraged and helped in this practice. There are specific kinds of confusions that can be clarified by teachers:

a. *Anaphora.* Anaphora refers to words or phrases that stand for other words, phrases, or passages. While pronouns such as *he, she,* and *they* cause some difficulty for students, abstract referents such as *that, this, which,* and *who* are more likely to cause confusion, especially when the referent stands for an idea rather than for a concrete object or person, or when the referent stands for a phrase or passage rather than for a single word. *Wh* questions may be constructed to give focus to the student's search for the antecedent. If these are not helpful, the passage can be simplified by blocking out all words not necessary to the pronoun-antecedent construction.

Another approach is to read the passage to the student, emphasizing through pitch, stress, and pause the relationship intended. Also charts can be constructed, moving from brief concrete referents to abstract, lengthy ones.

Example:

(1) mother = she
Jim = he
mother and Jim = they
Mother was the one who called me.

(2) Breaking my leg = that
Breaking my leg was the last straw. That made me give up skiing.

b. *Sentence Order.* Students need to be aware that sentence order can signal cumulative effects and causation. One way to help students see this is to change the order of sentences and discuss differences in meaning.

Example:

I hated him. He was kind. He was talented. He was popular.

vs.

He was kind. He was talented. He was popular. I hated him.

4. *Recovering Deep Structure.* Because the surface structure of a sen-

tence is not always sufficient to determine meaning, the student should be aware of underlying meanings that might be inferred. These can sometimes be obtained through oral reading. Example: He fed her dog food. The emphasis could be on *her* or *dog*. Another way to learn what the writer meant by the sentence is to read further. Example: He fed her dog food. She was insulted, (or) He fed her dog food. She barked for more. Another possibility is to provide a series of statements from which the student can select those with the same meanings and discuss his selections.

Example:
> She colored the tree orange.
> She colored the tree that was orange.
> She colored the orange tree.

Finally, context and previous experience need to be used to determine the intent of statements that are phrased in a contradictory fashion.

Example:
(1) Mary, I must have a loaf of bread right away.
    Do you want to go to the store for me? (The question is really a command.)
(2) Why, why must I do everything myself? Who can tell me? (No answer is required. The question is rhetorical.)

Oral reading by the teacher with appropriate inflections can help to convey the intended meanings of these statements. Or the student can be asked to choose among two or three interpretations that may alert him to the possibility of an implied rather than literal meaning. The student should be asked to offer support for his choice by giving examples from his own experiences.

SEMANTIC ABILITIES

Developing Semantic Knowledge and Abilities

A large vocabulary contributes greatly to comprehension, but the student should possess more than a large lexicon or store of words; he should also be aware of the changes in the meaning of words and ways of inferring meaning from context.[2] Though indirect learning can account for some vocabulary acquisition, there is evidence that vocabulary can be increased with conscious effort.

Selection of Vocabulary

1. *Student Selection.* Because it is difficult to anticipate which words are unknown, having the student skim through a passage to make a list or underline unknown words can be helpful. The student might also keep a vocabulary bookmarker to record unfamiliar words.
2. *Teacher Selection.* If the number of unknown words is large, the teacher can use the following criteria to select words for study:
   a. Those with high utility in daily life.
   b. Those necessary for comprehension in a specific subject area of interest to the student or needed by the student.
   c. Those that illustrate use of specific context clues or connotations.
   d. Those with affixes or roots that can unlock the meanings of many related words.

Instructional Procedures

1. *Classification by Semantic Features.* A student using this approach might be asked to classify words by some general feature: use, color, relationship, movement, and so on. Next the words might be classified by another feature and then another. Finally, words might be classified within categories. This procedure can be done in teams or singly. The advantage of using teams is that conversation and use of the words will occur, reinforcing the learning of the words. The reclassification fosters the extensiveness of meaning for the word.
   a. *Charts and Lists.* A student might be encouraged to collect words related to his special interests and record them on charts or lists. If the student's interest is cars, he might read or listen

---

[2] The reader is reminded that semantic knowledge cannot be separated from syntactic, conceptual, or other aspects of comprehension. The categories in this chapter are a convenience of presentation.

to car advertisements or read fiction related to racing or read mechanics' magazines and collect words he wants to add to his vocabulary. Some commercial materials are available that present words in high-interest categories: words to wear such as *beret, dashiki, turban*; or words to eat such as *omelet, parfait, ragout.* However, the student should be encouraged, in addition, to make his own list from menus, newspapers, advertisements, and catalogs. The next step is to practice the word orally in sentences and to write the word in sentences or short paragraphs so that it will be in the student's reading, speaking, and writing vocabulary.

b. *Word Cards.* Students can prepare cards with the word and its pronunciation on one side of the card and definitions and sentences containing the word on the other side. Students can team to hear each other's words, or a student can study independently. Language master cards can be prepared; or the teacher can make tapes that refer to the student's cards, requesting the student to find synonyms, pronounce the words, match definitions, and so forth.

2. *Remembering Words by Associations.* Students can be helped to remember words by associating them with ideas or experiences that have personal meaning. These associations can be jotted down on the list or cards or notebook kept by the student. The teacher can encourage students to think of associations by sharing her own associations. "When I think of *demolish,* I remember the headline, 'Western High School demolished Northern.' What do you think of when you see the word _____? Can you picture it in your mind? What do you see?" Labeling pictures, drawings, models, and objects can be useful. For example, magnetized cards can be used to label machine parts. Dramatizations, use of words in songs or quotations, association with objects, self, others, or experiences are all ways to learn new words by association.

3. *Roots and Affixes.* Care should be taken that the most frequently used affixes and roots with fairly consistent meanings are selected for study. Common prefixes include these:

un	dis	in	pre
re	de	anti	ex
pro	en	com	

Older students seeking to expand their vocabularies may learn the meanings of prefixes such as

mono	uni	multi	counter	im	a, an
bi	tri	auto	il	ir	ante
super	tele	homo	bene	trans	retro

However, students should be aware that some words containing letters common to affixes may not be affixed. One student remarked, on studying the prefix *mal*, that there wasn't anything bad about a mallard duck.

The study of roots and affixes has more utility if it is done in the context of a particular subject area. Because the words are likely to be used and encountered by the student within a field, retention will also be improved. Thus, *ideo, demos, anthro, polis, circum, geo*, and *scribe* are word parts that would be useful to study in social studies, whereas *osteo, neuro, micro, scope*, and *chron* are examples of word parts useful to study in science.

Matching exercises and grids can be used to study the transferability of word parts. Students might use lists of key roots and affixes to create new words and test each other on their ability to infer meaning.

4. *Context Clues.* A student should use the larger context—that beyond the word or the sentence—to comprehend unfamiliar words. Though there are several types of clues to meaning, there are some specific clues that might be taught. Practice with these can give confidence in inferential abilities so that the reader will be less likely to skip unknown words. To identify the types of context clues the student is encountering most frequently, the teacher should analyze the material the student is reading for content area subjects, as well as for leisure interests. In other words, context clues should be studied in context.

Some specific types of context clues are these:

> Comparison and contrast:
>> I'm not just pleased; I am *delighted.*
> Synonym or restatement:
>> I am pleased, *delighted,* to see you.

Circumstance or experience:

How good to see you. I am *delighted.*

Definition or direct explanation:

Delighted means to be highly pleased.

Cloze activities and nonsense words can be useful in teaching students to use context. The most important part of the instructional activity, however, is having the student discuss his reasons for the definition he selects. The teacher might be familiar with the "Jabberwocky" ("Twas brillig and the slithy toves did gyre and gimble in the wabe") to illustrate one's ability to obtain meaning from word order, setting, and function words. Context clues are not infallible, and the reader needs to be flexible in using them. To emphasize this, one might use the following examples:

That statue is beautiful, but his one is *frumgump,*

But might suggest the opposite of beautiful.

On the other hand, consider the following:

I don't know which to choose. That statue is beautiful, but this one is *frumgump,* too.

Other ways of teaching context clues include (1) underlining words that give clues to meaning. Example: I like *card games.* I'm looking forward to learning to play *canasta.* (2) Diagrams, an example of which follows:

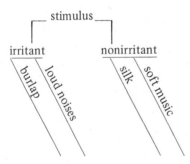

(3) Self-correcting exercises. Example: We visited many churches on

our tour. In the Middle East we saw many m $\underline{\ }$ $\_$ $\_$ $\_$ $\_$ $\underline{s}$. (models, mountains, mosques)

5. *Connotation.* Some students give the impression of being insensitive to connotation. When one boy said, "She is fat," he was asked if *heavy* would be a better word to use. "Why?" he asked, "She is fat, isn't she?" But when asked if he would want people to call him *skinny* or *slim,* he began to see the difference. Other students react strongly to connotation but are not aware that words have both literal and suggested meanings. Some problems can arise in reading content area material when students confuse denotation and connotation for words such as *scientific, experiment, democracy, socialism,* and *communism.* Some instructional procedures are these:

a. *Classification* of words under positive, neutral, and negative headings. These words and phrases might be drawn from the content of a particular subject area and displayed in the classroom on a chart to which students add words, or a student might keep such a chart in his notebook. Example:

Positive (good feeling)	Neutral (not good or bad)	Negative (bad feeling)

For older students, words such as the following might be put on the chart:

thrifty	reformer	slum child
pride	stingy	economically disadvantaged child
secret	describe	backward country
arrogant	flatter	underdeveloped nation
clandestine	praise	evolving nation
private	agitator	culturally different child

Younger students may sort words such as these:

fat	cold	slow	walk	rest	stay home
hot	thin	fast	run	help	go out
sleep	nap	sit	work	try	get up

An important part of the classification process is discussion as to how connotative meanings have come about, changes in meaning over time, and differences in interpretation among individuals.

b. Substitution of words in a passage to create different effects. The teacher might select a neutral descriptive passage and have students substitute words to create a positive and then a negative description. Cloze procedures might be used. Example:

Every morning the woman walks to the store to buy a
    paper.
At the last minute the hag hobbles to the dime store
    to grab the daily rag.
____ the _____ to the ____ to ____ a ____.(Create a
    positive description.)

c. *Selection* of words within a sentence to obtain appropriate effects. Example:

I think of myself as _____ with money.
    (generous, a spendthrift, careless, stingy, careful,
    tight)
With regard to studying, you could say I'm _____.
    (disciplined, carefree, lazy, compulsive,
    inconsistent)

d. *Analogy and Figures of Speech.* Analogy and figures of speech might be identified by the teacher or the student, and alternative analogies or figures of speech might be created. Advertisements, literature, and essays are all fertile sources. *Mad* magazine provides humorous examples that expose subtle attempts to use connotation.

e.   *Inferences in Long Selections.* At times connotation is studied as devices in sentences or passages whereas the building of effects or the culmination of devices is ignored. Care should be taken to study connotation in both nonfiction and fictional books.

6.   *Derivation.* The origin of words might be studied as a device to create interest in studying word meaning or assist memory if the student finds this activity appealing. Some commercial materials are available, but the teacher should collect words within a particular subject area that lend themselves to etymological study. Another place to start is with the origin of the names of the students and locations with which they are familiar.

7.   *Dictionary.* One cannot take for granted that students know how to use the dictionary or that they are aware of the kinds of information contained therein. Some students don't know the alphabet; others are not aware that the dictionary is arranged alphabetically; many cannot use the key to pronunciation or guide words on each page.

Care should be taken that use of the dictionary not be drudgery. If dictionary use is integrated into instruction naturally, the student is more apt to perceive its usefulness. Games such as Scrabble and crossword puzzles are a positive way to provide word study and opportunities for recourse to the dictionary. The thesaurus should also be introduced to the student as an aid to word choices for speaking and writing.

8.   *Reading and Listening.* By listening to material read aloud and following the text, the student can learn the pronunciation of words that may be in his reading vocabulary but not his speaking vocabulary. Those words that are not in either the student's reading or speaking vocabulary can be enhanced by hearing them pronounced in context because tone, pitch, stress, and pause provide additional clues to the meanings of words in both a literal and connotative sense. Commercial materials—tapes and records—are available for this purpose, and the teacher can, of course, read directly to students or make her own tapes. Because of the richness of context clues aided by vocalization, the student will be able to experience far more difficult materials, enjoyably than he can read independently. In this, as in other activities, the student should be encouraged to *use* the words—say them and write them in a variety of contexts.

REASONING ABILITIES

Growth in Reasoning Abilities

Reasoning abilities can be improved if the student is provided with settings rich in opportunities created by a supportive teacher whose role is to reflect, clarify, and question. *Consciousness of abstracting* is the critical insight for growth in reasoning abilities. Though one can accept ideas such as "we can never know *all* about anything" or "words are not the events but symbols for the events," being mindful and applying these notions are difficult tasks. Therefore, activities related to logic or critical thinking should be incorporated whenever possible in instructional situations. Composing in speech and writing can demonstrate *abstracting to communicate,* and comprehending speech and writing can demonstrate *abstracting to understand.*

Instructional Procedures

1. *Awareness of Egocentricity.* Direct experiences with differences among people as to how information is perceived, expressed, abstracted, and interpreted can serve as referents or reminders not to assume that everyone experiences things the same way. Such group activities as tasting food, witnessing a staged incident involving a violent argument, hearing conflicting trial testimony, and viewing tachistoscope presentations of pictures and then comparing one's impressions and interpretations can help make the point that people's senses are inadequate, that past experiences help to determine what they will select and deselect in abstracting information, and that the same words may have different meanings for different people. The teacher may wish to keep objects, pictures, or charts associated with the experiences, displayed prominently as reminders of the foregoing concepts so that students or the teacher can refer to them as necessary. Not only should the difficulties associated with differences be stressed, but also the positive elements resulting in creativity and expansion of one's views.

2. *Identification of Sources of Common Errors in Reasoning.* Students might review and list problems in reasoning such as the following and

search for instances of serious violations in their own and others' expressions:

a. *Allness* statements (such as "All women are inferior," "All minorities are alike," "All dogs are loyal") should be analyzed and practice given in using qualifiers: *some, a few, many, most, once in a while, possibly. Implied* "all" should also be examined. "A dog is loyal" implies "dog=loyalty," but dogs may only *appear* to be loyal.

b. *Is* of identify should be analyzed as not meaning "equal to." Practice should be given in qualifiers such as it *appears* to me at this time, it *seems* to be, it *might* be.

c. Either-or arguments should be analyzed in terms of false choices, shades of gray rather than black and white, conditions, and alternative choices.

d. False premises in if-then arguments should be tested. Example: "Rabbits have two ears; you have two ears; you are a rabbit" can be restated in a syllogism, "*If* all creatures with two ears are rabbits, and *if* you have two ears, *then* you are a rabbit." Students might be given practice in recognizing, constructing, and testing syllogisms.

e. Inconsistencies might be examined to evaluate conclusions.

f. Fact needs to be discriminated from opinion by listing the source, descriptive characteristics, and purposes of both kinds of statements.

g. Propaganda devices can be listed in the student's terminology and instances found of each device by using selections such as advertisements and political speeches.

  The teacher might make a file of clippings that lend themselves to analysis by students in order to detect problems associated with the preceding list. These can be duplicated for group analysis and discussion. Another useful activity is coding. The student might code each loaded word, value judgment, generalization, false premise, or propaganda device in a selection. Students may be asked to bring in their own selections for analysis by other students. Their interactions can be recorded and played back for group analysis.

h. Oversimplification (in instances such as attributing a result to a single cause, going beyond the facts to make an unsupportable generalization, and depending on inadequate information and authorities) needs to be identified in reading and listening.

3. *Seeing Relationships.* As relationships may be implicit or explicit, students will need experiences with both. The explicit relationships are often easier to perceive; therefore, it may be useful to start with these and use them as points of reference. Relationships may later be analyzed through:

a. Selection of logical statements.

$$
\begin{Bmatrix} \text{All} \\ \text{Some} \\ \text{No} \end{Bmatrix} \text{girls} \begin{Bmatrix} \text{are} \\ \text{were} \\ \text{seem to be} \end{Bmatrix} \text{athletes.}
$$

b. Uses of *is*.
   (1) ascribes—is beautiful.
   (2) identifies—is my mother.
   (3) indicates existence—man is.
   (4) involves—to live is to suffer.
   (5) relates—is better.

c. Conjunctions.
   (1) coordinate—*and, or, but*
   (2) subordinate—*since, because, when, which, if*

d. Sequence.
   (1) to imply conditionality—ice cream will be served. I will be there.
   (2) to imply causation—I didn't eat breakfast. I'm hungry.

e. Transitional words.
   (1) order and sequence—*first, next, finally*
   (2) cause and effect—*therefore, as a result*
   (3) comparison and contrast—*on the other hand, but, similarly*

f. Syllogisms: *if, then* statements.

g. Categorial statements.
   (1) identify—"These were _____ ."
   (2) exclusion—"None of them were _____ ."
   (3) inclusion—"All _____ were _____ ."
   (4) disjunction—"Some _____ were _____ ."

Instructional activities might include reading and writing detective stories; creating or using syllogisms provided by the teacher to build theories; playing games such as *Wiff and Proof* and card games in which categories must be inferred or created; solving brain teasers;

using material such as *Reading for Understanding* or *Test Lessons in Reading Reasoning* in which inferences must be drawn from implied relationships and discussing the student's reasons for his answer; asking questions about material such as, How did the writer organize his ideas? Why? Does this result *always* occur? What else might have been a cause? and so forth.

4. *Evaluating Adequacy and Accuracy of Information.*
    a. Paragraphs might be analyzed by listing statements of main idea and proof to determine adequacy.
    b. Longer selections might be analyzed by outlining the writer's conclusions; listing his proof, purpose for writing, and sources of information; and critiquing each element.
    c. The teacher might model questions that the students can later ask themselves and others:
        (1) What are the writer's qualifications?
        (2) Why did he write this? For whom?
        (3) How recent is this information? Is the date important?
        (4) What are the writer's main points?
        (5) Did he leave out important information?
        (6) What kinds of information did he omit? Why?
        (7) Are his conclusions reasonable?
        (8) Did he sufficiently use qualifiers?
        (9) Is there evidence of propaganda devices?
        (10) How do his conclusions and presentation compare with other writers on this subject?
        (11) How might one account for discrepancies?
        (12) Did the writer use half-truths?

COGNITIVE LEVELS OF COMPREHENSION

Knowing Through Manipulating

There appear to be levels of knowing. When we recognize something, we say we know it, yet this may be a superficial kind of knowing. But when we experience something in a variety of contexts, our knowledge is likely to be more extensive and to have more depth. To the extent that we can manipulate things and ideas with some degree of skill and insight, we can reach a more profound level of knowing. Thus, a reader might understand on a literal level, but he may not be able to interpret or evaluate or apply what he has read. The reverse may be true. A child read *The Scarlet Letter* at an early age. She could interpret some of the feelings and the cultural boundaries of the main characters, but she did not know what the precipitating event was. Though literal comprehension often underlies interpretive comprehension, this may not always be true.

The task of the teacher is to assess the extent of the student's comprehension and to provide experiences in manipulating ideas that will help him grow.

Instructional Procedures

1. *Reconstructing literal meaning* is not necessarily an easy task. If most readers were asked to paraphrase a chapter in a text on nuclear physics, they would find the task demanding. Factors relating to difficulty in literal comprehension include knowledge of concepts, terminology, complexity of syntax, abstractness, tense, and organization. In addition, the reader must know what is expected of him or what he expects of himself. When asked to tell what he read, a child replied, "I don't know; I wasn't listening to me."

    The task of the teacher is to provide experiences appropriate to the individual and to assist the individual in his personal quest for comprehension, but in both instances with the learner's awareness of the purpose and utility of the procedure.

    a. *Recognizing* information in paraphrase is one of the easier tasks that can be suggested. Though a large quantity of commercial material is available, the teacher can construct his own paraphrased choices tailored to the student's ability in material of special interest to that student. In addition, the student may skim to find details or put a series of cards depicting events into chronological order or match a speaker with his dialog or characteristics. If the student cannot recognize paraphrased information, he might work through several language experience sequences culminating in his rephrasing his own ideas. If the student's problem is severe, he might match the information to a photograph or drawing.

    b. *Translating* information requires a different set of abilities (production) from that needed in recognizing information (association). Those with severe difficulties might pantomime, act out, or perform a task; or they might draw a picture or diagram to indicate their comprehension nonverbally. Others may be given tasks such as, "Tell me in your own words," to translate information verbally. Other verbal production experiences include:

1. Completing paraphrased cloze sentences.
2. Reducing content to telegraph length.
3. Rewriting prose into dialog (or vice versa).
4. Outlining key points.
5. Filling in partially completed outlines.
6. Rewriting in another tense.
7. Rewriting in other literary forms: poems, diaries, news accounts, letters, cartoons, and so forth.
8. Making summaries of events.
9. Making summaries of ideas.
10. Reconstructing a sequence of events.
11. Following directions.
12. Locating summarizing statements or paragraphs.

2. *Interpretive reading* can and should be developed with literal comprehension. Abstractness and complexity, along with the reader's maturity and experience, influence his interpretive abilities. But even a young child can respond to questions such as, "What do you think will happen next?" and "Do you think this really happened?" Some other approaches include:

a. *Relating to Personal Experience.* (1) Prior to reading the teacher might ask questions such as, "Can you remember a situation in which you felt you had to try, but were afraid of failure?" or "What are some reasons why people are afraid of failing?" After discussing these the teacher might say, "Here is a story about the feelings a man had as he attempted an almost impossible task. Let's read it and then discuss how he seemed to feel." (2) After reading the teacher might encourage introspection or reflection with respect to matters such as universality or cultural influences. "Do you think a man who had never experienced poverty would have felt the same way? Why?"

b. *Moving Toward Higher Levels of Abstraction.* In this procedure the teacher begins with questions to clarify the physical setting and events; then moves to questions about the feelings of the characters, then their rationale or code, then the social-psychological implications, and, finally, the theme and its implications for the reader and for mankind.

c.   *Absorbing Background.* The teacher provides an opportunity to prepare for the reading of fiction by a study of history, preceding events, social customs, classes, architecture, music, paintings, decor, education, and so forth so that the student can be better able to remove himself to some extent from his own cultural perspective. Conversely, with nonfiction such study can help the student understand how the writer came to hold his views and what the impact of his writing was. The goal is to help the student be less judgmental and trapped by his own experiences. In fact, judgment should be withheld until exhaustive efforts have been made to understand and interpret the writer's intent.

d.   *Discriminating Between Descriptive and Ascriptive Statements.* In both reading and writing, students should understand and recognize the difference between observation and inference. Statements such as the following might be used for practice:

O = Observation: something you can see.
I = Inference: something you think is so.
    O   (1)   The man trembled.
    I   (2)   The man was afraid.
    O   (3)   The man staggered.
    I   (4)   The man was drunk.

Later, students might search for such statements in their own writing and that of others. Detective stories can provide instances of observation and influence.

Example:
    "The man's hands were stained green and black (observation). He might have been working with the chemical _____ (inference), which is used in making _____ (observation). Therefore, we will look for him in a _____ factory." (Unstated inference: "He might work in a _____ factory.")

e. *Marking Books.* Printed materials owned by the student or reproduced for him by the teacher can be marked in various ways to provide a dialog between the reader and the author. Students might exchange marked materials with someone of their own choice as a way of sharing personal questions, insights, and feelings.

f. *Inferring Relationships.* Students might be asked to compare or contrast ideas or characters, look for cause and effect, or discuss the implications of a sequence in order to interpret the nature of relationships. Another possibility would be to ask students how the selection would be changed if a particular idea or character had not been introduced. Finally, the student might analyze the effect of alternate forms of organization of the selection.

g. *Analyzing Assumptions.* In order to interpret information, one needs to be aware, particularly, of unstated assumptions. Students might first be made acquainted with the pro- and anti-slavery views of people living in the seventeenth and eighteenth centuries and then read tracts to determine the writer's point of view. Next students might analyze more subtle assumptions underlying current nonfiction and fiction. They might be asked, "What beliefs about government are not stated, but implied in this writing?" "What values are assumed by the writer to be shared by the reader?"

3. *Synthesizing information* can involve observing, recording, classifying, weighing, comparing, outlining, and summarizing. Students may need experiences in both structural summaries and conceptual summaries. These experiences can lead to a synthesis of the information with the understandings or beliefs or the values of the individual.

a. Structural summaries are those that follow the form employed by the writer: his organization and mode of presentation. Students may outline by headings and subheadings or by following the sequence of paragraph types (introductory, definitional, illustrative, and so forth).

b. Conceptual summaries are those that condense the most important ideas within a selection. Students can develop their skills by paraphrasing what another student has stated orally to the speaker's satisfaction; then by summarizing what the speaker has said to his satisfaction. The same sequence can be repeated with the writing of another student. (This interaction is most helpful because it is unlikely that the student can receive feedback from most authors.) Finally, the students might summarize written selections independently and compare them.

On a more difficult level, the student might summarize the shape of a writer's argument and compare it to that of other writers.

4. *Evaluating Information.* One usually evaluates something by comparison or by utility. A presentation might be judged to be better organized, more original, more interesting, more complete, less biased than another. Or a presentation might be judged as satisfactory with respect to a particular need. These are some of the judgments a reader might be asked to make or wish to make as he evaluates.

    a. For an in-depth evaluation of a book, the reader might skim all of the books he can find on a particular subject. Then he might select those relevant for comparison to the book of interest. The reader should then skim these books to find relevant ideas and passages. Next he should decide the questions or issues that need to be addressed in order to explore the topic. Finally, he should develop criteria for adequate or superior presentations. The reader is now ready to compare his evaluation.

    b. Students who are not ready for such sophisticated evaluation might be provided with outlines for the evaluation of fiction or nonfiction, or they may share their impressions with each other informally.

    c. On a personal level the student might evaluate a selection empathetically. Whether others dislike the selection or not should not be an issue. The teacher should serve as a model by valuing the student's right to his opinion and not imposing other values on him. The teacher may help the student clarify his personal reactions through reflective statements.

5. *Problem solving and creativity* require self-directedness on the part of the student. If the teacher defines the problem and directs the hypothesizing, collecting, and organization of information, the student is engaged in performing a task, not solving a problem. The teacher can, however, create situations that encourage creative abilities and problem-solving abilities, and the teacher can help the student identify factors that inhibit or facilitate his skills. The teacher can also promote favorable attitudes toward oneself and others as

being creative or having the potential to be an effective problem-solver.

a.   *Promoting New Insights Through Reading in Supposedly Unrelated Fields.* Recently, a book appeared describing relationships among historical events, epidemics, and the physical ailments of major historical figures. This unusual interpretation of history was the result of combining knowledge of history with knowledge of a supposedly unrelated field, medicine. The teacher can set the stage for new interpretations by helping students think of unlikely combinations and finding information to be read and analyzed from a new perspective. This procedure, along with similar activities, can help students develop awareness of functional fixedness and ways to combat being limited by old associations and solutions.

b.   *Applying Old Insights to New Problems.* To some extent this may be viewed as the opposite of the preceding objective, but both abilities are important. By providing a variety of new situations that call for the application of previously learned principles, the teacher can facilitate the rate of acquisition of a learning set and its transfer to new situations. Example: "A chef wishes to prepare a particular dish, but one ingredient, baking soda, is not available. What should the chef do?" Aside from the answer, "He can make something else," students will need to review the function of baking soda in a recipe and read to discover a suitable substitute. This procedure can be repeated in other settings calling for the application of principles from chemistry or math or other fields.

c.   *Collecting and Organizing Information.* To the extent the student decides which categories of information are to be collected and how the information will be organized, he will be engaged in a problem-solving activity. The teacher may help by suggesting the student keep category options open while an exploration of the problem takes place. She may show students how to write categories on slips of paper and shift them about in order to examine alternative forms of organization. Students might also experiment with analogies—learning a new language is like fixing dinner, growing plants is like driving a car, and so on—as a way of discovering new categories and ways of organizing.

d.   *Defining Problems.* One of the most important and often ne-

glected part of the problem-solving process is defining the problem. The student may be helped somewhat by being given a list
of the traditional guidelines such as the following: Is the problem too broad? Is the statement clear? Is the problem manage-
able? Defining the problem requires much support from the
teacher for some students. The teacher might help by asking the
student what it is he doesn't know, whether or not there might
be more than one solution to the problem, whether the problem
can be stated as a question, what the student means by his
statements, and so on. The teacher should not give the problem
statement to the student but might suggest areas of exploration.

RATE OF PROCESSING

Factors related to rate of processing in oral and written speech include familiarity with content and form of presentation, purposes for attending,
flexibility, attitude, concentration, and practice. The reader's rate is further
influenced by his word recognition abilities (does he have a sufficient store
of words that he can instantly recognize?), phrasing, and lack of inhibiting
behaviors such as unnecessary and excessive subvocalization and regression.
Work with phrasing and word recognition should precede concentrated attention to rate and, especially, speed reading.

INSTRUCTIONAL PROCEDURES

1. *Dealing with Inhibiting Beliefs.* Some readers do not know whether
    or not they have the ability to read faster; others feel sure that they
    cannot; some are compulsive in their need to read every word. The
    teacher needs to assess the student's knowledge and attitudes about
    rates of reading, demonstrate the skills that can be acquired, dis-
    cuss their positive and negative aspects, and, above all, help the
    students prove to themselves that they can increase their reading
    rate for specific purposes in particular kinds of materials. Mechani-
    cal devices, if they are available, may be used to demonstrate vari-
    ous rates and to help the reader realize that he can read faster without
    substantial loss of comprehension for some kinds of materials. The
    teacher should tell the student to look over some fairly easy selec-

tions, choose one, and read so that he can answer some general questions about the content. The mechanical device should be set at the student's usual rate. (This can be determined through formal testing or by having the student try various rates and choose one where he feels comfortable.) Next the teacher can gradually increase the rate while continuing to evaluate comprehension. Most students will discover they can read faster. If mechanical devices are not available, the teacher can practice pushing a card over the page while timing herself in order to learn to approximate various rates.

The major question is the student's *need* to read faster. If the student's rate is so slow that it interferes with his vocational or academic achievement, he should be encouraged to acquire more techniques for reading faster. If such is not the case, the choice of increasing rates of reading should be left to the student. He may be encouraged, however, to experiment with skimming techniques for a while before making his decision.

2. *Discouraging Inhibiting Behaviors.* Even good readers regress and subvocalize when material is difficult for them. The teacher needs to learn whether the student is using finger-pointing, regression, whispering, and lip-moving because such crutches are needed to understand the content or whether these are unnecessary—possibly habits acquired at a word decoding stage that have not been discarded or habits fixed by the student's continual placement in materials too difficult for him.

The teacher should help the student find easy, interesting materials for reading, explain the need to avoid unnecessary crutches, and provide regular practice sessions. If the student finds devices such as hand-pacing or holding a pencil in his mouth helpful, he might use them. Mechanical devices can also be used to help the student practice reading without regression. It should be understood, however, that some regression is helpful and that many people need to use subvocalizing occasionally.

3. *Increasing Prediction Abilities.* Students need to be encouraged to increase their knowledge of ways to predict what might be said and to apply their knowledge. The following activities may be useful.

    a. Reading passages with all words except subjects and verbs blocked out, then summarizing content, and finally checking summary with unblocked, original passage.

    b. Reading only parts of selections: title and first and last para-

graphs, first lines of paragraphs, summarizing statements (omitting illustrations and examples), subheadings, and so forth.
These activities may be followed by briefly summarizing ideas
and/or the writer's form of organization, then confirming one's
prediction of content and structure by reading the entire
passage, chapter or book.

4. *Matching Rate to Purpose and Familiarity with Material.* After he
has completed an overview of the material, the student should consider his own familiarity with the content, the organization (well-
organized information can be read faster), and his purpose for reading
(to recall details, analyze the discussion, follow the plot, and so on)
so that he can select an appropriate rate or rates for reading. The student may need to read everything slowly, to skim, or to skim some
parts and study others. Many readers unconsciously read everything
from adventure stories to physics texts at the same rate. The teacher
can foster flexibility by providing materials on a range of topics,
engaging the student in discussion of his overview, selection of purpose and rate/s, and providing practice for reading at various rates.

5. *Developing Skimming and Scanning Abilities.* The following practices can be helpful in increasing rate:

   a. Frequent timed reading of easy material followed by a brief
   summary of what was read or by answering comprehension
   questions. Keeping a graph of progress in rate with comprehension.

   b. Depending upon the individual, hand-pacing, pushing a card
   over the page, or using mechanical devices. These are motivational for some students. If mechanical devices are used, two
   graphs should be kept: one for practice with the device and
   one for practice without it. This will help insure transfer.

   c. Scanning to find a date, name, or section of material where an
   idea is discussed.

   d. Nonlinear processing: practicing on material whose content is
   quite familiar to the reader—association of information presented in nonlinear form. The teacher might read a list of words,
   such as *late, law, children, guide, time, responsibility, complaints,
   violence, television, increase, parents, legislature, protest,* and ask
   the student what he thinks is in the passage and what were
   the bases of his guesses. After practice in this, the teacher
   might use unrelated phrases intermixed with nonessential
   words and phrases to discuss possible content. Next the student

might preview material and then practice various eye-movement patterns such as ↓, ⟨, ⟨ and attempt free recall.·

Nonlinear processing requires much concentration, flexibility, and content background. Many students will not want to attempt it or be able to be very successful with it.

RECALL OF INFORMATION

Recall is influenced by attention, clear sensory reception, intention to remember, meaningfulness to the receiver, organization of the information, interference or repression, vividness, assimilation into organization of previously acquired information, rehearsal of information, and application of information. When a student appears to have difficulty in remembering, the aforementioned factors should be carefully reviewed with the learner and adjustments made to the teaching/learning process.

Instructional Procedures

1. *Severe Retrieval Problems.* Some students may be helped by tracing, or revisualization, or reauditorization procedures such as those described in Chapter 3. Those who have difficulty recalling the content of long sentences may practice reading and repeating aloud sentence expansions. (Ex.: I ran. I ran quickly. I ran quickly down the street. I ran quickly down the street to the drugstore.) Some may need stimulus pictures or questions from the teacher: "Did what? Ran how? Ran where?" Students with problems recalling nonphonetic words might be helped by a series of promptings in one part of the word and then in another. Example:

```
f i g h t
_ i g h t          (Student's task is to fill in the missing letters.)
f i g h _
_ _ g h t
f _ _ _ t
_ i g h _
_ _ _ _ _
```

Each student should be studied to determine the kinds of things he has difficulty in retrieving and the prompting that seem to work best for him. The student should know that frequent practice is a must and why. He will need much support and some survival strategies for social, academic, and vocational situations that are likely to arise. For example, the student may need to carry his phone number and address, key words relating to assignments, a spelling dictionary, a daily and weekly schedule book, or a brief diary of daily events, depending on his age, abilities, and situation. The student may be helped by sharing his ideas with others who have similar problems or have had them in the past.

2. *Attention.* If the material is perceived by the learner as boring, unimportant, too long, too difficult, or at variance with his beliefs, he is more likely to be inattentive. These factors should be discussed with the learner in an open, nonjudgmental fashion. The teacher should seek to learn from the student what his perceptions are as to how he best remembers and which factors seem to be inhibiting. The teacher might offer suggestions to be tried as an experiment and jointly evaluated. These might include the following:

    a. Selective attention. Looking only for a few important ideas instead of trying to remember everything.

    b. Working with material selected on the basis of learner interest and knowledge of concepts with uncomplicated vocabulary and syntactic structure.

    c. Using brief selections with short, simple recall tasks.

    d. Taking short breaks instead of pretending to attend.

    e. Being active while reading: underlining key ideas, remembering points made in discussion, making marginal notes or vertical slashes, outlining and/or talking back to the author.

    f. Actively intending to recall. Stating reasons why he wishes to remember the key points before starting to read.

    g. Looking for organizational clues: headings and subheadings, italicized words, organizational structure words, color highlighting, and/or numbered sets of ideas.

    h. Preparing for reading or listening by participating in experiences related to the topic; exploring audiovisual presentations; and/or reading easier fiction or nonfiction passages, short selections, or books related to the topic.

    i. Rewarding oneself for attention with breaks, alternative activities, food, or whatever is rewarding for the individual concerned. Keep a graph of increasing attention span.

j. Scheduling and sequencing demanding or less desirable tasks when the individual is most alert.

k. Using time limits. Example: giving oneself five minutes to find the main points of the author.

l. Adapting and practicing SQ3R strategies.

m. Avoiding a distracting atmosphere.

3. *Organization, Association, and Assimilation.* Information is more easily remembered if it is organized in a meaningful fashion and related to what has been previously learned. Some suggestions include these:

a. *Classifying and Grouping Ideas under a Category or Label.*

Examples:
    Three results of colonization
    Characteristics of pagodas
    Uses of flagstone

b. *Using Numbers, Letters, Pictures, or Rhymes as Mnemonic Devices.* Examples:

(1) Code numbers to letters:

0 1 2 3 4 5 6 7 8 9
a b c d e f g h i j

(a) 1 0 6 6 = b a g g–picture William the Conquerer carrying a K-Mart shopping bag.
If the letters are not pronounceable, key them to a set of words:

(b) 1 4 9 2 = b e j c *b*ig *e*lephants *j*umping over *Co*lumbus–picture the scene

(2) Using rhymes and/or alteration:

(a) The Japanese phrase *sumimasen* means "Excuse me." Associate it with "Sue me! My sin."

(b) Presidents: Wash, Ad, Mad, Jeff, and so forth.

c. *Mapping or Diagraming.* Key concepts from a chapter or book can be remembered by putting them into a pattern. The *student* should make the map or diagram, not the teacher, for the thinking and sorting process is a valuable aid to memory. Each word or phrase should be placed on a slip of paper. These can be shifted about to make the pattern. Students who have difficulty getting started might be helped by using *who, when, where, why, what, how* questions. Teaming to make maps and diagrams is helpful because students will be forced to *verbalize* the concepts and their relationships. This is another important aid to recall. Later, they should be encouraged to close their eyes and visualize their diagrams. Example:

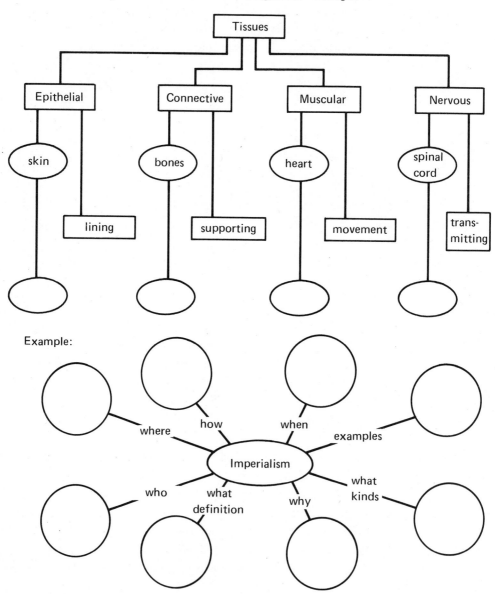

Other examples might include these: mapping the parts of English government on a symbol such as the king or queen, mapping elements of communication theory onto a network of highways or a diagram of a telephone hookup or mapping the parts of the United States government onto a line drawing of Uncle Sam. Example:

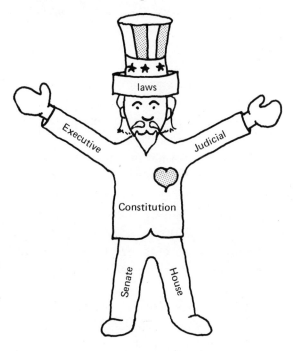

d.   *Analogy.* One of the most effective ways to remember a set of abstract, complex relationships is through analogy. Some examples of working with analogies are these:

(1)   Role playing. Students assume the parts of Lincoln, Grant, Lee in the Civil War.

(2)   Simulation. Students solve problems through in-basket techniques. Answer letters as an advice columnist might.

(3)   Comparing. Students may be asked how various types of human dwellings compare to those of certain animal species or how the Roman government compared to ours.

(4)   Projection. Another useful approach for some students is to imagine their actions or feelings in a situation. Example: You are an antibody who has just been notified of an invasion. Another example: You are a South American representative to the World Food Crisis Conference in

1966. What are your chief concerns? Outline them in a brief diary entry or a letter to your family.

(5) Association. The teacher may ask questions to help students relate new information: "What does this remind you of? In what ways?" Students can learn ways of association that may not have occurred to them through sharing. Later they can be encouraged to ask themselves similar questions: "Where have I seen or heard something like this before?" "How does this new information confirm or disconfirm what I knew or believed?"

4. *Rehearsal to Retrieve Information.* Several activities have been found useful to practice information in short-term memory so that it is more likely to be retained for a long period of time. These include the following:

a. *Reciting.* Verbal information is best retained if the learner speaks aloud or writes. Thinking about the words is much less effective. The learner should recite in the same manner in which the material will be used. (The recite step in SQ3R is one of the most important components in the sequence.) Reciting is more effective than rereading, for recall. Nonverbal information might be rehearsed through drawing, diagraming, or performing.

b. *Reviewing.* Brief, frequent periods of review are much more effective than one or two lengthy sessions. Some students find it helpful to make fact cards: Cut 3 by 5 cards in half; write the question on one side and the answer on the other. Hold these together with a rubber band, and keep them available for review at odd moments: waiting for a bus, riding in a car, and/or waiting in lines. Another possibility is to have students quiz each other or to make examinations and take them.

Overlearning, continuing to review or practice after one has learned the material, results in better recall over a longer period of time than stopping when one considers he has learned the material. Most learning becomes less available over time when no practice or application has occurred.

c. *Avoiding Interference.* Studying before going to sleep is a way to avoid the interference of new information. Scheduling the content of learning so that similar forms, sounds, and ideas do not interfere is also effective. Students should be helped to schedule their studying so that minimal interference will occur. They also should be aware that many people have difficulty in remembering things that are unpleasant or that disagree with their views. Therefore, they should learn to give special attention to these situations. One possibility is to make comparative lists of ideas, characteristics, events so that the less pleasant concept will be tied to the more pleasant one.

A SYNTHESIS OF INSTRUCTION IN COMPREHENSION: AN ILLUSTRATION

In constructing a plan of instruction, the teacher needs to consider the student's feelings and interests, as well as his abilities. The emphasis too often in instruction has been on the weaknesses of the student. This is unfortunate because the student's strengths are equally important. In fact, they may be highly significant as potential for growth, a place from which to build and to obtain clues to functioning. Another area, often neglected, is the student's need to cope with demands from his environment that cannot be ameliorated. Many subject-area teachers will not change their texts or their methods. Printed matter used in daily, social, and business exchanges needs to be confronted. Therefore, the instructional plan needs to include feelings, interests, needs, strengths, and weaknesses.

The student should be involved to a high degree in determining the form and content of the plan. Through constant feedback and discussion, the student should also be involved in adjusting the plan.

An Example

The teacher is considering the needs and interests of Richard. She has interviewed Richard; he has completed a Student Priorities Form; she has collected records and comments from other teachers, and she has administered some informal, open book assessment tests.

Richard is in eleventh grade. He reads *generally* on a junior high level, but he has good comprehension of material pertaining to auto mechanics. His grades in biology and social science are very poor. He wants to attend the local community college after high school to complete a two-year degree in an area pertaining to mechanics. His low grades embarrass him, and he wants to improve his reading and study skills.

In order to get a better picture of Richard's strengths and weaknesses, the teacher profiles Richard's abilities (Figure 8.2). After sharing the profile with Richard and reflecting on his comments, she makes an initial plan that seems to fit his needs (Figure 8.3). Although this plan doesn't use commercial materials, she does intend to use some judiciously in order to illustrate a principle or provide practice. (A list of materials is presented in Figure 8.6 at the end of this chapter.)

FIGURE 8.2.   Strengths and needs in comprehension

Richard

(student)

Comprehension Factors:	Areas of Interest or Concern:			
	Personal Reading Interests: detective stories western adventures	Subject Area Reading	Vocational Reading	Social-Business Reading
1. Conceptual Knowledge		Biology. concept development below average	strong in mechanical areas	
2. Perceptual Abilities	Can easily follow plot in detective stories	Problem in setting purpose and shifting set in social science	Able to concentrate in auto-mechanics books	
3. Syntactic Abilities	Problems with anaphoras	Loses thought in complex sentences in social science		

FIGURE 8.2.   Continued

Comprehension Factors:	Areas of Interest or Concern:			
	Personal Reading Interests: detective stories western adventures	Subject Area Reading	Vocational Reading	Social-Business Reading
4. Semantic Knowledge	Difficulty with connotation		Good on associative level for mechanical terms	Limited general vocabulary; doesn't understand abbreviations in bus schedules
5. Reasoning Abilities	Good in predicting outcome in detective stories	Difficulty recognizing propaganda devices in social science		Can recognize and use qualifiers in reading and discussing sports articles
6. Cognitive Levels of Comprehension	Difficulty drawing inferences in character interpretation		Can do problem solving in auto repair	
7. Rate of Processing	Generally slow		Scanning skills good in auto-mechanics indexes	
8. Recall of Information		Poor in biology and social science	Generally good for mechanic manuals	

FIGURE 8.3. Excerpts from initial plan to improve comprehension

Richard

(student)

Materials	Purpose	Reading Levels	Projected Activities	Schedule
Auto-mechanics: books periodicals	Power in comprehension	High school	Keeping a vocabulary notebook, making a personal reference guide	
Detective stories, Western adventures	Fluency	Upper elementary junior high	Skimming, recalling content	Individual sessions 30 min M W F
Biology texts, films, tapes	Conceptual growth	Upper elementary junior high school	Listening and viewing, making charts, discussion	Group sessions 20 min M W F
Social science texts	Study skills, syntactic-semantic processes	Junior high high school	SQ3R, mapping, recasting sentences	Home practice 30 min daily (min.)
Newspapers	Vocabulary, logical reasoning		Making vocabulary cards with examples of slanted language, discussion	

The teacher thinks of levels, not level, of reading difficulty in selecting materials for Richard. First, an easy level to build fluency. Second, a level suited to his present functioning to manipulate ideas and develop skill in attending and in flexibility of set. Third, a level that is somewhat difficult, but within his grasp, to promote growth. Finally, she examines the materials he must use in other classes or outside school in order to look for ways to help him achieve some success with them.

A Reminder

This chapter has been presented with the realization that the categories discussed overlap and interact in various situations. However, because of the
difficulty many teachers have had in the diagnostic/prescriptive aspects of
comprehension, the separate categories have been presented to clarify the
comprehension prerequisites and processes so that teachers may more easily
conceptualize them.

Figures 8.4 and 8.5 may be used for practice with simulations or for
instructional planning.

FIGURE 8.4.   Tentative analysis of strengths and needs in comprehension

(student)

Comprehension Factors:	Areas of Interest or Concern:			
	Personal Reading Interests: (list)	Subject Area Reading	Vocational Reading	Social-Business Reading
1. Conceptual Knowledge				
2. Perceptual Abilities				
3. Syntactic Abilities				
4. Semantic Knowledge				
5. Reasoning Abilities				

FIGURE 8.4.   Continued

Comprehension Factors:	Areas of Interest or Concern:			
	Personal Reading Interests:	Subject Area Reading	Vocational Reading	Social- Business Reading
6. Cognitive Levels of Comprehension				
7. Rate of Processing				
8. Recall of Information				

FIGURE 8.5.   Tentative plan to improve comprehension

(student)

Materials	Purpose	Reading Levels	Projected Activities	Schedule

FIGURE 8.6.   Instructional materials

I. Intermediate and Secondary Reading Levels (4–12)

Title	Interest Level	Publisher
Be a Better Reader	Elementary and Secondary	Prentice-Hall
Breaking the Reading Barrier	Secondary	Prentice-Hall
Design for Good Reading	Secondary and Adult	Harcourt Brace Jovanovich
Gates-Peardon Reading Exercises	Elementary and Junior High	Teachers College Press
How to Study	Secondary and Adult	Science Research Associates
Listen and Think	Elementary and Secondary	Educational Developmental Laboratories
My Weekly Reader	Elementary	American Educational Publications
New Reading Skill Builder Series	Elementary, Secondary and Adult	Reader's Digest
Picto-Cabulary Series	Elementary, Secondary, and Adult	Barnell Loft
Plays for Echo Reading	Elementary	Harcourt Brace Jovanovich
Psychotechnics Radio Reading	Secondary and Adult	Psychotechnics
Reading for Understanding (Senior and Junior)	Elementary, Secondary, and Adult	Science Research Associates
Reading Line	Secondary	Cambridge
R.S.V.P., I & II	Secondary and Adult	AMSCO
Silly Sentences	Elementary	Houghton Mifflin
Specific Skills Series	Elementary, Secondary, and Adult	Barnell Loft
S.R.A. Reading Laboratories	Elementary, Secondary, and Adult	Science Research Associates
Standard Test Lessons in Reading	Elementary and Secondary	Teachers College Press
Tactics in Reading	Secondary	Scott Foresman
Test Lessons in Reading Reasoning	Secondary and Adult	Teachers College Press
Think Programs	Secondary	Innovative Sciences
Thinking Box	Junior High	Benefic
Troubleshooters	Secondary and Adult	Houghton Mifflin
Word Clues	Secondary and Adult	Educational Developmental Laboratories

FIGURE 8.4.   Continued

I. Intermediate and Secondary Reading Levels (4–12)

Title	Interest Level	Publisher
Wordcraft Vocabulary	Elementary, Secondary, and Adult	Communicad

II. Equipment

Title	Type	Source
AVR Reading Ratiometer	Shutter descends over page. Electrical	Audio-Visual Research
Controlled Reader, Junior and Senior	Projects lines of print	Educational Developmental Laboratories
Reader Mate	Projects lines of print	Singer Graflex
Shadowscope Reading Pacer	Beam of light descends over page	Psychotechnics
S.R.A. Reading Accelerator	Shutter descends over page. Mechanical	Science Research Associates
Tachomatic 500 Filmstrip Projector	Projects lines of print	Psychotechnics

CHAPTER 9

A Diagnostic Sequence

The chart incorporated in this chapter suggests a sequence that might be followed by those who are taking their first course in reading diagnosis or who are beginning to work with students on an individual basis.

This chapter explores a sequence to be followed in diagnosing areas of difficulty. The diagnostic sequence one might use depends upon a number of factors: the background and experience of the teacher; the nature and severity of the reading difficulties of the student or students with whom she is working; the time available for working with each student; and the setting in which the diagnosis takes place—classroom, reading center, or clinic.

THE READING DIAGNOSIS FLOWCHART

The sequence[1] illustrated in the chart (Figure 9.1) might be followed by beginning teachers as a means of familiarizing themselves with a logical order of procedure. More experienced teachers may also find the chart useful as a

[1] *Note:* The writer collaborated with Eldon E. Ekwall on the construction of a diagnostic sequence and wishes to acknowledge his contributions to her thinking, although she accepts the responsibility for the sequence and explanations presented in this chapter.

179

FIGURE 9.1. Reading Diagnosis: Scope and Sequence. [Lois A. Bader, *Reading Diagnosis and Remediation in Classroom and Clinic* (New York: Macmillan Publishing Co., 1980).]

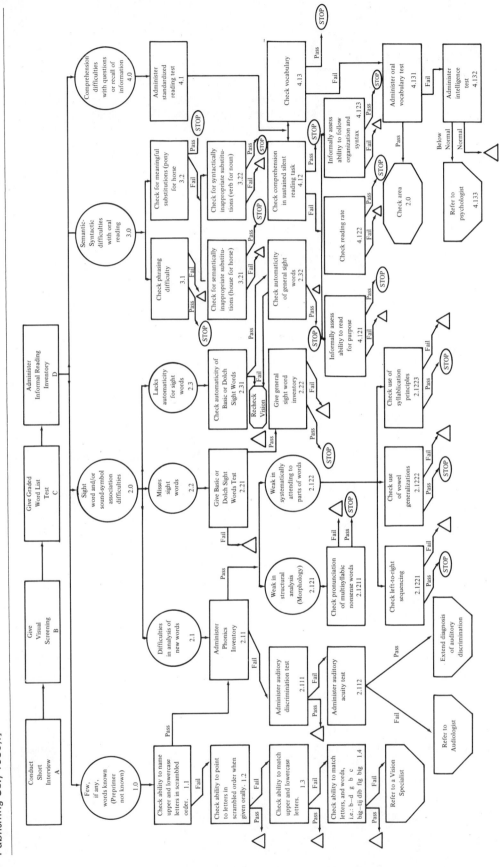

quick reinforcement of their own decision making. A list of suggested tests, keyed to the chart, is given at the end of this chapter.

Although the chart suggests divisions between areas, these are only artifacts necessitated by the effort to clarify a complex procedure. Comprehension, for example, is not removed from word recognition, as a careful reading of this chapter will indicate. Many interconnecting lines could have been drawn in the chart, but they may have been confusing to those new to reading diagnosis. There are actually far fewer tests suggested than would appear by looking at the chart, for after the Informal Reading Inventory (IRI) has been administered, information is collected only in the areas indicated by consideration of IRI and Word List Test findings. The large circles refer to decision points, that is, points at which it has been determined that deficiencies have been revealed. The rectangles indicate which additional cue collection method might be used, the triangles identify where to begin remediation, and the octagonal figures suggest which other areas to consider.

FLOWCHART CATEGORIES AND SEQUENCE

The remainder of this chapter is devoted to a step-by-step discussion of the areas of the chart. The preliminary four steps lay the groundwork for everything that follows and should be conducted with care. They are the short interview, visual screening, graded word list test, and informal reading inventory.

Short Interview (A)

The major purposes of the interview are to establish rapport with the student and to acquire information that might be pertinent to diagnosis and/or remediation. One should prepare for the interview (1) by learning as much as possible about the student from various sources: parents, referral forms, school records, and so forth, and (2) by having on hand items to stimulate conversation. These might include interesting photographs, figures, and models, as well as priority checklists, interest inventories, and unfinished sentence tests. Much can be learned from an interview. A major consideration should be an *informal* assessment of the student's language facility. More on interviewing techniques can be found in Chapters 2–5.

Visual Screening (B)

Visual screening should be accomplished with a stereoscopic instrument, accompanied by tests of near-point and far-point acuity, fusion, stereopsis, and accommodation-convergence. Because many disabled readers have visual problems, screening should be a routine part of diagnosis. Fortunately, the tests are neither difficult nor time-consuming to give. As with the administration of any tests, the diagnostician must be a keen observer and be able to relate findings to instruction. One child, as he was being given a test of near-point acuity, was asked, "Where is the ball?" (The correct answer was, "Over the pig's head.") He replied, however, "I don't know; it's still moving. [pause] Oh, now it's over the pig's head." The child's teacher said, ". . . and I've been flashing sight words for him!" With practice under qualified supervision, a teacher or clinician can learn to make appropriate referrals to vision specialists. Schools with financial problems might appeal to service organizations such as the Lions Club to assist in purchasing a visual screening device.

Graded Word List Test (C)

The next step is to have the student read from a graded word list test. From this the teacher can obtain an estimate of the student's (1) level, (2) sound-symbol associations, (3) structural analysis skills, (4) sight words, (5) automaticity, and (6) word recognition approaches. In addition, the teacher can ask the student to give the meanings of some of the words he has missed in order to learn more about his vocabulary level. (See earlier chapters for detailed observational cues for these and other elements referred to in this chapter.) Teachers should prepare for the administration of a word list test by adding spaces to record the student's response beside each word. Example:

	Student Response	
	Flash	
Test Item	*Presentation*	*Analysis*
helm	help	c
joke	jump	jack
guess	gū	geese
argue	na	na

c = correct
na = not attempted

Informal Reading Inventory (D)

Graded paragraphs from a published test or from graded reading materials can be used informally. The student should be asked to begin reading orally from his estimated *independent level,* as indicated by the graded word list test, and continue to his *frustration level,* which is indicated by the number and quality of miscues, the time he takes to read, and his recall of information or response to questions. Next the student should begin to read silently from his highest independent oral reading level to his silent reading comprehension, frustration level as indicated by time and recall of information or response to questions. Finally, the student should listen to the reading of graded paragraphs from his highest independent silent reading level to his listening comprehension frustration level as indicated by his recall of information or response to questions.

From the informal reading inventory the teacher can (1) obtain an estimate of the student's independent, instructional, and frustration reading levels for oral, silent, and listening comprehension; (2) observe the student's use of context to process phonemic-graphemic (sound-symbol), syntactic (word order), and semantic (word meaning) information; (3) learn more about the student's graphemic associations; (4) discover the number of sight words he recognizes; and (5) determine his rate of processing information.

Decision Point

Is the Student a Disabled Reader?   At this point the diagnostician should have enough information to make a judgment as to whether the student might be a disabled reader in terms of the interview, the evaluations, and his age/grade placement.

Consider Four Conditions.   If the student does appear to be a disabled reader, the diagnostician needs to consider student performance on the word list and IRI to determine which of four conditions need to be investigated more thoroughly in the diagnosis. The four conditions are represented in the chart as:

Strand 1.0—Few, if any, words known.
Strand 2.0—Sight word and/or sound-symbol association difficulties.
Strand 3.0—Semantic-syntactic difficulties with oral reading.
Strand 4.0—Comprehension difficulties with questions or recall of information.

Each strand is expanded into successive areas in sequence, so that if a student passes a testing area, he is directed elsewhere. If the student fails, he is taken further along the strand in an effort to pinpoint his major area(s) of difficulty. The student's performance in each area is examined in isolation *and* in conjunction with other areas. For example, his ability to recognize words and his reading rate are among the factors related to his comprehension of different materials. Whenever testing reveals a problem, remediation is begun in a trial teaching mode.

Strand 1.0—Few, If Any, Words Known

The student's ability to recognize preprimer words in the graded word list test and first paragraphs of the IRI should be noted. In addition, the teacher should assess the student's ability to recognize potent words and abbreviations in his environment, such as his own name, K-Mart, Woolco, Coke, stop, TV. If few or no words are known, the following abilities should be assessed:

1.1 Naming Letters.   Although one can learn to read without being able to name letters, the ability to do so is revealing. It indicates attentional, associative, perceptual (auditory and visual), and oral production capabilities. In addition, being able to name letters enables one to talk about the symbols used to represent the language more easily. If the names of most letters are known, the student's sound-symbol associations should be assessed by administering a phonics test.

1.2 Pointing to Letters.   By having the student point to letters when given orally by the examiner, one might gain information to suggest (a) that the student's difficulty with oral production might make him unable to demonstrate his knowledge, (b) that he is in an early stage of acquiring letter-name associations, or (c) that he has had auditory discrimination problems. One child who was asked to point to letters asked, "Where is minto? You know, k, l, minto, p." He did not hear l, m, n, o, p.

1.3 Matching Upper and Lowercase Letters.   The task of matching upper and lowercase letters assesses the student's associative knowledge for upper and lowercase letters, as well as his visual discrimination of letters.

1.4 Matching Letters and Words.   The task of matching letters and words is a visual one that requires the student to be able to discriminate fine differences. If the student is unable to match letters and words, he would appear to have a problem with visual perception or visual acuity and should be referred to a vision specialist who is capable of determining the nature of the difficulty. However, before making the referral, one should determine whether the student understood what he was to do, was attending to the task, was putting forth reasonable effort, and had had previous opportunities to note letter differences and also if (in the latter case) he could respond to trial teaching.

Strand 2.0—Sight Word and/or Sound-Symbol Association Difficulties

The next condition that needs to be considered for students beyond the pre-primer level is sight word and/or sound-symbol association difficulties. Sound-symbol knowledge does not appear to be indispensable to reading. We know that there are excellent readers who cannot demonstrate a knowledge of phonics. Yet an assessment of the sound-symbol associations of poor readers can be quite helpful. Just as letter-naming, which is not necessary to reading, is revealing in a number of ways, so is a phonics inventory revealing for some students, as will be explained in the following sections.

2.1 Difficulties in Analysis of New Words. If the student had difficulty with a large number of words that were new to him (but were in his meaning vocabulary) in isolation (word list) and in context (oral reading in the IRI), he should be given a phonics inventory. Section 2.11, *Phonics Inventory (Failed),* is presented with the sequence to be followed if the student fails the inventory, Section 2.111. Section 2.11, *Phonics Inventory (Passed),* suggests related areas to consider if he is successful with the inventory, Sections 2.121 and 2.122.

2.11 Phonics Inventory (Failed). The phonics inventory should assess the student's recognition of phonemes and common syllables and his ability to blend phonemes with common syllables. The diagnostician should integrate the student's responses to the inventory with the student's previous reading of the word list and oral paragraphs in order to confirm the diagnosis. In addition to checking the student's associations and blending abilities, the examiner should note tendencies for careful or wild guessing and inconsistency of behavior, which may suggest partial learning or faulty problem-solving applications.

2.111 Auditory Discrimination. If the student did not do well on the phonics inventory, he should be given an auditory discrimination test to determine his ability to make fine sound discriminations. Because a student is often asked on such tests whether two sounds are the same or different (example: *bat-bet* or *hat-bat*), the examiner should be sure the student understands the *concepts* of *same* and *different*. In addition, the examiner should consider whether language background contributes to sound confusion. For example, to some students with a Spanish background, both *pin* and *pen* sound like /pēn/. Finally, as some students with poor auditory discrimination may depend on lip-reading, the teacher should remember to have the student face away from the teacher if the teacher is pronouncing words aloud rather than using an auditory discrimination tape.

An analysis of the student's spelling from dictation should also be considered at this time: Was the student able to produce all of the sounds in the word (even though the word may have been incorrect, technically, *kat* for *cat*)? Did the student produce the sounds in correct order (not *aminal* but *animal*)?

2.112 Auditory Acuity.   An auditory acuity test should be administered to those who have difficulty with auditory discrimination tests. An audiometer should be used under proper testing conditions. A quiet room is essential. Students should not be tested when they have colds or other congestive problems. Care must be taken to have the audiometer calibrated frequently. The auditory screening (like the visual screening) can be given by a teacher or clinician who has had some instruction by a qualified audiologist. Audiometers used in screening are generally of the pure-tone type. A 30 decible response indicates a mild hearing loss that should be tested further with a speech-type hearing test conducted by an audiologist. A high frequency loss may cause the student to miss voice inflections, which might affect his understanding of syntactic patterns. In addition, a high frequency loss may affect the student's hearing of some consonants and their combinations. Examples: *s, l, t.* A low frequency loss may cause the student to have difficulty with vowel sounds, consonants such as *g, m, b,* and their combinations. However, the specific nature of the problem and its effect on the student's reading should be determined by a specialist in auditory-speech sciences.

If the student does not have a problem in auditory acuity, the diagnosis of auditory discrimination should be extended. In this area, as in visual discrimination, inattention may be a factor. Or the student may be naïve with respect to the *concepts* of letter sounds (phonemes) in words and *words* as entities. To some, *cup of coffee* is one word, pronounced *cupacoffee.* This may be due to poor articulation on the part of the speaker, or it may be that the student does not know what a *word* is. Naivety might extend to the use of pitch, pause, intonation, and inflection as indicators of meaning. Dialect need not be a problem because speakers are usually consistent in their pronunciations. As long as the teacher and student can understand each other, there is no need for standardization of speech sounds.

2.11 Phonics Inventory (Passed). If the student who appears to have difficulty in the analysis of new words does well on the phonics inventory, the next areas to consider are skill in structural analysis, evidence of effective, systematic attending to parts of words, and use of context to confirm word recognition. The student's performance on the preliminary word list test and IRI may have indicated that the student did quite well in these areas. Perhaps he lacked sound-symbol associations for combinations such as *ph* and for some silent letter phonograms such as *ight,* but he may have successfully pronounced many multisyllabic words. In that case, further testing in this area of word analysis may stop at this point. However, if that is not true, testing should continue within this strand of the chart.

2.121 Structural Analysis. Confirmation of difficulties in this area may be obtained by having the student pronounce multisyllabic nonsense words. These can be found in Chapter 4 or in some of the word analysis tests, keyed to the flowchart and listed at the end of this chapter, or the examiner may construct her own list. The purpose of using nonsense words is to rule out the possibility of the student's having the test words in his sight vocabulary. By careful selection of stimulus words, one can determine a student's visual recognition of compound words and common roots and affixes. In evaluating the response, one should look for recognition of alternative syllabic units rather than one correct pronunciation. For example, faced with the task of pronouncing *redontion,* a student could say, "Re-dón-tion" or "Réd-on-tion." Attempts that give evidence of word structure knowledge should be considered positively.

2.122 Attending to Word Parts. An analysis of the student's pronunciation of words on the word list test and oral paragraphs may reveal that the student omits beginning, middle or ending letters or syllables, even though his performance on the phonics tests indicates that he has appropriate sound-symbol associations.

2.1221 Left-to-Right Sequencing. Difficulty in left-to-right sequencing (example: saying *stop* for *spot* or *on* for *no*) should be assessed as to whether the student's problem is due to habit or confused orientation. In addition to analysis of word list and oral paragraph performance, the teacher may have the student quickly read a list of commonly confused words. If he seems to have difficulty in left-to-right sequencing, the student should be given trial lessons with aids such as color highlighting or movement of a pencil or finger in a left-to-right fashion. A student who responds quickly to the trial lessons may simply have acquired faulty habits, but one who does not respond quickly may need more intensive perceptual training or a method of teaching that requires a holistic, as opposed to a letter-by-letter, approach to word recognition.

2.1222 Vowel Generalizations. The *use* of vowel generalizations should be checked rather than recitations of rules. A vowel at the end of a word containing only one vowel usually has the long (glided) sound. By having the student pronounce nonsense words, such as *fla, ki, mo,* and by considering his word list and oral reading performance, the teacher can assess the student's knowledge of this generalization. Other generalizations might be similarly checked. Care should be taken not to be concerned with generalizations that have limited usefulness. Probably more important than the use of a generalization is the student's flexibility in context. If the long (glided) sounds of a vowel don't result in his pronouncing a word he can recognize in his listening vocabulary, then the student should attempt the pronunciation with a short (unglided) sound, or vice versa. The question is, Can the student shift vowel sounds and accents and check his attempts with context?

2.1223 Syllabication Principles. The application of syllabication principles should be assessed similarly to the application of vowel principles. The utility of the student's approach and his flexibility are important. For example, a student might try to apply the principle that when there is a consonant between two vowels, the consonant usually goes with the second vowel (*pa/per*); but when, in the case of a word such as *nev/er,* the application of the principle does not yield the pronunciation of a word in his listening vocabulary that makes sense in context, the student should try an alternative division of the word. Also, a student should pronounce words with double consonants as */litt/le* rather than */lit/tle,* for we do not pronounce two distinct *t*'s when we speak. However, performance is the key. If dividing the word as *lit/tle* on paper helps the student recognize the word as *litt/le,* there would seem to be no need to be concerned. In fact, correct writing form requires word division between consonants at the end of a line.

2.0 Sight Word Recognition.   Sight words are defined here as those words that are recognized without phonetic or structural analysis. Beginning readers are expected to acquire a stock of words most frequently encountered in print, such as *the, of, and.* These have been referred to as service words, instant words, basic words, and Dolch words—those words selected by Dolch as the most common English words, exclusive of nouns. A sight word is usually acquired by repetition in context. However, some students have difficulty, perhaps because of an insufficient number of repetitions, a slower learning rate for words, inattention, or a physical problem. Also, the basic words are generally low in meaningfulness or interest. *Of* doesn't have the impact of words such as *Coca-Cola, snake,* or *dinosaur.* Therefore, previous instruction that emphasized drill in isolation may have contributed to the problem.

2.21 Basic, or Dolch Words.   If the student appeared to miss many basic sight words within the word list and oral paragraphs, he may be tested with the Dolch list (Garrard Publishing Company) or a similar list to evaluate his knowledge of these words. The words may be printed on cards and presented to the students one at a time while the teacher records responses on a separate sheet. The teacher should analyze the nature of the errors. A tendency to sound-out many of the words may indicate that the student is being overanalytic in his approach. In order to assess the student's ability to use context as a word recognition aid, the failed words should be presented in sentences.

To determine the best method for teaching the basic words, administer a test-teaching sequence such as the *Mills Learning Modality Test.* If the Mills test is not available, two or three teaching sequences that would seem to have potential for effectiveness may be devised. Ten words may be taught in each sequence for about fifteen minutes for each session. Then, to discover which methods seems most effective, one should check the number of words retained from each method. Isolated drill on words low in meaningfulness should be avoided.

2.22 General Sight Words.   General sight words are defined as instantly known words other than the high-utility basic words. For students using a graded reading series such as a basal, words frequently encountered within the series might be used to obtain an estimate of general sight word level. Those words are usually listed in a glossary within each book.

For students who have not been using a series, a list of words encountered in daily life such as *stop, exit, ladies, gentlemen, men, women, danger, no ad-*

mittance, bus, and so forth, might be employed as a check. Other possibilities are (1) to ask the student to list words he feels he can recognize and then write each word on a card, shuffle the cards, and have him read the words, and (2) to ask the student to bring in printed material he nas been attempting to read, select high impact words, write them on cards, and have the student read them.

2.3 Lacks Automaticity for Sight Words.   If a student hesitates before pronouncing a word he has previously encountered and then correctly pronounces it, he would seem to have a problem with automaticity. To the extent that a student can instantly recognize a large number of words, he will be better able to concentrate and attend to meaning. The teacher may have observed a lack of automaticity in the word list test, the oral paragraphs, or one of the sight word tests. Possible causes include visual problems or instructional difficulties, as listed under the previous section. Some students may require more time to focus visually. Others may lose their place as they read a line of print or move to the next line, thereby missing words they easily recognized in isolation.

2.31 Automaticity of Basic or Dolch Words.   Automaticity for the basic words may be tested by flashing them for the student on cards at a rate of one second per exposure. Mechanical or electrical tachistoscopes may be used, if they are available. If students instantly recognize the basic words in isolation, they should be checked on their ability to recognize the words quickly in the context of phrases, sentences, and paragraphs. Cards can be made or purchased that contain common phrases, such as *down the hill, from the store, boy and girl,* and so forth. Further assessment should continue in the context of short, easy paragraphs. If the student misses easy or known words, note whether the student seems to have difficulty in visual tracking (keeping his place as he reads each line). If so, test to see if his performance improves by putting a card under each line as he reads. Further visual testing may be required. The *Spache Binocular Reading Test* may be used, if available.

Students who recognize the basic words when permitted to study them, but miss the words in a flash presentation, may have a problem in fusion in that they cannot effortlessly get a clear image of a word and require a longer exposure time. If this is so, further visual testing may be required. Other causes may be lack of practice, tendency to be overanalytical, confusion of similar words, confused orientation, boring drill, lack of meaningful context, and inattention to distinctive features (ascending and descending letters).

2.32 Automaticity for General Sight Words.   As in Section 2.31, basal or high intensity words might be used to assess automaticity for words other than the basic, or Dolch, words. And as in Section 2.31, the words should be flashed in isolation, then in context to check automaticity. Because these words are more meaningful than the basic words and may have more distinctive forms (*jello* vs. *come*), they tend to be more quickly recognized in isolation.

3.0 Semantic-Syntactic Difficulties with Oral Reading. In this portion of the chart the major consideration is the student's ability to process what he reads rather than his ability to recognize words. The teacher should analyze the student's performance on the oral paragraphs to evaluate his abilities in this area. For example, a student who uses dialect reads, "I be goin" for "I am going." In order to have said, "I be goin," he obviously understands, "I am going." Therefore, this facet of his performance does not indicate a reading problem. Another example: A student reads, "a large leader" for "a great ruler." This student also demonstrates syntactic-semantic competence.

A final example: Two students read similar passages. One reads in a halting, word-by-word fashion, with flat intonation and a disregard for punctuation. He makes no errors in pronouncing words. When he finishes, he remembers little of what he read, even when prompted. The other student reads smoothly, with appropriate intonation, and responds to punctuation. She miscalls three words: *jumped* for *leaped, stopped* for *halted,* and *men* for *soldiers.* She inserts one word: "in *the* winter" for "in winter." She is able to recall the major events in the paragraph. Of course, the latter is the better reader. She is later asked to read *leaped, halted,* and *soldiers* in isolation and is able to pronounce the first two words, indicating that she is not lacking in word recognition ability, but may have substituted *jumped* and *stopped* because she is more accustomed to using them in her oral vocabulary. The first student is given an unfinished sentence test to learn more about his view of the reading process. Some of the unfinished sentences and his responses are these:

> When I read . . . I sound out words.
> My mother helps me . . . sound out words.

This student perceives reading as pronouncing words rather than understanding meaning.

Although oral reading is used as one indicator of reading ability, it should not be considered the only indicator. Some readers do very poorly in oral reading, but have excellent comprehension of what they have read silently. In these cases it is pointless to attach too much significance to oral reading performance or to work toward improvement in oral reading, unless the student wishes to improve in oral interpretation. Silent reading comprehension is the goal.

3.1 Phrasing Difficulty. In addition to having a student read aloud, one can assess phrasing ability by having the student insert slash marks in material that he has read silently. He should respond to presentation, as well as sentence patterns. Example:

On the shelf / over the clock / my sister Mary / keeps her diary.

Those who are unable to do so should next be given the task of inserting the slashes as the teacher reads aloud with slight exaggeration of pause and inflection in order to see whether the student can discriminate speech cues that relate to visual word patterns. A high frequency hearing loss may contribute to a problem with phrasing.

Some readers may not have the *concept* of phrasing or of punctuating. After trial teaching, one girl responded, "Oh, I didn't know I was supposed to read that way. I'll change." She was able to do so without further assistance.

3.2 Meaningful Substitutions. The ability to make meaningful substitutions, as previously discussed, is usually an indication that the student's syntactic-semantic processing is satisfactory. However, if there is an inordinate quantity of substitutions, there may be a problem within Strand 2.0, *Sight Words and/or Sound-Symbol Associations,* or within Strand 4.0, *Comprehension*; that is, a student with a good understanding of the reading process and good language facility may be compensating for a problem in another area.

3.21 Semantically Inappropriate Substitutions. A student who reads, "The cowboy got on his house and rode out of town," may be confusing *house* with *horse,* but, more important, he is disregarding meaning. His behavior may have been caused by his perception that word recognition is primary. The teacher who has observed semantically inappropriate substitutions in oral reading might say, "Here is another passage to read; if you come to a word you don't know, just put in a word that makes sense." The student should also be encouraged to reread the passage if he wants to change his first guess. Or the teacher might give the student some cloze sentences composed of words he can recognize:

Before you write, sharpen your _____ .
I forgot my umbrella, and it is starting to _____ .

The content of the sentences must reflect the conceptual knowledge of the student. When a student makes an incorrect choice, ask him why he made the choice. A man related that he once "rode out of town on a house"—in a flood! One may find logical reasons for seemingly illogical responses.

3.22 Syntactically Inappropriate Substitutions.   A student who reads, "The was is on the table," for "The wallet is on the table" is making a substitution that is not only semantically inappropriate, but also syntactically inappropriate. *The* should be a signal to the reader that a noun or pronoun or possibly an adjective (the small ___) should appear. In addition to analysis of the student's oral reading behavior, the teacher can confirm the problem by using cloze sentences that signal certain parts of speech:

> (noun)   The man closed the _____ .
> (adverb)   The man closed the box _____ .
> (adjective)   The _____ man closed the box quickly.

Students who are not successful may have the sentences read to them or may be given choices:

> The man closed the _____ .
> ___ box   ___ any
> ___ was   ___ drawer
> ___ door   ___ seeing
> (Directions: Check the words that might be used in the blank.)

Some students may be able to understand simple sentence patterns, but not those that are complex. These, too, may be checked with cloze passages. In addition, questions may be constructed:

> The girl who is a good friend of my sister is standing at the end of
>   the line.
> Who is standing at the end of the line?

Frequently, readers seem to have difficulty with patterns (such as the preceding) with embeddings between subject and verb, long left embeddings, and constructions using referents such as *who, whom, which,* and *that.*

Another way to determine the effect of syntactic complexity on a student's comprehension is to rewrite a complex passage, using language patterns familiar to the student as indicated by a sample of his speech or his writing. Have the student read complex passages and answer questions. Compare the results.

Teachers working with students who have English as a second language should start their assessment with comprehension of sentence patterns that are common to both languages, then proceed to dissimilar patterns.

4.0 Comprehension Difficulties. In this section of the chart a sequence is suggested for assessing comprehension difficulties that may have been indicated by the interview (for example, reported problems in reading assignments) and/or by the Individual Reading Inventory.

Generally, those reading beyond the second or third grade level will comprehend better after silent reading than after oral reading, whereas the condition is often reversed for beginning readers. This happens because auditory vocabulary may exceed visual recognition of words and spoken language is rich in syntactic-semantic clues. The beginning reader may be expected to have a higher level of listening comprehension than silent reading comprehension. A not uncommon response of young developing readers, asked about what they have just read aloud, is, "I don't know. I wasn't listening to me." Adults, too, can read aloud to others for extended periods without attending to meaning. In addition, oral reading is stressful for some. Teachers should not be concerned if they find better recall after silent reading than after oral reading. However, the entire assessment, not just the oral reading part, may have been stressful to the student. In this case, a silent reading test can provide an opportunity for the student to work alone and perhaps do better, if it is administered in a manner that makes him feel comfortable.

4.1 Standardized Reading Test. Although some experienced teachers may prefer constructing their own tests, many busy teachers and most inexperienced teachers prefer using published tests that have been standardized so that comparisons can be made with respect to performance (grade) level. Tests containing vocabulary and comprehension sections can yield further information because the subtests offer a point of comparison. A reader whose vocabulary score is significantly higher than his comprehension score may have problems with (1) rate, (2) syntactic patterns, (3) organizational patterns, (4) conceptual knowledge, and/or (5) interest. Conversely, if the comprehension score is significantly higher than the vocabulary score, the reader may be giving indications that he is comprehending about as well as can be expected given his present vocabulary level, but that improvement in vocabulary might be likely to improve comprehension. However, one must keep in mind in analyzing the above hypotheses that performance on a test is only one sample of behavior that must be confirmed by further observation. In addition, care should be taken to consult the test manual for a table that displays significant differences between scores because apparent differences may be due to measurement error.

Guessing can occur on group standardized tests. Therefore, the teacher should observe students closely, but unobtrusively, to identify this behavior. As stated earlier, more than one sample of a student's silent reading should be obtained.

4.12 Comprehension in Sustained Silent Reading. The content of the comprehension passages should be within the conceptual knowledge of the student, reasonably interesting, and suitable to his maturation level. Otherwise, the aforementioned factors may result in the student's earning a spuriously low score.

A test that requires sustained silent reading over several paragraphs is preferred to one that calls for responses after a short passage, for the former more closely approximates the reading the student is required to do in content area subjects. Some students have difficulty with comprehension only when they have to sustain their attention and follow the writer's organizational pattern.

The test should be given according to directions with one exception. The examiner should mark the last item the student completed when time was called and then have the student finish the test, if he is able to do so. In this way a judgment can be made with tests that become progressively difficult as to whether rate strongly influenced the results. Another way to estimate the effect of rate is to compare the number of items attempted with the number correct.

If the questions accompanying the reading passages appear to require different kinds of reasoning, the examiner might categorize them and analyze the responses to discover if any particular kinds of questions seem to have been missed. Categories might include questions requiring the student to (1) find or recall something explicitly stated such as a name, date, or place or (2) see relationships between or among ideas or (3) interpret ideas or figurative language. A cloze test can also be used to look at different kinds of comprehension. Deletions of structural words can measure comprehension of detail, and deletions of nouns can measure comprehension of major ideas. As a rough guide to construction, consider frequent deletions (every five or six words as difficult and every nine or ten words as easy). About 50 percent correct completions indicates 80 percent comprehension.

4.121 Reading for a Purpose. Because attending to ideas is a problem for many with poor comprehension, the next step is to determine whether a student can comprehend if he is given a purpose for reading. The student should be provided passages of varying lengths and asked to read first to find information explicitly stated, then to respond to organizational patterns (sequence, comparison, cause and effect), and finally to summarize.

If the student is able to succeed in reading for purposes stated by the teacher, he should be given additional passages and asked to make his own questions after surveying the material.

4.122 Reading Rate. Although some tests contain subtests to evaluate rate, these are often quite superficial and fail to do an adequate job of (1) sampling various rates for reading for different purposes, (2) testing flexibility of rate, or (3) evaluating the student's ability to select a rate appropriate to his purpose. Although some information can be obtained about the student's rate from the IRI and the standardized reading tests, it may be necessary for the teacher to construct informal tests of rate and ask the student to skim for a general overview or read slowly to recall details, and so forth, in order to discover the nature of the rate difficulty, if it exists. A rate score or report in words-per-minute is useless unless accompanied by information about the student's comprehension. Consequently, informal rate tests must include an evaluation of the student's recall of information, either prompted or free.

A comparison of comprehension and rate can yield some hypothesis with regard to the student's needs. High speed and low comprehension may mean that (1) the student has the habit of reading quickly and superficially or (2) he is inflexible and does not slow down to analyze an unfamiliar word or idea, or (3) he may be nervous under testing conditions and rush ahead unable to think. Low speed and high comprehension may mean that (1) the student believes that it is impossible for him to read faster with adequate comprehension, or (2) he reads everything slowly and does not realize that he should skim portions of a text he understands easily and slow down for other parts.

Some test-teaching sessions in which the student is counseled with regard to selecting rates to fit his purpose for reading and is given practice should reveal more about his ability to learn to read appropriately for his needs.

Low speed and low comprehension may mean (1) a low sight vocabulary, (2) difficulty in processing sentence patterns, or (3) unfamiliar content.

4.123 Following Organizational and Syntactic Patterns. Another area that might need to be evaluated is the student's ability to read materials of varying complexity with regard to the writer's organization and his sentence patterns. The instructor can rewrite passages the student failed to comprehend, emphasizing the ordering of ideas and simplifying sentences to discover whether either or both of these factors appear to have contributed to the student's comprehension difficulties.

These skills can also be evaluated by (1) constructing questions appropriate to sequencing, cause and effect, and comparison, or (2) writing disorganized passages and asking the student if he sees anything wrong with them.

Comprehension of complex sentences can be further checked (1) by presenting stimulus sentences with paraphrased sentences and asking the student to mark the one that is the best paraphrase or (2) by asking questions concerning ideas embedded in the complex sentences.

4.13 Vocabulary. The vocabulary section of a standardized test may be useful in diagnosis for comparative purposes as earlier described. However, the vocabulary test samples only a limited number of words and may not be a very accurate reflection of the *size* of a student's vocabulary. This would be especially true for students who have not read extensively in areas from which the words were taken and for culturally different students. Reading rate can affect vocabulary scores; a low score may mean that the student could have scored higher if given more time to finish. Poor recognition of words in his listening vocabulary can affect performance, too. In this case, if the incorrect items are read to the student, he may do better.

Because experience strongly influences vocabulary size, an effort should be made to learn whether the student has read widely in any particular areas and what kind of exposure he has had to others who possess a large speaking vocabulary. A comparison should be made between the school or standard vocabulary versus specialized and nonstandard vocabularies.

In evaluating school vocabulary, teachers should informally check:

1. Knowledge of directions. Examples:

    Put a *cross* over the incorrect word.
    Underline the best answer.
    Circle the word that doesn't fit.

2. Meanings of abstract structural words. Examples:

    About the time of George IV.
    I can't go, *for* I will be busy.

3. Meanings of words specific to content areas.

4.   Common figurative language that may be unfamiliar to those from different cultural and/or language backgrounds.

In evaluating nonstandard reading vocabulary, the teacher might have the student define words from his hobby or occupational reading. For example, some students who are quite low in the vocabulary found in their literature books, may recognize and define large numbers of technical words in electronic manuals.

4.131 Oral Vocabulary.   The oral vocabulary test suggested here is the type in which the student listens to a word pronounced by the teacher and points to one of four pictures that represents the word. This procedure has the advantage of checking vocabulary in a nonreading situation as well as providing an opportunity to respond without speaking. This makes the test desirable for those with articulation problems, physical handicaps, or auditory retrieval difficulties. Another advantage is that tests are available that have been normed. However, these norms may not be suitable for special populations, and the teacher may have to use informal measures as described earlier.

If the student did well on the oral vocabulary test but not on the reading vocabulary test, his word recognition, word analysis, and/or syntactic comprehension abilities should be assessed.

Those significantly below level on the oral vocabulary test whose performances do not seem to reflect cultural differences should be given an opportunity to demonstrate their ability to respond to instruction through some trial teaching sequences planned to engage their interest. If the response is poor, they may be given an intelligence test or referred to a psychologist.

4.132 Intelligence Test.   Intelligence tests have been under attack with much justification, for they may be culturally biased, carelessly administered, or used to make unwarranted judgments about children and adults. In this diagnostic sequence, however, a test is suggested for the purpose of either ruling out a low verbal intelligence or for making a referral to a psychologist.

If the teacher is qualified to give an individual battery that evaluates verbal and performance abilities, she may do so. Otherwise, she may give a test such as the *Slosson Intelligence Test,* which has a high correlation to the major batteries.

Note: The preceding sequence has been suggested as an aid to systemize the diagnostic sequence for those new to diagnosis. As the examiners gain in experience, they will probably learn to adjust their procedures by constructing their own tests, using their own test-teaching sequences, obtaining a maximum amount of information from a minimum amount of data, omitting or adding parts as needed, and changing the order in which they collect information to fit the diagnostic-remedial setting.

Tests Keyed to Reading Diagnosis and Remediation Flowchart

Note: Number in Parentheses Refers to Publishers' List.

- B.   Visual Screening Instruments
    1.   Bausch and Lomb Orthorater (3)
    2.   Bausch and Lomb School Vision Tester (3)
    3.   Keystone Visual Survey Telebinocular (15)
- C.   Graded Word Lists
    1.   Classroom Reading Inventory (Word List Section) (5)
    2.   Diagnostic Reading Scales (Word List Section) (6)
    3.   Ekwall Reading Inventory (Word List Section) (1)
    4.   San Diego Quick Assessment (16)
    5.   Slosson Oral Reading Test (19)
    6.   Sucher-Allred Reading Placement Inventory (Word List Section) (8)
- D.   Informal Reading Inventories (graded paragraphs that can be used in administering an informal reading inventory)
    1.   Classroom Reading Inventory (Silvaroli) (5)
    2.   Diagnostic Reading Scales (Spache) (6)
    3.   Durrell Analysis of Reading Difficulties (11)
    4.   Ekwall Reading Inventory (1)
    5.   Sucher-Allred Reading Placement Inventory (8)
- 2.11   Phonics Tests
    1.   Botel Reading Inventory (9)
    2.   El Paso Phonics Survey (1)
    3.   Gates-McKillop Reading Diagnostic Tests (20)
    4.   Phonics Knowledge Survey (Durkin) (20)
    5.   Woodcock Reading Mastery Tests (2)
- 2.111   Auditory Discrimination Tests
    1.   Goldman-Fristoe-Woodcock Test of Auditory Discrimination (2)

  2. Lindamood Auditory Comprehension Test (21)
  3. MAP Word List (13)
  4. Wepman Auditory Discrimination Test (18)
2.112 Auditory Screening Instruments
  1. Beltone, Model 9D (4)
  2. Eckstein, Model 60 (7)
  3. Maico, Model MA-12 or MA-19 (17)
 2.21 Basic Word Tests
  1. Dolch Basic Sight Words (10)
  2. Ekwall Basic Sight Words (1)
  3. Harris-Jacobson List (12)
 4.1 Standardized Silent Reading Tests (timed vocabulary and comprehension and rate sections)
  1. Gates-MacGinitie Reading Tests (2)
  2. Iowa Test of Basic Skills (14)
  3. Metropolitan Reading Tests (11)
  4. Nelson-Denny Reading Tests (14)
  5. Nelson Reading Test (14)
  6. Stanford Achievement Tests (11)
  7. Stanford Diagnostic Reading Tests (11)
4.131 Oral Vocabulary Tests
  1. Gates-McKillop Diagnostic Reading Tests (Oral Vocabulary Section) (20)
  2. Peabody Individual Achievement Test (2)
  3. Peabody Picture Vocabulary Test (2)
  4. Wechsler Intelligence Scales (Oral Vocabulary Section) (18)
4.132 Intelligence Assessments
  1. Stanford-Binet Intelligence Test (14)
  2. Slosson Intelligence Test (19)
  3. Wechsler Intelligence Scales (18)

Flowchart
Test Publishers List

 1. Allyn & Bacon, 1977
  470 Atlantic Avenue
  Boston, MA 02210

2. American Guidance Service, Inc.
   Publisher's Building
   Circle Pines, MN 55014
3. Bausch and Lomb Optical Company
   Rochester, NY 14802
4. Beltone, Electronics Corporation
   4201 West Victoria Street
   Chicago, IL 60646
5. Wm. C. Brown Co. Publishers
   135 South Locust Street
   Dubuque, IA 52001
6. California Test Bureau
   Del Monte Research Park
   Monterey, CA 93940
7. Eckstein Bros., Inc.
   4807 West 118th Place
   Hawthorn, CA 90250
8. The Economy Company
   P.O. Box 25308
   Oklahoma City, OK 73125
9. Follett Educational Corporation
   1010 W. Washington Boulevard
   Chicago, IL 60607
10. Garrard Publishing Company
    2 Overhill Road
    Scarsdale, NY 10583
11. Harcourt Brace Jovanovich, Inc.
    757 Third Avenue
    New York, NY 10017
12. Harris, Albert J., and Jacobson, Milton D. "Basic Vocabulary for Beginning Reading." *The Reading Teacher,* 26 (January 1973): 392–395.
13. Haspul, George, and Bloomer, Richard. "Maximum Auditory Perception (MAP) Word List." *Journal of Speech and Hearing Disorders,* 26 (May 1961): 156–163.
14. Houghton Mifflin Company
    Two Park Street
    Boston, MA 02107

15. Keystone View Company
    2212 East 12 Street
    Davenport, IA   52803

16. LaPray, Margaret, and Ross, Ramon. "The Graded Word List: Quick Gauge of Reading Ability." *Journal of Reading,* Vol. 12 (January, 1969): 305–307.

17. Maico Hearing Instruments
    7573 Bush Lake Road
    Minneapolis, MN   55435

18. The Psychological Corporation
    575 Third Avenue
    New York, NY   10017

19. Slosson Educational Publications
    140 Pine Street
    East Aurora, NY   14052

20. Teachers College Press
    1234 Amsterdam Avenue
    New York, NY   10027

21. Teaching Resources
    100 Boylston Street
    Boston, MA   02116

CHAPTER 10

Teacher-Constructed Tests

Suggestions are provided here to help diagnosticians and teachers construct their own assessment tests, using instructional materials available to them.

Because a major objective in testing is to assess the levels of students' reading for the purpose of placing them in materials, it is reasonable for teachers to use the instructional materials available to them to construct their own tests rather than hope for a match of levels between a purchased test and their instructional materials. The following kinds of tests are suggested for teacher construction:

1. Graded word recognition tests.
2. Graded paragraph tests.
3. Open book assessment tests.
4. Cloze tests.

GRADED WORD RECOGNITION TESTS

Description. Graded word recognition tests are composed of lists of words that are typically encountered in leveled reading material with designated, controlled vocabularies.

Purposes. The purposes of the graded word list tests are (1) to estimate the highest reading level at which the student can easily recognize almost all of the words he encounters, (2) to determine the degree of automaticity, or quickness, with which words are recognized, (3) to analyze sound-symbol association knowledge, and (4) to understand the student's method of approaching an unknown word.

Construction. Words are selected at random from the set of graded materials that serves as the basic series in the reading program. On the elementary level the basic series will probably be a set of basal readers; on secondary and adult levels the basic series may be graded materials such as controlled reader books, a set of stories and essays leveled from beginning through upper reading levels.

If there is a glossary for each level or book, a sample of twenty words might be taken at random from this list; otherwise, a sample of twenty words per level can be obtained by selecting every tenth word from the content, not including repetitions, proper nouns, and unusual words, such as those found in idiomatic expressions or foreign phrases. Depending on the purpose of the examiner, an abbreviated list of ten words per level (short form) may suffice as a rough indicator of level. A shorter test is less reliable but saves testing time.

In order to use the list for conditions of automaticity (instant recognition) and analysis, the teacher might have each word typed on a 3 by 5 card to be exposed rapidly by her, or a hand tachistoscope might be made as in Figure 10.1. Each word is typed in triple spacing on oaktag board or heavy paper, which is pulled at the desired speed through a window opening in a larger piece of oaktag board.

FIGURE 10.1. A strip tachistoscope.

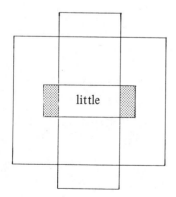

The Flash-X, a mechanical device by Educational Developmental Laboratories, can also be used by obtaining blank cards made by the company and typing or printing the words on them for timed and untimed exposure.

Finally, score sheets are prepared and duplicated so that the students' responses may be recorded, as in Figure 10.2.

Administration. Say to the student, "I am going to show you some words like this [demonstrate flashing]. Say as many as you can. If you don't know a word right away, I will give you time to study it." For demonstration purposes, use a card with a word that is not used on the test.

Proceed to flash each word, putting a check after each correct response, an *na* after each word not attempted, and a *C* after each response that is cor-

FIGURE 10.2.   Score sheet

Jim	10/5
Name	Date

Graded Word List

(short form)

	PP	*Flash*	*Analysis*
1.	little	✔	
☆2.	is	it C ✔	
3.	like	na	look
4.	and	✔	
5.	can	car	✔
6.	said	ss	say
7.	man	may	✔
8.	you	✔	
9.	the	✔	
10.	help	he	him

Correct:
(☆ = corrected
error)   5   2   F + A = 7

	P		
1.	some		
2.	house		

rected on flash and analysis. Record incorrect responses phonetically if they are nonwords. (See Figure 10.3.) Have the student proceed through each level until he misses three words he is unable to identify on analysis on the short form (ten words) and six words on the long form (twenty words). More information can be obtained by returning to words the student missed after being given time for analysis and asking him what the words mean or by observing his response to coaching. For example, the teacher might uncover the word slowly from left-right and ask the student to attempt its pronunciation, as she might cover the *b* in *bring* to see if the student could recognize *ring*. Then, if he could, the teacher would uncover the *b* and ask the student to attempt the word.

Scoring. Generally, a score below 80 per cent on the flash, or timed, portion of the test indicates a deficient sight vocabulary for that level.

Analysis. An analysis of the student's errors is quite important. (See Chapter 4 for checklists relating to word recognition in isolation.) Some teachers may wish to construct a chart for tabulating errors (Figure 10.3). In addition, comments should be recorded with regard to understanding word meaning, response to coaching, or attitudinal factors.

Other Graded Word Lists. A procedure similar to the one just described can be developed for a list of basic service words, such as the Dolch list.

GRADED PARAGRAPH TESTS

Description. Graded paragraph tests are often called informal reading inventories, or IRI's, but because many types of tests are described as "informal inventories," the more specific title, Graded Paragraph Tests, is used here. These tests, as their name implies, consist of sets of paragraphs taken from basals or other carefully graded material. The student reads orally, then silently, from easy to more difficult levels until the material becomes frustrating because of problems in word recognition and/or comprehension. Finally, the student listens to progressively more difficult passages. After oral and silent reading and after listening, the student is asked to respond to questions about the content or to restate the content. Graded paragraph tests are widely used and generally considered one of the most valuable tools of the diagnostician. An obvious advantage of those constructed from classroom reading materials is that they are likely to be more accurate for placement purposes than com-

FIGURE 10.3. Graded word list analysis

	Graded Word List Analysis			Jimmy		11/14	

Beginning Consonants and Consonant Combinations		Medial Vowels and Vowel Combinations		Final Consonants, Consonant Combinations, Inflectional endings		Reversals (Words and letters)		Prefixes and Suffixes		Multisyllabic Words		Silent Letter Phonograms	
said	for	said	for	said	for	said	for	said	for	said	for	said	for
fat	pat	bat	bit	risk rest dress dresses		spot stop cool look		rent return		faster factory		fit fight that through	

Comments: Jimmy became very upset as words became more difficult and refused to continue. He was able to pronounce both reversed words when teacher pointed to first letter.

207

mercially published tests because basals vary in equivalence of reading grade levels.

Purpose.   The purposes of these tests are as follows:

1.   To estimate the reading levels of the student for the purpose of placement in graded instructional materials.
2.   To observe the student's use of context in recognizing words.
3.   To estimate the student's sight vocabulary.
4.   To observe the student's fluency in reading.
5.   To estimate the student's ability to comprehend material.

Construction

1.   For elementary school children, obtain the basals or other comparable graded materials that will be used for instruction. For secondary students or adults, obtain the graded materials that will be most frequently used in instruction.
2.   Choose selections from a book on each level that appear to be most typical in word choice, sentence construction, organization, and concepts. Elementary series will probably include preprimer and primer books and books from the first through the sixth or eighth grade levels. Secondary and adult series may or may not include preprimer or primer books or books in 2.5 and 3.5 levels.

     As with the graded word list test, the teacher may elect to construct short and/or long forms of the tests. Longer forms may be more reliable, but may fatigue the student and take more time to administer. Passages in the preprimer, primer, and first grade levels should be at least 50 words long; on the second through fourth grade levels, about 100 words; and on fifth grade levels and above, about 150 words.
3.   On each level three passages should be selected: one for oral reading, one for silent reading, and one for listening. The teacher may wish to construct alternative forms of the test to assess progress. (Students have been known to memorize test passages.) Care should be taken that the passages a student is given to read are in clear, readable print. Grade level designations should be removed. An examiner's copy of the passages should be reproduced with sufficient space between the lines so that oral reading behaviors can be coded.

4. The examiner may elect to use short-answer questions or a free response format. Both approaches have strengths and limitations. Appropriate questions are difficult to construct but can elicit literal and inferential responses. The free response format doesn't lead the student as questions might, but a shy student may be reluctant to reply as fully as he is capable. The following guidelines are offered for constructing questions:

    a. Short answer questions should be passage-dependent; that is, students should not be able to answer the questions without reading the passage.

    b. Yes/no questions should be avoided.

    c. Questions should be stated briefly and clearly in the language of the passage.

    d. Five to ten questions may be asked for each selection.

        The following types of questions may be used:
        Recall of details to test literal comprehension.
        1) Where did the man go?
        2) What did he find at the park?
        3) Who went with Jim?
        4) When did they see the plane?
        Vocabulary to test understanding of word use.
        1) What does *test the water* mean in this story?
        2) What does *capacity* mean?
        3) What does an *umpire* do?
        Inferential items to test ability to follow the logic of the selection.

        Example:
        Everyone at the party could play a musical instrument. If one could not play the piano, he could play a stringed instrument or a horn. Mike, Sue, Jim, and Linda enjoyed the party. Jim said he wished he could play the piano and some kind of stringed instrument.

        1) Did Sue play a musical instrument?
        2) What kind of instrument did Jim play?

    e. Most items should be in the literal recall category because the length of the test prohibits adequate testing of other facets of comprehension.

        If a free-response format is used, each concept should be listed in short phrases on the examiner's copy for ease in checking each item as it is mentioned. A sample selection is illustrated by Figure 10.4.

Finally, the test constructor should give the test to *average* readers on each grade level to observe a range of typical oral reading behaviors, time to read each selection, and responses to questions or free-recall. Revisions should be made as needed in content or questions. These data on average readers in each grade can provide a basis of comparison in future administrations of the tests.

FIGURE 10.4.   Recorded retelling of selection

Mary had been walking for a long time
when she came to a small lake. There
were trees around most of the lake,
but on one side was a cornfield. She
stopped to talk with two boys who were
fishing. Mary wanted to ask them
where she could buy some food.

	Memories:	*Example of Student's Retelling;*
✓	Mary	"A girl
___	walking a long time	
✓	came to a small lake	came to a lake
✓	trees around most of lake	with trees around it.
___	cornfield on one side	
✓	stopped to talk	She talked with
✓	two boys fishing	some boys fishing
✓	Mary wanted to ask	so she could ask
___	where she could buy food	them something."

Yes   No

Yes	No	
✓	___	Sequence of events were generally retold in same order of original selection.
✓	___	Generally used language of original selection rather than paraphrase.
✓	___	Minor details generally omitted.
6	out of 9	reported memories.

Administration

1. If a graded word list test has been given, the student might be asked to start reading on a level at which at least 80 percent of the words were recognized. Otherwise, the teacher should select a level that, according to her judgment from information obtained in the interview, would be a level near the student's independent reading level.

2. The examiner should introduce each selection by mentioning the topic and asking the reader about his experiences with the subject. This helps to put the reader at ease and helps the teacher learn whether the student's concepts are adequate for comprehending the content.

3. Assessment should start with the set of oral paragraphs. The student should be told to do his best and that he will be asked about what he has read when he is finished. Then the student should read orally with the examiner recording his oral reading behaviors in a code similar to the following:

a.	Substitutions and mispronunciations	Write the response above the word.	was I saw it. swā I saw it.
b.	Omissions and partial omissions	Cross out word or word part.	He did ~~not~~ go. It was forgot~~ten~~.
c.	Words pronounced by examiner	Write a *P* above words pronounced by examiner.	They saw a P large horse.
d.	Words repeated	Write an *R* above the word repeated.	He saw the R strange animal.
e.	Hesitations	Put a check over the word on which the hesitation occurred.	It was a long ✔ voyage
f.	Insertions	Use a caret and write in insertion.	We went the in ^ summer.

g.	Self-corrections	Put a *C* over words corrected.	They saw a c little large horse.
h.	Ignored punctuation	Cross out ignored punctuation.	Are you coming? After he left/we
i.	Phrasing	Use slash lines to indicate phrasing.	waited for his call./

Note any unusual behavior such as whispering, finger pointing, unusual book position, head tilting, squinting, and so forth.

The examiner should refrain from correcting the student or pronouncing a word for him until the student has had a reasonable length of time to attempt it himself. If possible, a tape recorder should be used to verify the accuracy of coding the reading behaviors. After the student has finished, the passage is taken from him, and he is asked about its content.

The procedure should continue until the student reaches his frustration level, which is determined by a large number of inaccuracies in word recognition, poor comprehension, and a very slow reading rate. At this point the examiner should drop down one level and administer the silent reading paragraphs, preparing the student for each one and asking about content as in the oral paragraphs. Unusual behavior or responses should be recorded.

When frustration level has been reached on the silent reading paragraphs, the examiner should again drop down one paragraph and administer the listening paragraphs with preparation and response to content, noting unusual behavior or responses.

Scoring. Both quantity and type of inaccuracies in word recognition as well as difficulties in comprehension and reading rate need to be considered in making a determination about independent, instructional, and frustration levels. If the examiner permits the reader to read silently before reading orally, more accuracy should be expected than if the reader reads without preparation. A general guide appears in Figure 10.5. The first column (1) suggests criteria for prepared readers; the second (2) suggests criteria for reading at sight.

Analysis. Major questions in making a decision as to level are these: What constitutes an error? Are some errors more serious than others? Though all ob-

FIGURE 10.5.   General guide to estimating level

Estimated Level	=	Accuracy in Word Recognition		+	Comprehension	
		(1)	(2)		(1)	(2)
Independent		99%	95%		90%	80%
Instructional		95%	90%		80%	70%
Frustration		90%	85%		60%	60%

servable behaviors of a reader are recorded, not all behaviors should be considered errors or equally serious. One also needs to consider the purpose for estimating level, that is, placement in materials.

1. Interpreting inaccuracies in word recognition.
    a. Inaccuracies that probably do not reflect lack of ability to recognize words include those that are a result of habitual oral language use. Examples:

    the   the
(1) We went to á   lake in ^   summer.

    Children and adults who often go to a particular lake usually refer to "the lake." "In the summer" is a phrase used more often by some people than "in summer."

    be goin tamara
(2) I am going tomorrow.

    The substitution of *be* for *am*, the omission of the ending of *going*, and the mispronunciation of *tomorrow* are all dialectical and do not indicate difficulties in recognizing words. These should not be considered errors.
    b. Other behaviors that are not "wrong" but may reflect a problem include hesitations, repetitions, and self-corrections.

        R   R✓ big
    (1) He saw a large dog.

    The reader was not having a problem with *he, saw,* or *a,* but with recognizing the word *large*. By repeating himself, the reader was filling in time he needed to try to recognize the unknown word. The reader's substitution was semantically and syntactically correct, indicating that his comprehension was satisfactory even though he could not recognize *large*. But what if the missed word were not *large*, but *huge* or *enormous*? Because these are less common words, the examiner would have to ask the reader, after he finished the passage, what the missed word meant. If the reader did not know, the inaccuracy would be classed as a vocabulary difficulty rather than a word recognition difficulty.

(2)   He took his dog, ~~Skipper~~, for a walk.

√SK-SK P
Skipper wanted to run in the weeds.

      the dog
When ~~Skipper~~ saw a cat he ran after it.

   He
~~Skipper~~ would not . . .

The reader of the above passage felt uncomfortable about attempting the word *Skipper,* even after it had been pronounced for him. He continued to make appropriate substitutions throughout the selection. This repeated inaccuracy should be considered as only *one* missed word.

     C   C
    saw   five
(3)   It was a fine day for a swim. Sue

     C
    him
met her friends.

The reader of the above selection missed several words but always corrected herself. In this instance, the *quantity* of self-corrections indicated a problem—possibly visual in nature. An occasional inaccuracy that is self-corrected is not considered an error. Similarly, reading behavior that appears to be a result of lack of oral fluency, rather than inability to recognize words, is not considered a reading problem.

c. An inaccuracy in oral reading that is more clearly an error is a word substitution that is inappropriate to the meaning of the passage: "They went to the game after school. Tim rode on a bus, but Don *wall* to the game." Another error that should be scored is pronunciation of a word for the reader *after* he has had a reasonable length of time to attempt the word. In these instances, the reader's behavior would seem to indicate that he was having difficulty with word recognition.

d. One way to consider both quality and quantity of inaccuracies in oral reading is to count as one error an inaccuracy that appears to be a result of inability to recognize a word and count as one-half any reading behavior that appears to reflect lack of ease and automaticity in recognizing words. Do not score behaviors that do not fit into the aforementioned categories. Obviously, examiner judgment is extremely important, and the percentages in Figure 10.5 are meant only as a guide. Furthermore, the diagnostician needs to remember that only a small sample of behavior is obtained on limited content and that verification of examiner judgment will need to be made as instruction proceeds.

An in-depth analysis of oral reading behavior can be made by preparing a chart similar to that in Figure 10.3, using the checklist in Chapter 7, and comparing word recognition behavior in isolation and in context. This can be helpful to those learning to diagnose or to a researcher but may be too time-consuming for a busy teacher.

2. Interpreting behavior related to comprehension. Oral reading behavior reflects comprehension through appropriate phrasing, inflection and intonation, and syntactic-semantic substitutions. However, such behaviors can become automatic, as experienced readers who have read aloud to other for extended periods without attending to meaning can testify.

Response to questions or free recall after oral reading reflects both comprehension and attending behavior. However, in this area, too, there are many judgments that must be made by the examiner: students may be so familiar with the topic that they may correctly guess the answers; others may lack concepts necessary to under-

stand the material, although they could read material of similar complexity if it were within their range of experience; some students
may be too shy or tense to do their best; some may not have understood their task; some may be affected by the length of the selection,
taking advantage of more information presented in longer selections
to predict content; and still others have difficulty retaining information or following the organization of the passage.

Another phenomenon, not infrequently observed, is the ability
of a reader to do better on a more difficult (higher grade level)
passage than on one that is supposedly easier. This may reflect greater
reader interest in some passages or may be due to several other
factors. Again, teacher judgment will have to play a part in estimating *comprehension level,* and the guidelines in Figure 10.5 are not so
clearly a matter of computing percentages.

Finally, because oral reading can be distracting to those who are
not on a beginning reading level, more weight should be given to responses after silent reading than after oral reading. Readers beyond
the second grade level whose oral reading comprehension is higher
than their silent reading comprehension level should be considered as
handicapped because silent reading is required for most reading
tasks.

3. Determining reading level. A major purpose of administering a graded
paragraph test, constructed from classroom materials, is to make a
judgment on appropriate placement. As word recognition, comprehension, and their interaction influence performance, teachers
need to keep these factors in mind as they consider the instructional
decisions they have to make with regard to placement. For example,
two students, Tim and Bill, may have the same profile:

TABLE 10.1.

Reader Level	% Accuracy	% Comprehension
2.5	100	100
3.0	95	100
3.5	90	80
4.0	85	80

However, an examination of word recognition errors may reveal that most of Bill's errors were with multisyllabic words, whereas Tim missed basic sight words and made semantically inappropriate substitutions. Bill might be placed in the 3.5 reader and given help with affixes and syllabication, whereas Tim might be placed in the 3.0 reader and given more basic instruction before moving to material containing multisyllabic words and more complex sentence structure. For Tim and Bill, identical profiles did not result in identical instructional levels.

OPEN BOOK READING ASSESSMENTS

Description. Open Book Reading Assessments (OBRA's) are informal silent reading assessments employing questions to be answered or tasks to be performed by the reader with the selection before him. The material is taken from academic material or daily-life reading. The skills tested by questions or tasks may reflect course goals or life competencies. OBRA's are most appropriate for those reading above the third grade level. They may be used with individuals or with groups.

Purposes. The purposes of the open book tests are (1) to obtain specific information on students' abilities to understand and use content area, vocational, or daily-life reading materials; (2) to plan instruction; and (3) to confirm or supplement other diagnostic data.

Construction

1. Portions of material considered to be typical reading for the student within particular areas of emphasis should be selected. For content areas this might include textbooks, periodicals, or pamphlets; for vocational areas, manuals, indexes, or directories; and for other life-role areas, newspapers, schedules, and catalogs. Passage length will depend on the reading ability of the student.

2. To determine the skills to be evaluated, one must give consideration to (a) the nature of the tasks to be performed with the material and the levels of comprehension required and (b) the enabling skills required to perform the tasks or comprehend the information. With regard to tasks and levels, will the reader need to interpret graphs

and maps? Follow directions? Identify summarizing or main idea statements? Evaluate information? When the main objectives of using the material have been determined, the test constructor can then turn to the enabling objectives. For example, will the reader be able to understand the technical and general vocabulary? Skim to find specific items of information? To perceive the organization of the information?

3. Multiple choice, matching, or short-answer test items should be constructed rather than those requiring the student to express the answer in his own words. This will result in ease of scoring, but, more importantly, it will evaluate the student's ability to understand what he has read rather than his ability to express himself (a higher level of functioning). This is not to say that expression should not be tested but that the underlying ability, comprehension, should be tested separately. In this way, the diagnostician can separate those students who comprehend but cannot express themselves verbally from those who cannot comprehend *and* cannot express themselves verbally.

On the elementary level, if self-contained classrooms are used, the teacher should reflect on his objectives for using the content area material and construct the test accordingly. But on secondary-adult levels or in other situations where the reading teacher does not determine course objectives, those teachers who do determine the objectives and teach with the materials should be consulted about test construction.

4. Page and paragraph numbers should be provided for each question, unless vocational skills are being tested. The more items within a category, the more reliable the test. At least five or six items per category should be constructed. The test should be piloted on a sample of average readers, and poor items should be rewritten or discarded. Many text books on tests and measurement present guidelines for constructing test items.

5. Sample categories and questions from various content areas:

Technical Vocabulary
(1) fossil (page 230, paragraph 2)
    (a) A rock shaped by wind or water into the form of an animal.
    (b) A trace of an animal or plant that lived long ago.

    (c)   A search for animals that lived in the ice age.

    (d)   A plan to reconstruct animals from the ice age.

    (e)   I don't know.

(2) composing room (page 22, paragraph 1)

    (a)   Where news is set in type.

    (b)   Where news articles are written.

    (c)   Where news items are selected.

    (d)   Where news policy is established.

    (e)   I don't know.

General Vocabulary

(1) distinguish (page 50, paragraph 5)

    (a)   Group together.

    (b)   Twist out of shape.

    (c)   Tell apart.

    (d)   Find a total.

    (e)   I don't know.

(2) dwells (page 6, paragraph 6)

    (a)   Eats.

    (b)   Dives.

    (c)   Walks.

    (d)   Lives.

    (e)   I don't know.

Specific Context Clues to Vocabulary

(1) coagulates (page 42) The acid thickens or *coagulates* the proteins of milk.

    (a)   Makes larger quantity.

    (b)   Makes more dense.

    (c)   Makes more digestible.

    (d)   Makes sour tasting.

    (e)   I don't know.

(2) opaque (page 40) You can see through glass, but wood is *opaque.*

    (a)   Can't be melted.

    (b)   Can't break it.

    (c)   Can't be bent.

    (d)   Can't look through it.

    (e)   I don't know.

Main Ideas

(1) the main idea (important principle) on page 22 is:
   (a) Winds blow across the water.
   (b) Evaporation lowers air temperature.
   (c) Moisture is removed from the air.
   (d) Refrigerators can help preserve food.
   (e) I don't know.

(2) The main idea (statement of theory) on page 108 is:
   (a) The United States is in the temperate zone.
   (b) Countries that are in temperate zones make greater progress than those that are not.
   (c) Progress is measured by gross national product.
   (d) Climate affects the course of world history.
   (e) I don't know.

Literal Details

(1) Circle three examples of an amphibian. (pages 29 and 30)
   (a) frog   (d) turtle   (g) salamander
   (b) bird   (e) toad   (h) water buffalo
   (c) fish   (f) alligator   (i) snake

(2) The new stars of 1600 and 1604 were observed by (page 32)
   (a) Galileo
   (b) Copernicus
   (c) Kepler
   (d) Tycho Brahe
   (e) I don't know.

Interpretation

(1) Match the following statements to the diagrams:

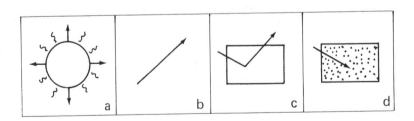

_____ Light can be bent. (p. 40)
_____ Light can be reflected. (p. 41)

____ Light travels in straight lines. (p. 40)
____ Light can be absorbed. (p. 42)
____ Light can travel through space. (p. 42)

(2) Sam's mother appeared to be (pp. 80–82)
   (a) worried (b) disappointed (c) angry
   (d) pleased (e) not concerned
   about his new job.

Using Charts

(1) Olefin is cleaned by _____ . (p. 57)
   (a) washing in warm water
   (b) washing in hot water
   (c) dry cleaning
   (d) brushing with cornstarch
   (e) I don't know.

(2) The distance from Lansing to Central City is _____ .
   (See map grid.)
   (a) 62 miles
   (b) 72 miles
   (c) 86 miles
   (d) 59 miles
   (e) I don't know.

Using Book Parts

In my textbook, to find quickly:	I would turn to:	on page:
____ ____ A definition of a technical word	(a) table of contents	(1) ii
____ ____ Pages that mention a particular person's name	(b) preface	(2) 390
____ ____ A statement of why the author wrote the book	(c) the glossary	(3) iii
____ ____ Name of book's publisher	(d) title page	(4) vii
____ ____ Outline of what is in the book	(e) index	(5) 385

Administration. Students should be given a generous amount of time, although those who take much longer than others should be noted as they may require further testing. The OBRA may be given in sections so that students who are unable to concentrate for a sustained period will not be inclined to guess or mark answers without reading the material. As with all test administration, students should be given clear, explicit instructions, encouraged to do their best, and observed for evidence of inattention to the task or confusion over test directions.

Scoring.   As a general guide, 80 per cent may be considered adequate for most categories. If several students are tested, the results might be charted as in Table 10.2.

TABLE 10.2.

	Literal Details						Technical Vocabulary						Main Ideas						And so on
	1	*2*	*3*	*4*	*5*	*6*	*7*	*8*	*9*	*10*	*11*	*12*	*13*	*14*	*15*	*16*	*17*	*18*	
Jim	✔	✔		✔	✔		✔	✔		✔	✔	✔			✔		✔		
Sue	✔	✔	✔	✔	✔	✔	✔	✔	✔	✔	✔	✔	✔						
Donald	✔	✔		✔						✔	✔						✔		
Linda	✔	✔	✔	✔	✔	✔	✔	✔	✔	✔	✔	✔	✔	✔	✔		✔	✔	
And so on																			

The number refers to the test item; a check mark indicates a correct answer.

Analysis.   An analysis of the results can provide information on specific strengths and weaknesses. If the chart is read vertically, it can reveal group needs; if read horizontally, it can indicate individual needs. Jim, for example, needs help in identifying main ideas in his textbook, whereas Donald's low performance in one of the easier sections of the test, literal comprehension, suggests the need for further evaluation in the areas of general vocabulary and underlying concepts. If these are low, he should not be required to use this text. If these are satisfactory, Donald's listening comprehension of the material should be evaluated to see whether he can have the textbook read to him while instruction is provided to improve his technical vocabulary and comprehension.

Students should be given feedback on their performance. This can be done by photocopying the chart, cutting it into strips, and giving each student his results. Then the teacher can explain the reasoning processes and knowledge required by each category. This might be the first time some of the students have gotten any insight as to what their comprehension skills are and what kinds of reasoning need to be done to comprehend various kinds of printed matter.

The OBRA can be extended over grade levels by constructing additional tests for material on higher and lower grade levels. Donald might be evaluated on easier material, whereas Linda might be evaluated on more challenging material. Students have a level at which they can function fairly well, but within that level they have strengths and weaknesses.

The teacher can develop a file of OBRA's on materials on different levels in various areas over a period of time that can be used to supplement a diagnostic battery or to place students in materials.

CLOZE TESTS

Description. Cloze tests are composed of reading passages with every nth word omitted. The omitted words may be chosen randomly or at spaced intervals, or they may be selected on the basis of a language factor such as parts of speech.

Difficulty may be manipulated by (1) passage selection, (2) distance between omissions (every fifth word or seventh word or tenth word), (3) complete or incomplete word deletion (I need a loaf of b _____ d. vs I need a loaf of _____ .), (4) provision of word choices to fill in the blanks (*bead, bread, basket*), (5) deliberate deletion of words that appear frequently in particular phrases or in a particular word order (pass the salt and _____). Several examples are given in Appendix E.

Depending on their construction, cloze tests may be given to groups or to individuals.

Purposes. Cloze tests have been used (1) to place students at their instructional or independent reading levels in materials, (2) to estimate reading levels of materials, (3) to obtain information about a student's ability to respond to specific aspects of syntactic-semantic structure, and (4) to assess knowledge of content in a particular subject area.

Construction. In order to construct a cloze test to estimate the students' frustration, instructional, and independent levels in a particular set of graded materials, one should take the test passages from the set of basals or similar materials that will be used for instruction. The passages should be representative of the material in the books from which they were taken.

The guide in Table 10.3 might be used to select passage length:

TABLE 10.3.

Text Level	Approximate Passage Length (Words)
PP	40–50
P	50–75
1	75–100
2	100–125
3	125–150
4	150–200
5	200–250
6	250

The passages should be taken from the beginning of an article or story, and the first sentence should be left intact. The test constructor can experiment with five or seven word deletions to see which is more desirable with sets of materials at various levels.

The deletions should be replaced with numbered lines of equal length.

Example:
Tim and Sue were walking to the bus stop.
They saw a small (1) _____ sitting near
a bench. (2) _____ was wearing a collar
(3) _____ a leash attached to (4) _____ .

If the students taking the test are able to write, a response sheet can be constructed with numbers to match those before the blank lines in the passages. Then a key can be prepared to line up with the students' answers.

If transferring answers to a response sheet is too difficult for those taking the test, they might be permitted to write their answers in the blanks within the passages. A key can be prepared on plastic or with cut-out sections to place over the students' papers. Example:

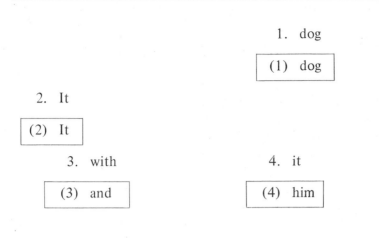

Administration.   The test may be administered in a group situation if all of the students are able to write. Those who cannot may read their passages aloud to the examiner. There is no time limit. However, those who take a much longer time than others should be noted and evaluated further.

To insure that students understand the task, they should be told that they are to guess the word that was removed from the blank and given practice in doing so before being given the test passages. They should be reminded that they will need only one word for each blank.

Scoring.   If exact words omitted are counted correct and synonyms are not accepted, greater interscorer reliability may result. However, teachers may agree on acceptable synonyms in advance of test administration and list these on the key. Incorrect spelling is not penalized.

Table 10.4. is a general guide to reading levels:

TABLE 10.4

60–100%	Independent Level
40–60%	Instructional Level
below 40%	Frustration Level

Analysis.   Cloze tests, like other tests described in this section, are only samples of behavior. Results must be considered along with other observations, and consideration should be given to the nature of the task.

The cloze procedure appears to test associational fluency along with familiarity with particular writing styles and topics. If a student does not do well, these factors should be considered along with his other reading skills.

To determine the accuracy of the cloze test for placement purposes, the teacher should test a sample of students on the cloze and another measure, such as the graded paragraph test, and compare results. If the cloze test seems to overplace or underplace students with regard to level, the percentage needed for placement can be adjusted or the test can be revised.

SUMMARY

Teacher-made tests can be quite valuable. If they are based on materials to be used for instruction, they can provide more pertinent information than commercial tests that may contain quite different concepts and language patterns from those in the instructional materials the students will use. Also, students are apt to do better in materials in which they have an interest and in those that contain familiar concepts. Teachers can take these factors into consideration as they construct their tests, so that a more accurate appraisal of student abilities can be obtained.

Finally, the experience of constructing tests can help teachers be more aware of the strengths and weaknesses of commercial tests so that they can learn to use them wisely.

CHAPTER 11

Dynamics of Diagnosis and Remediation, Case Studies

Included are selected cases that describe the general flow of procedures and some of the thought processes of experienced diagnosticians and classroom teachers.

Teachers working in a classroom may not have time to administer individual test batteries. They need to rely on skillful interviewing, informal testing, and trial teaching in a more parsimonious manner than a teacher working in a one-to-one situation. On the other hand, those working in a clinical setting also need to be careful of overtesting and inefficient use of time.

The goal for teachers in both individual and group settings is to learn what the student is capable of doing and how he responds to instruction. They may feel fairly confident about their knowledge of assessment procedures and remedial approaches but feel uneasy about the actual exchanges with a student. They know they cannot expect all students to be comfortable, motivated, and open, for many are aware that they have fallen behind their peers and may be defensive and insecure. Such students may have difficulty in attending or doing their best and may be putting forth only enough effort to get by. This means teachers have to observe carefully, note differences in the student's performance as he becomes tense or his attention wanders, and shift procedures accordingly.

It is apparent that people having difficulty in reading may be found on elementary, junior high, high school, and adult levels. The examples in the following narratives include two elementary school children, one junior high student, and one high school drop-out enrolled in a community college. These narratives illustrate the interaction between teacher and student as teachers adjust their techniques to students' needs. Knowledgeable teachers are able to hypothesize quickly about their students' needs and abilities and swiftly confirm or rule out their ideas with brief, informal tests or trial teaching. They may look at the flowchart or a list of skills to refresh their thinking, but they no longer need to rely on such aids. Scores are less important to these professionals than student processing behaviors, interests and attitudes, and the ability to learn.

MARK

Mark, a second grade student, was referred to the reading teacher in March. There was a question as to whether Mark should be promoted to third grade because of difficulties he was having in reading and other areas.

Procedures	Narrative	Hypotheses and Findings
	Session 1	
Reflection	Although this was my first meeting with Mark, I had seen him before, a muscular, freckle-faced boy, often dashing about, frequently being told to walk and watch where he was going. I had certainly heard about him. He was variously described as immature, spoiled, and emotionally disturbed. He had been given social promotions the previous two years.	
Interview	"Well, here I am. I guess you've heard of me. I'm Mark and my teacher thinks I'm stupid." These were Mark's opening remarks. As we talked, it became apparent by his command and use of words that Mark was quite bright. He also was quite upset about his lack of ability in reading, writing, and arithmetic. He frequently said he didn't want to do "baby" work.	Appeared to be an intelligent boy who was very disturbed about his lack of basic skills.

Procedures	Narrative	Hypotheses and Findings
Visual Tests	Although his record indicated he had successfully passed a visual screening in kindergarten, I administered the binocular battery I had. A few times I found Mark ignoring my instructions to keep both eyes open. His responses seemed slow. He failed some tests at near-point fusion but passed them a second time. I asked Mark to look at a pencil tip as I brought it slowly toward the space between his eyes from a distance of three feet. When the tip was almost seven inches from his face, his left eye wiggled, then rolled to the left.	Difficulty with fusion tests and informal convergence test. Needs to be referred to visual specialist.
Interview	I had noticed that Mark had some black mud spattered on his pant legs and shoes and asked about it. He said he had stopped at the pond on the way to school to look for turtles to add to his collection. I mentioned that I could find a book with pictures of turtles that we would use to look up the names of the ones he had caught. He said he would like to see them, but he hoped they were not "baby books."	Interested in hunting turtles.
Test	As Mark seemed to be unwilling to try to read for me, I showed him a set of cards on which I had pasted some words from popular products and typed some preprimer words and product names. I asked him to try them. He did not know any preprimer words. He was able to recognize a cereal name and a soda-pop name as they appear on labels in color, but he could not recognize them, when I showed them to him, typed on cards. Next I asked Mark to name some letters in scrambled order. He was only able to recognize consistently X and O. We stopped and chatted some more about his turtle hunting, for it was apparent that Mark was becoming upset. (Once when I showed him a card, Mark flinched and turned his head, as	Did not know any words. Could recognize only letters X and O.

Procedures	Narrative	Hypotheses and Findings
	though being offered a bad-tasting medicine.) I felt that no further work should be done until a report had been received from a visual specialist.	
	Interval	
	Two notes were received from the visual specialist. The first note confirmed that Mark had a visual problem, which was being treated with eye exercises. Some weeks later the second note stated that Mark was ready for instruction.	Visual problem was confirmed and corrected.
	Session 2	
Discussion	When Mark appeared the second time, two months later, he understood that his visual difficulty had contributed to his inability to learn to read, but his memory of reading instruction remained a disagreeable one, and he still seemed to question whether he was "too stupid," as he put it, to learn to read. He also said he didn't want to go back to "baby books." I reassured Mark about his prospects and the materials we would use.	Mark continues to be upset.
Instruction	I had some books on turtles, tracing paper, and a notebook. I explained to Mark that he could begin by writing and reading his own book about turtles. He agreed. I wanted to work with Mark's interests, but I felt he needed to do some tracing, matching, and copying to improve his visual discrimination of letters and words because his previous condition had caused him to make many errors in writing and copying. Mark found the pictures of three kinds of turtles he had caught and drew a picture of each on a separate piece of paper. Then he traced the name of each kind under its picture. As Mark worked on the last picture, I typed the three names in primer type on gummed labels. When he finished, I asked him to match the labels to the correct page and attach them. Then I showed	Mark was successful in the tracing-matching tasks.

Procedures	Narrative	Hypotheses and Findings
	Mark how to use a template to make three circles at the edges of his papers so that he could punch holes and insert his papers in a binder. We planned to continue to work on his book. For homework, I gave Mark three small cards with a label containing the name of a turtle on each and showed him how to learn to recognize each name and check his answer with his book. We made a pocket inside his notebook for his cards. . . .	He was interested and willing to try.
	After several more sessions, I recommended that Mark should be provided with regular, intensive tutoring throughout the summer and that he not be retained. His age was eight years and five months. He seemed to be making very good progress, and I felt that failure to be promoted might be so disturbing to him that his progress might be adversely affected. A nearby school was operating a nongraded primary. I further suggested that this might be considered as an option for Mark.	Prognosis is good.

SUZY

Suzy entered a third-grade class in November as a new student. Her mother said, as she registered Suzy, that she didn't think she was doing well in reading.

Procedures	Narrative	Hypotheses and Findings
Interview	The principal brought Suzy to my third grade classroom in the middle of the afternoon as the children were working independently or in small groups. I asked Suzy privately if she saw any activities or displays that interested her. She said	

Procedures	Narrative	Hypotheses and Findings
	she liked the learning center on comparing weights. When asked why, she explained that her grandmother had to weigh her food sometimes because she had diabetes and she wanted to help her. I told her that she could start working on the center that afternoon, if she wished.	Child appeared to be fairly comfortable in the new setting. Her speech was fluent. She appeared to have a good vocabulary.
Reflection	In order to learn whether Suzy's previous instruction was in a basal reader and, if so, which one, I next asked her if she remembered the names of the children in the books used in her reading group. She readily mentioned the names and told me the color of the book she had been using. With this information I knew I would be able to find a copy of the book she had been using in our storage room, if her information was accurate. (We had been using another series supplemented with the language experience approach, but because of frequent student transfers our reading committee had made a chart of basals that included titles, reading levels, skills sequences, and names of central characters. If I did not have a particular book available, I could find one of equivalent difficulty.)	

Session 2

| Testing | The next morning while the other students were working on their word charts and story tapes, I asked Suzy if I had found the book she had been using when she moved. It was a basal in the 2.0–2.5 level range. She said it was the same book. I asked her to read a page of her choice silently and then to read it aloud to me when she was ready. | Previous placement appeared to be in a 2.0–2.5 reader. |
| | Suzy read smoothly from a story in the beginning of the book with appropriate intonation and phrasing, but she appeared to have memorized the story. Next I asked Suzy to read a page from the last half of the book after first reading | |

Procedures	Narrative	*Hypotheses and Findings*
	silently. She read very slowly, almost word-by-word. She made no errors with basic sight words or with other words that had been previously introduced and repeated in the series; however, she was not able to recognize new words. When she attempted them in context, her substitutions were generally semantically and syntactically acceptable. After we talked about the story, I wrote the missed words on cards, shuffled them, and asked her to try to pronounce them. She was unsuccessful with all of them. Her approach with most of the words was to call another word beginning with the same letter. I felt I needed to know if Suzy lacked knowledge of sound-symbol associations or if she was not applying the knowledge she had. As time was short, I planned to do so the next day.	Seems able to learn and retain sight words. Language processing and comprehension appear not to be a problem. Seems to have a problem with analysis of new words.
	Session 3	
Observation	Suzy appeared to be making friends with the other children. Her work in mathematics was quite good, and she seemed to select math-related learning centers over other activities. Her oral communication skills were excellent.	Peer group adjustment good. Reconfirmed verbal abilities.
Testing	I gave Suzy an abbreviated, informal phonics inventory. As she had given evidence of having appropriate sound-symbol associations for consonants and consonant combinations, I checked her knowledge of long and short vowels, vowel combinations, and structural analysis. She did well with all but a couple of vowel combinations, but aside from compound words she did poorly with structural analysis. I felt that Suzy had fairly adequate sound-symbol knowledge and that she had not learned to attend to new words systematically, blending sounds and syllables from left-to-right.	Child appeared to have sound-symbol knowledge she was not applying.

Procedures	Narrative	Hypotheses and Findings
Trial Teaching	I asked Suzy to say words she had missed the previous day as I slowly uncovered them with a 3 by 5 card in a left-to-right fashion. After a few attempts, she was quite successful. Next she read words as I pointed from left-to-right with my pencil under them. She was successful. I asked Suzy to read a short paragraph silently and, when she came to a word she didn't know, to try to say it while she moved her finger under it from left-to-right. With her ability in contextual analysis to aid her recognition, Suzy checked her identification of the word. Again she was successful.	Good response to instruction in left-to-right sequencing.
Instructional planning.	I intend to have Suzy continue to practice her new technique and to participate in some language experience activities involving writing so that she can reinforce her sound-symbol sequencing skills in a meaningful context. In addition, she will be asked to help make charts, emphasizing word structure. Example:	Able to use context to confirm pronunciation. Therefore, will not need to teach this skill—simply encourage its use.

ing words	un words
singing	unable
talking	until
running	unopen

	For the present, I will place Suzy in the 2.0–2.5 basal we are using, but I think she should be moved to the 2.5–3.0 basal in about a month. With her ability to use context, acquire sight words, and learn new skills, she should make rapid progress in reading this year.	Prognosis is good. As the student has good verbal skills and responds well to instruction, she should soon be reading as well as, or better than, her peers.

NORMAN

Procedures	Narrative	Hypotheses and Findings
	Session 1	
Interview	Norman was one of a group of eighth graders who came into the reading laboratory in September. The group informally discussed some things they wanted to learn. Norman said he had been a "real good reader" in sixth grade, but last year he had had trouble remembering what he read, even if he read the material a second time. He mentioned that he had had a newspaper route for two years and liked to read comic books. I had a hunch that "real good reader" might mean that Norman had little difficulty in word recognition. His difficulty in remembering could be a result of comprehension difficulties or ineffective study skills.	Seemed to be a responsible boy. Problem may be in comprehension or study skills rather than word recognition.
	Session 2	
Informal Testing	I asked Norman to read aloud a short passage from his social science text that contained several multisyllable words and complex sentence structure. He had no difficulty. Phrasing, intonation, rate, and word recognition were good. His recall of the material was satisfactory. Then I asked him to read silently the next passage, which was much longer, and to tell me about it when he was ready. His rate was very slow. Norman's recall after silent reading was poor. His response was fragmented and poorly organized. What he did remember were phrases in the exact words of the text. I asked him to explain the meaning of some of the words and ideas. He was able to do so. As I had to meet with other students, I told Norman that he was right about needing help in remembering what he read, but he did do well in recognizing words	Ruled out word recognition and fluency as problems. Able to comprehend short eighth grade level passage after oral reading. Poor recall after silent reading. No difficulty with concepts or vocabulary

Procedures	Narrative	Hypotheses and Findings
Interview	and understanding short passages, and I felt sure that he could learn to read better. I asked if there were any textbooks he wanted to be able to read better. He replied that he would like to stay with the social science text and do some work with that. He added that he would like to read faster. Norman went to browse through the paperback book collection in the reading center.	Student goals were comprehension and recall of social science material and increased reading speed.

Session 3

	Four other students had needs and interests similar to Norman's, so I met with all five.	
Trial Teaching	I asked the group, after some preliminary discussion, to read a passage from the social science text that dealt with aid to developing nations in order to find three ways aid was given and to number and underline them on pieces of plastic that fitted over the pages. When they finished, they compared and discussed results. One student, Mike, had listed "supplying tools and equipment for farming" as *two* different ways, but the others explained why the statement should be categorized as one way. Norman had correctly underlined the three categories. I asked the group to close their books and write in their own words three ways aid was given to developing countries. All were able to do so.	(I made a mental note to help Mike with categorizing tasks.) Norman was able to read for the purpose stated.
	Next we discussed whether the purpose given for reading was probably one their teacher would give them on a test and then whether the question was reasonable. Finally, the group concluded that being able to predict class discussion and test questions would be useful . . .	Group seemed to be motivated for further work.
Instructional Planning	I planned to work with the group on (1) recognition of signal words in organizational patterns, (2) inferring main ideas from organizational	Feel that outlook for Norman's

Procedures	Narrative	Hypotheses and Findings
	patterns, (3) finding summary statements, (4) raising questions on literal and interpretive levels after surveying, (5) setting their own purposes for reading, and (6) practicing memory strategies such as recitation and mnemonic devices.	improvement in comprehension and recall is good. Problem seemed to have been lack of insight and/or instruction in what to study and how to study.

CHIP

Chip went to the community college reading center at the suggestion of a counselor who talked with him during the admission process. At the center he was given an appointment with a diagnostician.

Procedures	Narrative	Hypotheses and Findings
	Session 1	
Interview	Chip and I talked awhile to get acquainted. He was nineteen and had dropped out of a local high school. He said he planned to take a course in trucking. He had been employed as a dishwasher, but driving a truck was his goal. I noted a speech difficulty. Chip is black (I am not), and I felt a need to determine if dialect or articulation or both impeded communication. I further noted that Chip wasn't very fluent in expression and didn't volunteer much information	Wanted employment as a truck driver.
		Dialect difference?
		Articulation problem?
	I asked Chip about previous help he had had in reading. From his description of the materials I inferred he had been given help in phonics and sight words. In describing the material he used, Chip said, "If you're right, a nice picture comes	Verbal fluency due to shyness? expression of concepts?

Procedures	Narrative	Hypotheses and Findings
	on." He referred to *27* as "two-seven" and defined *speed* as "45."	Had been given instruction in phonics and sight words. Might begin word list testing at third grade level. Possibility of retardation?
Testing: Dolch List, Slosson Oral Reading Test	We proceeded to informal testing with a sampling of the harder half of the Dolch words. As he knew them all without hesitation, I asked him to begin reading the Slosson (SORT) word list at level three. Chip's speech difficulty became more pronounced. I asked him to use a word in a sentence if I was unsure of his pronunciation. Dialect was not a problem; he had a drawl I could understand. He substituted *w* for *r* and *ch* for *st* as he defined words in sentences. Example: "He wan by the chop sign," for "He ran by the stop sign." Chip scored 3.5 on the Slosson Oral Reading Test.	Was able recognize all Dolch words without hesitation. (Indicative of at least third grade reading ability.)
	An analysis of his errors indicated he had sound-symbol associations for consonants, vowels, and consonant blends. He missed vowel combinations and the soft sounds of *c* and *g*.	Speech problem more pronounced under tension. Articulation difficulty: *w* for *r* and *ch* for *st*. Indicates a need to check hearing. Scored 3.5 in word recognition. Knew consonant combinations.
	He did not seem to have a strategy for syllabication. I asked Chip to give the meanings for words that I pronounced for him at random from the SORT. He had difficulty with word meaning above the third grade level.	Lacked: soft *c* and *g*, vowel combinations, and syllabication.

Procedures	Narrative	Hypotheses and Findings
		Appeared to be low in word meaning in isolation.
Oral Paragraph Reading	Next Chip read orally from a book written at the second grade level. He had little difficulty. At one point I told him a word (*office*). He became upset and said that he knew the word but had a hard time getting it out. As Chip was becoming	Possible retrieval problem?
Interview	tense, we returned from the testing situation to the informal interview setting by discussing parts of the Student Priority Checklist. Chip said his major reading concern was to improve his ability to read road signs, maps, and work orders. He does little reading on his own but said he likes to read comics.	Chip's specific objectives: read road signs, maps, and work orders.
Informal test of Listening Comprehension with Diagnostic Reading Scale	After a break, I asked Chip to listen to the *Diagnostic Reading Scale* paragraphs and answer questions about them. He had difficulty above the third grade level.	Little practice in reading.
	I promised to find some materials that pertained to trucking for our next session, and Chip said that he preferred to work on those rather than "school things."	Listening comprehension level about 3.5.
	After Chip left, I completed the Level A Inventory and the Personality Checklist. I suspected that Chip might be retarded, but I intended to use care in drawing that conclusion because of (1) his coming from a culturally different background; (2) his articulation problem, which might indicate a hearing loss; and (3) his language retrieval problem, which might mean he has appropriate associations for ideas but difficulty in expressing them orally.	

Session 2

Interview	Chip seemed a little more relaxed as reflected by more casual dress and manner. We talked about dinner arrangements, but he was definite in that	

Procedures	Narrative	Hypotheses and Findings
	he didn't want to deviate from his regular schedule. Chip agreed to take a hearing test, which he passed without difficulty. He does not appear to have a hearing loss at the present time, although he said he had earaches when he was in second grade.	Auditory acuity appeared not to be a problem.
Test: Slosson Intelligence Test	I administered the Slosson Intelligence Test (SIT) starting at eleven years ten months. He had difficulty, and we had to go back to eight. He missed math, vocabulary, and comparison questions. I thought that he would have difficulty in the Truck Driving Course without basic math facts. The SIT score was 63. As all tasks up to this point have depended on Chip's verbally producing an answer, rather than responding by identifying or associating information, I felt a need to assess Chip's abilities through tasks such as pointing to a correct choice. I planned to find and/or create material on associative level for the next session.	Intelligence test, listening test, and word recognition test are all indicating third grade level functioning. A question remains in contribution of retrieval difficulty to level of functioning.
Interview	We discussed the materials I had found for Chip: Road maps Newspaper help-wanted ads *Michigan Drivers' Manual* Functional vocabulary list Recreational reading materials He agreed that the above materials were suitable, and he said he also wanted motorcycle information.	Confirmed acceptability of instructional materials.
Trial teaching: word recognition and comprehension	We reviewed signs from the *Michigan Driver's Manual.* Chip read all of them without hesitation. He was also able to explain what the signs meant. He couldn't give examples of where you might find a *Do Not Pass* sign, but, given the situation (hill, curve), he could tell you why you shouldn't pass. Chip did not know the meaning	Had automatic processing of all traffic words, such as *pedestrian, caution,* and so forth.

Procedures	Narrative	Hypotheses and Findings
	of local, national, and interstate highways. He wanted to know the meaning of solid and broken lines marking a highway and was not reluctant to ask questions. He seemed pleased with what we were doing. However, as we talked, his speech problems became more pronounced with some stammering and difficulty in retrieval. He was unable to form the word *exit*. (Later, when we reviewed the list of functional words, Chip refused to try any words starting with *ex,* although he knew most of the other words on the list.)	Difficulty in retrieving categorical information. Lacked some concepts of highway designations. Seemed eager to learn. Will need to check on recall at the next session.
Trial teaching reading maps	When we looked at the map of Michigan, I asked Chip about the upper and lower peninsulas. He said he had never heard of them. He did know directions, major cities, and map symbols. Chip did not know how to use the scale or the grid. I delayed instruction on the former because of Slosson math difficulties. Chip quickly learned to use the grid. He also had no trouble reading the population numbers for the cities he looked up. I asked Chip to go to the Tourist Center in the Commerce Building	Speech difficulties seem to be impairing functioning. Should be referred to speech and hearing specialist. Uneven conceptual development.
Interview	to pick up some up-to-date maps for our next session. Chip intends to plan trips to Greenfield Village and Cedar Point.	Demonstrated ability to learn to use maps.
	The best approach with Chip seems to be functional reading with immediate feedback. When he encounters unfamiliar words, Chip seems to be using a configuration approach. I plan to give him some work on structural analysis by using word patterns created from the *Michigan's Driver's Manual* and road maps.	Indicates interest in applying his skills. Should continue to use functional reading tasks. Blend skill instruction with practical application.

Procedures	Narrative	Hypotheses and Findings
	Session 3	
Interview	Chip brought the maps he had obtained from the Commerce Center. He had marked a route to Greenfield Village and seemed to be looking forward to his trip.	Seemed to be interested and motivated.
Evaluation of trial-teaching procedures	We reviewed the work we did in the last session. Chip retained the ability to use the grid and the meanings of terms he had been given, as well as the ability to recognize words he had studied.	Good retention for simple procedures, word meanings, and word recognition
Trial-teaching	Next we looked at pictures in an article I had found on motorcycling in some high interest-low level junior-high school material. I helped Chip circle compound words and the affixes he could find in the multisyllabic words from the article. Then he read the article silently,	
Application and Practice Test	and we discussed it. Next we used a list of multisyllabic words of the same type as those from the article to extend practice in structural analysis.	Good literal comprehension and recall. Seems to be able to acquire structural analysis skills.
	In order to assess the effect of Chip's difficulty with speech production on his verbal intelligence, I gave Chip the *Peabody Picture Vocabulary Test,* which requires him to point to one of four pictures as a word is pronounced for him. Again he scored in the same IQ range, 64. (The SIT required him to make oral responses).	Oral production difficulties did not seem to affect verbal intelligence score.
Reflection	At this point we took a break. I'm pleased with Chip's interest and positive responses. I think that Chip might be mildly retarded, but he does have potential to learn at least on a concrete level, and he should become a better reader if instruction continues. Successful work in structural analysis should bring Chip up to a fifth or sixth grade level of literal comprehension in areas where he has adequate conceptual knowledge and interest.	Appears to be mildly retarded but has the ability and the interest to read better. Instruction should continue.

Commentary

These narratives serve to illustrate the dynamics of the interaction between student and teacher. In order to learn as much as possible about a student's abilities, the teacher needs to be sensitive to the student's feelings and to his interests. If teachers grind ahead with their own agendas, they may succeed in having their students perform, but whether their performance is indicative of their true abilities may be open to question. More than a few diagnosticians have been embarrassed to find that their "incapable" students have become successful in other settings. Perhaps the diagnostician was unaware that the student was bored, hostile, or afraid of failure. Perhaps the student did not understand what he was to do or see value in the task. Most students, whether retarded, disturbed, or normal, will probably do their best if they feel comfortable and are working in areas of interest. Therefore, sensitivity to students' verbal and nonverbal behavior is essential.

The teacher should also be aware that some students will try to avoid making an effort by using various excuses: "I'm tired"; "I don't like this"; "I don't feel well." Others will try to engage the instructor in conversation. An instructor who engages in lengthy "rap" sessions regularly may be filling a need students have for a sympathetic listener, but that is not her primary role. Those who need counseling should be referred. If a counselor is not available, time might be scheduled to talk with students, but this should be time spent in addition to instructional sessions, not in place of them. All poor readers *deserve* appropriate diagnosis and remediation. Social-psychological factors should not be used as an excuse for not providing educational assistance. Indeed, education may be one of the few ways of escape open to a student with social-emotional problems.

The diagnosticians in the narratives were able to maintain rapport and keep their students' attention by shifting activities and alternating between periods of intense concentration and casual discussion. They did not spend an unreasonable amount of time in talking with their students, but they listened carefully so that they could obtain important clues for diagnosis and remediation.

Another characteristic of the diagnosticians in the narratives is that they planned for each student by obtaining materials or preparing activities that they felt would be meaningful. Unspoken messages here are, "I *listened* to you," and "I cared enough about you to search for these things." Planning, of course, also was evident in their having a variety of tests, inventories, and other materials on hand in case there was a need to change direction or shift activities.

The diagnostic hypotheses were made quite early by the diagnosticians with a minimum of cues. This enabled them to proceed quickly without a great deal of testing. Care was taken to treat hypotheses about student needs and abilities as tentative, requiring confirmation. This was especially true of the student who appeared to be retarded. The teacher was not one who routinely gave intelligence tests and matched them to reading level:

> His word level score is third grade, and his mental age is eight, therefore, he is doing as well as can be expected and is not recommended for instruction.

Rather, although she was alert to those of his responses that suggested retardation, she realized that other factors could have influenced his behavior. She proceeded to discover whether or not he was capable of improvement in reading within a reasonable length of time. Most, if not all, tests results should be rechecked with trial teaching. The student's response to instruction is one of the best ways to confirm one's hypotheses with regard to needs, abilities, and appropriate remedial methods.

CHAPTER 12

Applications in Clinical Decision Making

In this chapter diagnosticians are given procedures to use in order to improve their reasoning abilities when confronted with specific data concerning students with reading disabilities.

INCREASING ABILITIES IN CLINICAL DECISION-MAKING

College instructors or those responsible for continuing professional development may wish to conduct sessions in which participants analyze a variety of cases and share their reasoning with regard to each aspect. There are several ways this might be done.

1. *Reviewing Case Studies in Various Stages of Completion.* In this first procedure, case study information, is given to two or more diagnosticians, who discuss their interpretations of the data and make recommendations for further data collection and trial teaching. This activity can provide a review of the cues associated with particular kinds of problems. When detailed case studies are given, the diagnosticians should propose plans for remediation and explain their selection of procedures in terms of the data.

2. *Responding to One Item of Case Information at a Time.* This second procedure can be used to develop hypothesizing abilities. For in-

245

stance, participants might be given a single item of information such as a sample of a student's writing *or* a tape of his oral reading and asked to list (a) what problems they have ruled out and why, (b) what difficulties they think the student might have and why, and (c) what information they would like to have next and why. Then another piece of information is provided with similar analysis, and so forth. There are many useful variations of this procedure: individual oral or written responses, group analysis, and conditions of time-press (having only twenty minutes, for example, to consider the data). Debriefing is an important part of these activities.

3. *Discussing Cases in Progress.* Participants are given some referral information such as age, grade placement, and report card information. They discuss the data they should collect and procedures they might use in the first session with the student. At their next meeting the diagnosticians discuss their observations and findings and plan for their next session with the student. This procedure continues through remediation and is enhanced by peer observations and critiques.

PREPARING CASES FOR CLINICAL INSTRUCTION

1. *Case content.* Cases can be developed for purposes of preservice and in-service teacher preparation and research that provide varied opportunities for detailed analysis. The diagnosis and remediation that form the case should be carried out by expert clinicians. They should collect as much data as possible: tape recordings of diagnostic and remedial sessions, work samples, informal and formal tests, detailed observations of student's work, background information, and so forth.

    The clinicians should *overtest,* that is, give more informal and formal tests than they normally would so that any information that a diagnostician might reasonably request would be available. These data, for ease of handling, should be placed in file folders labeled according to category and boxed (one case per box). As these materials will be handled extensively, they should be laminated or enclosed in plastic sleeves. The following categories have been found to be useful in filing the case information:

    Arithmetic
    Attitude/motivation

Auditory acuity
Auditory discrimination
Background information (home, school, other)
Graded paragraphs (oral, silent, listening)
Graded word lists
Language (oral expression, reception)
Perceptual test batteries
Remediation (log and lesson plans)
Spelling
Standardized test batteries
Trial teaching reports
Verbal, nonverbal intelligence
Visual acuity
Visual discrimination
Word analysis tests (phonics and structural analysis)
Work samples
Writing/copying (near- and far-point)
Writing/expression

2. *Case Summary.* A panel of expert clinicians should review all of the data independently and write their findings, which should be compared with those of the reporting clinician if the cases will be used for research purposes.

3. *Case Selection.* The types of cases selected for extensive development should be those that are most likely to be encountered in practice in both corrective and severe remedial categories. As graduate and undergraduate students may have direct experiences with only a limited number of children and adults with learning difficulties during their clinical training, the "boxed" or simulated cases can provide an opportunity to examine and interpret data on a full range of problem categories. The following categories are suggested:

Visual acuity (near-point fusion)
Auditory acuity (high frequency loss)
Visual perception (without acuity problems)
Auditory perception (without acuity problems)
Language development (slow maturation)
Mild mental retardation
English as a second language
Instructional problems (inappropriate or absent)
Emotional Problems

These cases can be developed over a period of time by a college clinic or special services division of a public or private school. Another possibility is for teachers in their local professional associations to develop cases to share with each other as a continuing education project for self-improvement.

4. *Categories to Consider in Case Studies.* The following outline is presented as an aid in preparing a diagnostic-prescriptive case study. The examiner should attempt an estimate of the status of each of the following:

    1.0 Elements of Reading
    - 1.1 Sight vocabulary
    - 1.2 Structural analyses
    - 1.3 Sound-symbol association
    - 1.4 Syntactic-semantic processing
    - 1.5 Rate
    - 1.6 Comprehension
    - 1.7 Levels of performance
    - 1.8 Problem-solving approaches
    - 1.9 Recall of information

    2.0 Language Development
    - 2.1 Articulation
    - 2.2 Maturity
    - 2.3 Expression
    - 2.4 Reception

    3.0 Writing
    - 3.1 Handwriting (including near-point and far-point copying)
    - 3.2 Mechanics
    - 3.3 Spelling
    - 3.4 Expression

    4.0 Physical Factors
    - 3.1 Visual acuity and perception
    - 3.2 Auditory acuity and perception
    - 3.3 Other physical factors

    5.0 Affect/Motivation
    6.0 Educational Factors
    7.0 Home/Community Factors
    8.0 Potential for Learning
    (immediate and long-range outlook that includes verbal abilities, learning-rate, and expectations for levels of achievement)

5. *Using the Cases.* Preservice and in-service teachers may individually

or in small groups examine some or all of the data in a case, write their diagnoses and recommendations for remediation, and then read the clinician's final report to compare their analyses.

In-service teachers and specialists might present one case at each of their staff meetings over a school year and discuss the implications for their program. Selected elements of a case can be presented to a large group by using transparencies and tapes.

These are several ways that the cases can be used, depending on the needs of those who wish to use them.

PRACTICE IN INTERPRETING AN ABSTRACTED CASE

Case Outline, Laura

Student:	Laura	Age:	Eight years, one month
School:	Public, Urban	Grade:	Two

Graded Word List

Primer Level: 16 words correct out of 20.

                 errors: *with* for *what*

                             mouse for *mother*

                             what for *want*

                             baby for *help*

First grade list: 6 words correct out of 20.

                 Sample errors: *come* for *came*

                   dārk for *dark*   *red* for *ride*

                   fīrst for *first*   *love* for *live*

                   foot for *food*   *rade* for *road*

Score Pp. grade level

Dolch List

Flash: Knew very few words when flashed, including those known on graded word list.

Analysis: Managed to identify correctly several words after laborious study.

Score: Would appear to be on 1.0 grade level. (Test stopped because of time required by the student to recognize each word.)

Problem-Solving Strategies for Words in Isolation

1. Would say the unrecognized word several times, trying various sounds for the vowel until the word was identified.
2. Would sometimes study a word before attempting it and give a rule such as, "The silent final *e* means the *o* says $\bar{o}$."
3. Would self-correct, as "on—I mean no"; "came—I mean come."
4. Would sometimes repeat a word's final consonant sound before and during the sounding of the word: "*t-t-th-tt-thă-th-ă-t—that.*"

Oral Paragraph Reading

Primer level: Very slow, word-by-word reading.
   3 words missed: omitted *little*,
   substituted *a* for *an* and *blue* for
   black.
All comprehension questions answered correctly.

Problem-Solving Strategies for Words in Context

1. Would usually substitute words that were acceptable to sentence structure and meaning.
2. Would often self-correct when miscalled words were not acceptable to structure or meaning.
3. Would rarely omit or insert words.
4. Would make many substitutions of words with similar beginning consonants and other graphic similarities.
5. Would make effort to sound out almost every word.

Silent Paragraph Reading

Laura attempted to read silently but whispered the words to herself. She knew she was not following directions and became upset with herself, saying, "I can't read without reading out loud."

Listening Comprehension

Laura was able to answer all questions correctly after listening to second and third grade level paragraphs. She missed three out of five questions on the fourth grade level paragraph and two out of five questions on the fifth grade level paragraph.

Picture Vocabulary Test
Score obtained was equivalent to seven years and one month.

Language Development
Laura expressed herself clearly and fluently. Her word choice and sentence patterns appeared to be typical of a child her age.

Physical Tests

Audiometric—no problems.
Telebinocular—no problems.
Hand-eye coordination—some directional difficulties.

Other Tests

Auditory Discrimination—missed six out of forty.
Health history—excellent health, rarely ill.
Home background—large family. Seems to be supportive, well integrated. No problems apparent.
Current instruction—self-contained second grade classroom. Placed in a 2.0 basal reader.

Laura: Your Impressions

Given the above information

1. What is your assessment of this student's abilities?
2. What instruction does she need?
3. What is the basis for your assessment?
4. How might you confirm or disconfirm your hypotheses?
5. Are there any problems you feel you want to rule out? Why? How would you proceed?
6. What else do you want to know? Why? How would you gather the information you want?
7. If you were going to work with this student, what would you plan to do in your first meeting? Why?
8. Outline a plan of remediation with two or three alternatives. How will you assess your instruction?
9. What is your prognosis?

PRACTICE IN EVALUATING INITIAL
REFERRAL INFORMATION

Often the diagnostician is given some information or has an opportunity to obtain data before the first meeting with the student. Though this information may be quite helpful in some instances, it may sometimes be misleading or inaccurate. The problem, then, is to use the information to construct some hypotheses for testing while at the same time to be cautious in interpreting and using records, data, and opinion until their implications are confirmed.

The following outlines contain information about students who were referred to special services for evaluation.

Referral, Melinda (Sixteen Years; Tenth Grade)

Report Card

Subject	Grade	Comments
Social Studies	D	"Doesn't participate in class discussions"
American Folk Tales	D	"Does not complete assignments; inattentive"
Math	C	"Computation satisfactory but needs improvement in problem solving"
Tailoring I	B	No comment
Science	D	"Seems withdrawn from peers; does not contribute to team"

Tests of Academic Progress

Reading   20 percentile
Math   40 percentile

Diagnostic Spelling Test

Level   4.0
Missed vowels and vowel combinations and word endings.

Handwriting Sample (Cursive)

Good, overall; letters well-formed; good spacing; neat.

Cumulative Record

Melinda has been described as well-behaved but withdrawn or shy. Appears to have little conversation with peers. Participation and achievement in physical education have been good. Long absences in second grade because of a variety of complaints: Cold, earaches, sore throats.

Referral, Bruce (Twelve Years; Seventh Grade)

Report Card

Subject	Grade	Comments
History	D	"Disruptive"
English	D	"Poor attitude"
Metal Shop	B	"Helps others"
Math	C	No comment
Outdoor Living	A	"Shows leadership"

Reading Tests

STANFORD DIAGNOSTIC READING TEST, LEVEL II

	Literal	Inf.	Total	Vocab.	Syll.	Sound Disc.	Blend-ing	Rate
	9	9	9	9	9	9	9	9
S	8	8	8	8	8	8	8	8
T	7	7	7	7	7	7	7	7
A	6	6	6	6	6	6	6	6
N	5	5	5	(5)	5	(5)	5	5
I	(4)	(4)	(4)	4	4	4	(4)	4
N	3	3	3	3	(3)	3	3	(3)
E	2	2	2	2	2	2	2	2
	1	1	1	1	1	1	1	1

Graded Reading Paragraphs

Instructional Level 5.0
Listening Comprehension Level 8.0

Had difficulty with silent letter phonograms. Used configuration to guess multisyllabic words.

Note: Student came to attention of Special Services because of behavior problems in history class. Parents requested conference.

Referral, Michael (Fifteen Years; Tenth Grade)

Psychologist's Report

Verbal Intelligence   120
Nonverbal Intelligence   90

Report Card

Subject	Grade	Comments
Algebra	C	"Seems to make careless errors; can do better"
History	C	"Group participation good; written reports need improvement"
English	C	"Mike is forgetful; absentminded"
Biology	B	No comment
Physical Education	C	"Needs to work on coordination"

Nelson-Denny Reading Test

Vocabulary	Comprehension	Total	Rate
80 percentile	54 percentile	69 percentile	33 percentile 216 WPM

Handwriting Sample (cursive)

Letters poorly formed; poor spacing. Many common words incorrectly spelled: *wen* for *when, wuz* for *was, no* for *know.* At times confuses *their, there; too, two, to.*

Note: Has a mild dilantin prescription.

Melinda, Bruce, Michael: Your Impressions

Given the above information

1. Do you see any evidence of problems in physical, emotional, or language development areas?
2. How might you confirm or rule out your hunches?
3. Are there any other data you would wish to obtain before meeting with the student?
4. What would you plan to do in your first meeting with the student? Why?

Looking at specific facets:

1. *Report Cards.* What skills and abilities are required in each subject? (examples: attending, listening, speaking, reading, writing, planning, following directions, working independently, working with peers, and so forth) How might you account for grade differences among subjects? What might account for comments made by the teachers? Have report card grades been consistent since first grade? When did a change occur? Why?
2. *Tests.* Were the tests administered to groups or individually? What are the differences between group and individual tests? What tasks were demanded by the tests? (reading and answering multiple choice questions, listening and matching sounds, matching synonyms, writing, and so on) Did the student finish? Did he lose his place? If the test shifted in print size or format, did the student begin to have difficulties? Who administered the tests? Why? Under what conditions? Have test scores been consistent since first grade? When did a change occur? Why?

3. *Other Work Samples.* Does the student have difficulty in copying accurately, forming letters, spacing, spelling? How long, in relation to others of his age, does he take to complete his work? Does the student seem to be making an effort? Can he recognize and correct his errors?

Health: Have there been irregularities in attendance since first grade? What instruction might have been missed? How could the missed instruction have affected the student's achievement? Could the health problems have affected auditory or visual abilities? What medication is being taken? For what purpose? Possible side effects of the medication?

CONSIDERING MOST PROBABLE DIFFICULTIES

Another procedure that contributes to parsimony in diagnosis is to consider the level on which the student is functioning in relation to years of instruction and the most probable cause of his lack of progress. The following charts list difficulties that should be considered under various conditions.

Reading at preprimer level after one or more years of instruction. Possible problems:

(1) Poor visual discrimination.
(2) Short attention span.
(3) Poor visual memory.
(4) Attending to inappropriate discriminators.
(5) Low meaningfulness of words and content.
(6) Lacks concept of sound-symbol association.
(7) Lacks concept of sound-symbol sequencing.
(8) Inadequate auditory discrimination of words and/or phonemes within words.
(9) Inadequate left-to-right sequencing.
(10) Lacks sound-symbol association for consonants.
(11) Poor auditory memory.
(12) Sensory difficulties.
(13) Inadequate drill and practice.
(14) Low motivation.
(15) Inappropriate material.

(16) Inappropriate pacing of instruction.

(17) Delayed language development.

Reading at primer level or first grade level after two or more years of instruction:

(1) Consider previous list and following possible problems.

(2) Recognition of few sight words.

(3) Lacks automaticity for sight words.

(4) Lacks sound-symbol association for

    (a)   consonant combinations

    (b)   short vowels

    (c)   long vowels

    (d)   vowel combinations.

(5) Unable to apply vowel rules.

(6) Doesn't know common phonograms.

(7) Difficulty in blending sounds.

(8) Inappropriate use, or no use, of context.

(9) Lacks ability to segment visually

    (a)   compound words

    (b)   inflectional endings

    (c)   contractions.

Reading at second grade level after three or more years of instruction:

(1) Consider previous lists and following possible problems.

(2) Inappropriate or overuse of letter-by-letter sounding.

(3) Does not attend to meaning.

(4) Lacks ability to chunk words in phrases.

(5) Lacks ability to segment visually prefixes and suffixes.

(6) Lacks ability to recognize and associate sounds of common silent letter phonograms.

(7) Unwilling to attempt unfamiliar words.

(8) Unable to shift accent and try alternative sound possibilities in words.

(9) Unable to use punctuation signals.

(10) Does not systematically apply sound-symbol knowledge.

Reading at third grade level after four or more years of instruction:

(1) Consider previous lists and following possible problems.

(2) Lacks ability to recognize multisyllabic words.

(3) Lacks fluency.

(4) Unable to recognize dependent clauses and see their relationships to rest of sentence.

(5) Unable to see relationships between pronouns and antecedents.

(6) Makes little or no use of context to confirm word recognition quickly.

(7) Lacks experiences to understand concepts presented in content.

(8) Lacks ability to comprehend figurative language.

Reading at fourth grade level after five or more years of instruction:

(1) Consider previous lists and following possible problems.

(2) Lacks ability to read for a purpose.

(3) Poor vocabulary.

(4) Lack of extensiveness of meaning for words.

(5) Inability to summarize long selections.

(6) Inability to recognize organizational patterns in short and/or long selections.

(7) Does not recognize organizational signal words and relate them to organizational pattern.

(8) Inability to recognize topic sentences or summarizing sentences.

(9) Inability to skip unfamiliar words in order to read for overall comprehension.

(10) Lack of practice (as earlier) to attain fluency.

Reading at fifth grade level after six or more years of instruction:

(1) Consider previous lists and following possible problems.

(2) Lacks technical vocabulary in content areas.

(3) Inability to skim.

(4) Inability to adjust rate to purpose.

(5) Inability to use basic references and parts of a book.

(6) Poor inferential comprehension.

(7) Difficulties interpreting analogies.

(8) Poor critical comprehension.

(9) Does not recognize statements of main ideas in content areas.

(10) Poor or no use of summarizing paragraphs.

(11) Does not preview material.

(12) Cannot set a purpose for reading.

Reading at sixth grade level after seven or more years of instruction:

(1) Consider previous lists and following possible problems.

(2) Poor general vocabulary.

(3) Difficulty in understanding words that describe thinking processes.

(4) Difficulty in comprehending lengthy passages using complicated syntax.

(5) Unable to relate and synthesize outside experiences with content of passage.

(6) Unable to recognize common paragraph types: introductory, explanatory, illustrative, summarizing, and so on.

(7) Unable to recognize expository patterns common to content areas.

(8) Unable to select important ideas and disregard detail.

(9) Unable to recognize propaganda.

(10) Unable to control concentration.

(11) Lacks knowledge of ways to retain information.

(12) Unable to engage in high speed skimming with adequate comprehension.

Using Reading Level/Years of Instruction Ratios

The preceding charts need to be used in conjunction with interview data and referral information to be of maximum value. For example, if one were asked to evaluate a fourteen-year-old student who reportedly was able to read on a fifth grade level, a reasonable procedure would be to quickly confirm his word recognition level by asking him to read four or five multisyllable words such as *impossible, phonograph, conclusion, national,* and *identify.* If he does well, word recognition is ruled out as a problem, and diagnosis can proceed in areas such as comprehension and rate. On the other hand, if one were to evaluate a seven-year-old student, reading on a preprimer level, there would be little value in giving him a syllabication test. It is important for a teacher to reason in this fashion because her time is limited and unnecessary testing is stressful for most students.

CHAPTER 13

Analysis and Use of Materials and Systems

This chapter attempts to guide the practitioner through the quantities of available material to be selected in implementing a remediation program.

Most classroom teachers and specialists are dependent on published materials for remediation. Classroom teachers, especially those on elementary levels, have responsibilities to teach many subjects in addition to reading: arithmetic, social studies, science, art, and physical education, as well as special areas of curriculum emphasis such as environmental education, global education, drug education, and career education. Often special teachers have to serve students and teachers in more than one school and have large case loads of students with severe disabilities. Both classroom teachers and specialists seem to have inadequate planning time to create their own materials and inadequate instructional time to sit with each student as he practices and extends his learning. Fortunately, there are quantities of excellent instructional materials available. In fact, the quantities of available material—good, bad, and mediocre—lead to another problem: material selection. Mistakes in purchasing can be quite costly in a financial sense as well as in a loss of effectiveness of the remedial program.

The goals of material purchase are to obtain materials (1) to meet the range of levels, interests, abilities, and specific skill needs of the students to be served and (2) to meet the organizational and management needs of the teachers carrying out remediation. Making the selections to meet these goals is a complex and time-consuming effort, and sufficient time should be allocated to the task.

An in-depth analysis of materials should involve consideration of the following factors.

1. *Readability Levels.* Are the reading levels advertised by the publisher accurate? Are a sufficient number of stories and articles available at all levels? Often materials advertised to span levels are insufficient at the lower end of the range. For example, only three or four exercises may be provided at the second grade level after which the remainder of the material is at the third through fifth levels, although the range advertised may have been "2.0 to 4.0."

2. *Age/Grade Levels.* Are the topics and format suitable to the age/grade levels of the readers? Older students are quickly turned off by large print and language, pictures and topics they consider babyish. On the other hand, younger students may need larger print and simple directions. They may be confused and bored by topics outside their areas of experience and interest.

3. *Motivational Factors.* Generally, students seem to like exercises that are short (about ten minutes) and are self-correcting so that they can obtain immediate feedback. They also seem to find satisfaction in working at a level that is challenging but permits success. They like to be able to chart or graph their progress and to make decisions with regard to story or article selections.

    However, there are many factors involved in motivation. If a decision needs to be made about a set of costly materials, it is good practice to visit other locations that have been using the program for some time (to permit the novelty effects to have worn off) to observe students using the materials and interview them and their teachers.

4. *Prescriptive Possibilities.* Is the material constructed so that a particular skill can be reviewed or practiced without going through extraneous presentations or exercises? Are the skills indexed for ease in writing prescriptions? Are there a sufficient number of practice items? Are items self-correcting? Are lessons brief enough to permit students to repeat them if necessary? Can the material serve several students? Often materials constructed for developmental reading programs contain lessons on a variety of factors that are unnecessary for the remedial student, and these lessons are often integrated in

such a manner that it is difficult to isolate the information or practice exercises needed by individual students.

5. *Nature of Skill Content in Beginning Reading Levels.*
   a. *Sight Words.* What is the nature of the "sight words"?
      (1) Are they the most common functional words (Dolch list)?
      (2) Are they common phonograms (*bat, hat, fat; pan, fan, man*)?
      (3) Are they a survival vocabulary (*men, ladies, danger, stop . . .*)?
      (4) Are they a controlled set of words, frequently repeated in context?
      (5) Are they a combination of any of these?
   b. *Word Recognition.* What approach or approaches are used to aid word recognition?
      (1) Repetition of whole words in isolation, phrases, sentences, and/or paragraphs?
      (2) Sound-symbol association in various forms?
         (a) sounds in isolation, keyed to pictures, letters, and/or words.
         (b) blending phonic elements: *fa-n, pa-n, ma-n.*
         (c) Initial sound substitution in word families: *cat, fat, hat, chat.*
      (3) Rule-Governed Approaches? Example: "Words that have a double *e* usually have the long *e* sound," and "In *ay* the *y* is silent and gives *a* its long sound."
      (4) Sentence Pattern Approaches? Example: "Tim saw a bird"; "Mother saw a bird"; "Sue saw a cat"; and "The man talked quickly"; "The man talked softly," and so on.
      (5) Structural Analysis?

Example:
   (a) take– taking   (b) elf– elves
       bake– _____   self– _____
       make– _____   leaf– _____

      (6) Integrated approaches that include listening, speaking, reading, and writing in structured or unstructured ways?
      (7) Combinations of any of the preceding?
   c. *Comprehension.* Is the material constructed so that compre-

hension, rather than sound-letter association or word recognition, is emphasized? In some materials the plan is to present a short passage, then an exercise, and, finally, another passage: begin in context, isolate to teach, return to context.

Example:
Slow Sue

(1) Sue eats her lunch slowly. Her friends always have to wait for her.

(2) *slow* + *ly* = slowly
Sue eats slowly.
Can you make other words and use them in a sentence?
slow + *er*   = _____
slow + *est*   = _____
slow + *ness* = _____

(3) Use words in the *slow* family to fill in the blanks.
"Why is Sue so _____ ?" asked Linda.
She is the _____ eater here. She is
even _____ than Mary."
        "Sue just likes to eat _____ ,"
answered John. "Why not? We are not in a
hurry. Her _____ doesn't matter."

Some plans may drill in isolation, but provide accompanying booklets that use the sounds and/or words taught in carefully controlled presentations. Other materials have accompanying readers that are unrelated to skills lessons.

There is a great variation in emphasis on comprehension that ranges from no use of context to no use of isolated skills.

A careful analysis of beginning reading materials will reveal quite different approaches. The question is, Which are likely to be more successful with particular populations? Because there is no best approach for all students, materials should be selected that reflect different approaches. If a student is given the same type of material with which he failed in the past, he may reject it for emotional reasons. Teachers need to have more than one type of instructional program available, and they should strive to be equally proficient and comfortable with each. Teacher enthusiasm, or lack of it, for a particular approach can affect the student.

(d) *Nature of Material Used for Comprehension and Rate Growth on Intermediate and Upper Levels.*

    (1) *Concepts.* Do the readers have experiential backgrounds sufficient to understand the content? Will the teacher need to spend much time providing readiness for the material? Are aids or suggestions provided for readiness? Does the content help to build students' conceptual backgrounds?

    (2) *Topics.* Are the topics likely to be interesting to the students who will be using the material? Are the topics suitable to the age and maturity of the readers? Is a sufficient variety of subjects available so that students can choose according to their interests?

    (3) *Purposeful Reading.* Are exercises constructed to provide practice in reading for a wide range of purposes: to read for major themes, principles, or theories; to read for specific details; to identify organizational patterns; to evaluate information; and so forth?

    (4) *Syntactic Comprehension.* Are activities designed to *involve* students in manipulation of sentence parts; identification of sentence components and their relationships?

    (5) *Vocabulary Development.* Are the words selected for study relevant to the students? Are the words likely to be encountered by the students? Are activities designed so that all language aspects are involved: listening, speaking, reading, writing? If not, can the teacher easily add the missing component(s)? Are words presented in meaningful contexts? Are only a few, related words presented at a time, with adequate repetition and provision for review?

    (6) *Critical Reading.* How extensive are the activities with regard to critical reading? Some possible areas include propaganda devices, logic, comparisons for accuracy or points of view, identification of statements of value, generalizations, ascription, connotations, inferences, and admissible and inadmissible evidence.

    (7) *Rate.* Is rate developed and tested *with* comprehension rather than in isolation? Do students practice adjusting their rate to their purpose for reading? Is flexibility of rate emphasized? Are methods included for previewing material? Are techniques for recall included? Are charts provided so that students graph their progress? If me-

chanical devices are used, is there provision to transfer rate skills to books and periodicals?

ANALYSIS OF SKILLS MANAGE-MENT SYSTEMS

Some schools purchase a skills management system for their developmental and/or remedial programs. These vary widely. The following factors need to be considered in selecting a system:

1. Intent of the system.
2. Range of reading/age levels for whom system is intended.
3. Adaptability of system to presently owned and preferred tests and materials.
4. Validity of objectives.
5. Number of objectives in the program (may range from 50 to 1,000).
6. Feasibility of selecting only desired objectives from the system.
7. Feasibility of adding objectives to the program.
8. Skill areas included, such as:

Readiness	Reference skills
Word recognition	Critical reading
Sentence comprehension	Content area reading
General comprehension	Rate
Study skills	Spelling
Vocabulary	Writing

9. Instructional activities. Variety, quality, and quantity of activities for each skill area. Provision for using instructional materials from other publishers and keying them to objectives.
10. Characteristics of tests, keyed to skills: time to administer, ease of administration and scoring, number of items for each skill, percent required correct for proficiency and/or for mastery, convenience of record-keeping of test results, and availability of scoring services and program evaluation.
11. Consulting services. Assistance in purchasing, organizing, and managing system. In-service for teachers. Troubleshooting after program has been purchased and is underway.

12. Research on the effectiveness of the system with populations similar to the one for whom the system is being considered.

CONSTRUCTING A MANAGEMENT SYSTEM

When a large number of students is in a remedial program and the number of professionals available to work with them is small, consideration may be given to constructing a management system. The goals of the system are these:

1. To monitor progress of students.
2. To insure adequate diagnosis.
3. To provide appropriate instruction and practice.
4. To use materials effectively and efficiently.

It should be kept in mind that incorporating materials already at hand will be more economical than selecting only new sets of materials.

1. Nature of the Population.   The first step is to survey the population to be served. Approximately how many will there be in each age/grade level? Of these how many will have severe reading disabilities (as defined by achievement significantly below expected level and complexity of problem)? How many will have mild reading problems? What is the expected range of reading levels and the expected number in each level?

Screening tests, past records, interview data, staff recommendations, and data from reading programs serving similar populations can be used to make estimates about the population.

2. Goals and Objectives.   The next step is to prepare the curriculum to meet the needs of the students with their ranges of strengths, weaknesses, and interests. This should first be done by broad statements of purposes and goals and then translated into specific objectives. Lists of objectives are available from many sources: state and local education departments, journals and texts, publishers of instructional materials, and various special projects of colleges of education. It may save time to review these and choose or adapt only the most desirable objectives rather than write them all. A caution: it is better to do a good job of keeping track of a few carefully selected objectives than a poor job of keeping track of many objectives or spending time on extensive record-keeping that would be better spent with students.

3. Criterion-Referenced Tests.   Criterion-referenced tests are tests that measure a person's ability to perform specific tasks in terms of mastery. A level of performance is set for passing each skill category. These tests are helpful in planning programs for individual students. Norm-referenced tests are designed to compare a person's performance with his or her peers. They are helpful as screening tests.

Criterion-referenced tests should be prepared to test for the selected objectives. These, too, may be available from the foregoing list of sources. However, if they are not available or if those available are not deemed suitable, tests will need to be constructed.

4. Instructional Activities.   Instructional activities need to be created and/or selected that will enable students to meet the goals and objectives of the program. Sources include reading and learning methods books, as well as activities kits, workbooks, and pamphlets on games, learning centers, and so forth. Activities need to be keyed to objectives.

5. Materials.   Instructional materials are then created and/or selected to be used with the instructional activities. First, materials on hand in school storage areas and classrooms are analyzed and charted by objective and level. Second, printed materials such as telephone books, catalogs, newspapers, maps, and schedules are charted. Third, the chart is analyzed for weak or missing areas of available materials. Fourth, materials are created and/or purchased as necessary.

The foregoing procedure is much more economical and effective than first buying materials and then constructing the program. When materials are purchased before the curriculum is outlined, the materials tend to dictate the program.

6. Organization and Management.   A management system is devised to individualize instruction, provide for student interaction with peers and teachers, and keep track of student progress. Rather than be overwhelmed by a host of individual and small-group instructional plans, a teacher new to management systems might do well to start with three to five groups and about six learning stations. Individual prescriptions or contracts can be added as the need is indicated. A schedule should be posted that allows for group and individual instruction and for preparation and record keeping. Checklists or cue-sort cards can be constructed for ease in keeping track of student growth. Room arrangement should provide for individual and small-group activities.

7. Evaluation.   A plan for ongoing evaluation of the system should be made before implementing the program. All components—objectives, tests, activities, materials, record-keeping, and grouping—should be reviewed and adjusted as necessary.

At various stages of the program students' suggestions and outside evaluations should be obtained because they provide insights that may well be missed by instructors involved in the day-to-day operation of the program.

PURCHASING INSTRUCTIONAL MATERIALS AND EQUIPMENT

The task of purchasing can be eased by maintaining a file of publisher's catalogs so that product descriptions, prices, order numbers, and addresses are readily at hand. A list of publishers' addresses is provided in Appendix D. One may send for catalogs or obtain them at publisher's displays at educational conferences.

Opportunities to examine materials or equipment for a brief period of time without obligation to buy can save costly errors. Obtaining samples is also helpful. Take care to read conditions of purchase statements. Schools often stamp materials as they are received. This usually results in their being unable to return the material.

Some enterprising, efficient staff members are aware that funds occasionally become available when budgets are readjusted during the school year or unexpected funds are provided by special state or federal sources. Realizing that there is often a deadline for submitting requests, they keep requisition forms on file. In some instances they may have completed the forms and have them ready for appropriate signatures.

Lists of instructional materials and equipment for use in reading remediation are provided at the ends of Chapter 5 and 8. A list of high-interest, low-level books is provided in Appendix B. In addition to these, every teacher should have a variety of appealing books, articles, news items, poems, and stories to read *to* students and should read to them often.

APPENDIXES

Appendix A

READING TERMINOLOGY

Part 1. Sounds and Letters

phone		gram	
phon	refer to sound	graph	refer to letters
phono		graphic	
		grapho	

grapheme — A letter. May be part of a word (*at* contains the graphemes *a* and *t*) or may be a word (in the phrase *I am a reader, I* and *a* are graphemes).

graphemic base or phonogram — A combination of letters often found in parts of syllables or words. Examples are: *ent, ive, ack, tion.*

phoneme — The smallest unit of sound in an utterance. For instance, the sound /p/ in *pat* or /b/ in *bat.*

grapheme-phoneme relationship or correspondence — Association between a written form and the sound that it represents. Thus p = /p/ Sometimes referred to as a language code.

encode	Putting into a code, as in spelling or writing.
decode	Translating a code, as in using knowledge of grapheme-phonemic relationships and other knowledge of language.
phonemic analyses or phonetic analysis	The use of grapheme-phoneme relationships to identify a printed word not recognized by sight.
phonic generalization	A rule or statement about sound-letter relationships in words. Percentage of occasions when rule applies is an important consideration.
phonetics	The study of speech sounds and their production.
phonics	The study of letter-sound relationships. A method of teaching reading that focuses on such relationships.

	Letters	*and*	*Sounds*
grapheme	A letter (defined earlier) that may stand for a sound	consonant	A sound produced with some degree of obstruction. May be classified
digraph	Two letters that stand for one sound. Example: *th*in loo*k* ma*sh*		in various ways: voiced—*b, d, v* unvoiced—*p, h, f* fricative—*f, s, v* labial—*p, m, b* sibilant—*s, z* single sound—*b, v, m* two or more sounds—*c, g, s*
cluster or consonant cluster	Adjacent letters that are pronounced so that a sound of each letter can be detected as: *str*eet, *dr*ess c*l*ue.	vowel	A sound produced without obstruction as *a, e, i, o, u* and sometimes *w* and *y.* A *breve* indicates a short vowel, as mặt. A macon indicates a long vowel, as *māte.*
silent letters	Those that do not represent a phoneme, as *e* in *kite* and *gh* in light.	diphthong	A composite sound that represents two or more vowels, as in *oi, oy, ou, ow*
		blend	A composite sound that represents two or more letters, as in consonant

clusters and diphthongs.
Also, to blend together
consonants and vowels
within a word.

Part 2. Words and Word Parts

morph		syllabic	
morphic	refer to units of	syllabication	refer to units of speech
morpho	meaning	syllabary	

morphology — The study of word meaning.

morpheme — The smallest meaningful unit within a word.

bound morpheme — A word part that carries meaning but cannot stand alone, as *re* in *rerun, ful* in *helpful.* Prefixes and suffixes are bound morphemes.

free morpheme — A word or word part that can stand alone. *Run* and *help* are free morphemes. Free morphemes are also called root words or base words. An affix (prefix or suffix) is attached to a free morpheme.

prefix + root + suffix   / /   The free morpheme is *turn.*

     re / turn / ing   / /   The bound morphemes are *re* and *ing.*

inflectional suffix — A word ending that may indicate tense, moods, person, number, gender, possession, or comparatives, for instance, *s, es, 's, ed; ing, by, er, est.*

derivational suffix — A word ending that gives new meaning to the base to which it is attached. Example: *shapeless* contains a derivational suffix; *shaped* contains an inflectional suffix.

etymology — The study of word origins.

syllable — A pronounceable unit containing a vowel sound that may form a word or a part of a word.

structural analysis or morphemic analyses — Study of word parts, as affixes and roots, and their relationships. Used as an aid to meaning and to word recognition.

Part 3. Sentences and Sentence Parts

syntax — Grammar. Sentence word order and the rules relating to order and word function.

phrase — A group of related words that are part of a sentence.

     Prepositional: I threw it *in the lake.*

Participial: The girl *swimming in the lake* is my sister
Gerund: *Swimming in the lake* is fun
Infinitive: *To swim in the lake* is fun.

clause — A group of words containing a subject and verb. An independent clause can stand alone as a sentence. A dependent or subordinate clause does not express a complete thought and is used as part of a sentence.
Adverb: I will play *when I can.*
Adjective: The girl *who won the prize* deserved it.
Noun: I know *what I should do.*

connective — A word that introduces a dependent caluse, such as *who, which, that, since, because, whenever, while.*

embedding — A phrase or dependent clause within a sentence.
Left embedding: The boy *who waved to Jill* was her brother.
Right embedding: He waved his hat *when he saw her.*

marker — A word that signals information about other words. For instance, noun markers (*a, an, the, her, then*) indicate a noun will follow.

content word — A word in a form or class that carries meaning somewhat independently of other words within a sentence. Examples: *house, large, run, justice.*

structure word
or
function word — A word that indicates relationships among other words within a sentence. Examples: *of, an, from, because.*

Appendix B

COLLECTIONS OF HIGH INTEREST, LOW-LEVEL READING BOOKS

Title	Reading Levels	Interest Levels[1]	Publisher
Action	2.0–5.0	Secondary	Scholastic
Action Libraries	2.0–4.0	Secondary	Scholastic
Adapted Classics	4.0–6.0	Upper Elementary and Secondary	Globe
American Adventures Series	2.0–6.0	Upper Elementary and Secondary	Harper & Row
Animal Adventure Series	PP–3.0	Elementary	Benefic
Animal Story Books	PP	Elementary	D. C. Heath
Beginner Books	1.5–2.5	Elementary	Random House
Box Car Children's Books	3.0–3.5	Upper Elementary	Scott Foresman
Checkered Flag Series	2.4–4.5	Upper Elementary Secondary	Field

Title	Reading Levels	Interest Levels[1]	Publisher
Contact	3.0–6.0	Secondary	Scholastic
Cowboy Sam Series	PP–6.0	Elementary	Benefic
Crossroads	4.0–9.0	Secondary	Noble and Noble
Deep Sea Adventure Series	1.8–5.0	Upper Elementary Secondary	Field
Dimensions—We Are Black (Boxed)	2.0–6.0	Secondary	S.R.A.
Dolch Four Step Reading Program	1.0–4.0	Elementary	Garrard
Doubleday Signal Books	4.0	Secondary	Doubleday
Happenings	4.2–4.6	Secondary	Field
Indians of America Books	2.0–4.0	Elementary	Children's Press
Monster Books	4.0–6.0	Upper Elementary Junior High	Bowman
Morgan Bay Mystery Series	2.3–4.1	Secondary	Field
Scope	4.0–6.0	Secondary	Scholastic
Simplified Classics	4.0–6.0	Upper Elementary Secondary	Scott Foresman
Sports Mystery Series	2.0–4.0	Upper Elementary Secondary	Benefic

[1] Some series designated as "Secondary" may be appealing to adults, depending on age and interests.

Appendix C

LISTS OF TESTS

The reader is encouraged to consult the test reviews, published in the *Mental Measurement Yearbooks,* O.K. Buros, ed., before purchasing any test. This is a basic reference found in most college libraries.

A full description of a particular test and current prices can be obtained by writing to the publishing company and requesting a test catalog.

Reading Readiness Tests

Title	Publisher
American School Reading Readiness Tests	Bobbs-Merrill
Gates-MacGinitie Readiness Skills Test	Teachers College Press
Harrison-Stroud Reading Readiness Profiles	Houghton Mifflin
Macmillan Reading Readiness Test (rev)	Macmillan

Title	Publisher
Metropolitan Readiness Tests (rev)	Harcourt
Monroe Reading Aptitude Tests	Houghton Mifflin
Murphy-Durrell Reading Readiness Analysis	Harcourt

Reading Tests, Group

Title	Reading Level	Publisher
Adult Basic Learning Examination	1-6	Harcourt
American School Achievement Tests	1-9	Bobbs-Merrill
Botel Reading Inventory	1-12	Follett
California Reading Test	1-College	CTB/McGraw-Hill
Cooperative Primary Tests	1-3	Educational Testing Service
Davis Reading Test	8-College	Psychological
Doren Diagnostic Reading Test	2-8	American Guidance
Durrell Reading–Listening Series	1-9	Harcourt
Gates-MacGinitie Reading Tests	1-12	Teachers College
Iowa Silent Reading Tests	6-College	Harcourt
Iowa Tests of Basic Skills	1-8	Harcourt
Metropolitan Reading Tests	K-9	Harcourt
Nelson Reading Test	3-9	Houghton Mifflin
McCullough Word Analysis Test	4-6	Ginn
Nelson-Denny Reading Tests	9-College	Houghton Mifflin
SRA Achievement Tests: Reading.	1-9	Science Research Associates
Stanford Achievement Test: Reading	1-9	Harcourt
Stanford Diagnostic Reading Test	2.5-8.5	Harcourt
Stanford Reading Tests	1.5-9.5	Harcourt
Tests of Reading: Inter-American Series	1-College	Guidance Testing

Reading Tests, Individual

Title	Reading Level	Publisher
Classroom Reading Inventory	2–10	Wm. C. Brown
Corrective Reading System	1–6	Psychotechnics
Diagnostic Reading Scales (Spache)	1–6	CTB/McGraw-Hill
Durkin-Meshaver Phonics Knowledge Survey	All	Teachers College
Durrell Analysis of Reading Difficulty	1–6	Harcourt
Fountain Valley Reading Skills Test	1–6	Zweig
Gates-McKillup Reading Diagnostic Test	1–7	Teachers College
Gilmore Oral Reading Test	1–8	Harcourt
Grey Standardized Oral Reading Paragraphs	1–8	Bobbs-Merrill
Peabody Individual Achievement Test	K–12	American Guidance
Reading Mesine Inventory		Macmillian
Sipay Word Analysis Tests	All	Educators
Slosson Oral Reading Test	1–12	Slosson
Wide Range Achievement Test	5–Adult	Psychological
Woodcock Reading Mastery Tests	K–12	American Guidance

Sensory, Language, and Motor Abilities Tests

Title	Age/Grade Level	Publisher
Beery-Buktenica Visual-Motor Integration Test	Ages 2–15	Follett
Bender Visual Motor Gestalt Test	Ages 7–11	Western
Benton Visual Retention Test	Ages 8–Adult	Psychological
Boehm Test of Basic Concepts	Grades K–2	Psychological

Title	Age/Grade Level	Publisher
Brown-Carlsen Listening Comprehension Test	Grades 9–12	Harcourt
Detroit Tests of Learning Aptitude	Ages 3–Adult	Bobbs-Merrill
Frostig Developmental Test of Visual Perception	Ages 4–9	Follett
Goldman-Fristoe Test of Articulation	Ages 2–Adult	American Guidance
Goldman-Fristoe-Woodcock Auditory Skills Battery	Ages 3–Adult	American Guidance
Illinois Test of Psycholinguistic Abilities	Grades 2–10	University of Illinois
Lindamood Auditory Comprehension Test	All	Teaching Resources
Northwestern Syntax Screening Test	Ages 3–8	Northwestern
Picture Story Language Test	Ages 7–17	Greene
Purdue Perceptual-Motor Survey	Ages 6–10	Merrill
Screening Test for Auditory Perception	Grades 2–6	Academic Therapy
Screening Tests for Identifying Children with Specific Language Disability (Slingerland)	Grades 1–8	Educators Publishing
Standardized Road Map Test of Direction Sense	Ages 7–Adult	Academic Therapy
Test for Auditory Comprehension of Language (English and Spanish versions)	Ages 3–7	Learning Concepts
Test of Language Development (TOLD)	Ages 4–9	Academic Therapy
Testing-Teaching Module of Auditory Discrimination	Grades K–6	Academic Therapy
Wepman Auditory Discrimination Test	Ages 5–8	Psychological

Intelligence or Scholastic Aptitude Tests

Title	Age/Grade Level	Publisher
Academic Promise Tests	Ages 6–9	Psychological
Ammons Full-Range Vocabulary Tests	PreK–Adult	Psychological
Arthur Point Scale of Performance Tests	Ages 4–Adult	Psychological
Cattell Culture Fair Intelligence Test	Ages 8–Adult	Bobbs-Merrill
California Test of Mental Maturity	Grades K–Adult	CTB/McGraw-Hill
Chicago Nonverbal Examination	Ages 6–Adult	Psychological
Cognitive Abilities Test	Grades K–12	Houghton Mifflin
Goodenough-Harris Drawing Test	Ages 3–12	Harcourt
Peabody Picture Vocabulary Test	Ages 2–18	American Guidance
Raven Progressive Matrices	Ages 5–Adult	Psychological
School and College Ability Tests, SCAT Series II	Grades K–14	Educational Testing
Slosson Intelligence Test	Ages 4–Adult	Slosson
Stanford-B Net Intelligence Scale (rev)	Ages 2–Adult	Houghton Mifflin
Wechsler Adult Intelligence Scale (WAIS)	Ages 16–Adult	Psychological
Wechsler Intelligence Scale for Children (rev) (WISC-R)	Ages 6–16	Psychological
Wechsler Preschool and Primary Scale of Intelligence (WIPPSI)	Ages 4–6	Psychological

Appendix D

PUBLISHERS AND ADDRESSES

Academic Therapy Publication
  1539 Fourth Street
  San Raphael, CA 94901

Addison-Wesley Publishing Co.
  2725 Sand Hill Road
  Menlo Park CA 94025

Allied Education Council
  P.O. Box 78
  Galien, MI 49113

Allyn & Bacon, Inc.
  470 Atlantic Avenue
  Boston, MA 02210

American Book Company
  450 West 33 Street
  New York, NY 10001

American Guidance Service, Inc.
  Publishers Building
  Circle Pines, MN 55014

AMSCO Publishing Co.
  315 Hudson Street
  New York, NY 10013

Barnell Loft, Ltd.
  958 Church Street
  Baldwin, NY 11510

Bausch & Lomb Optical Co.
Rochester, NY 14602

Behavioral Research Laboratories
Box 577
Palo Alto, CA 94302

Bell and Howell
7100 McCormick Road
Chicago, IL 60645

Benefic Press
10300 West Roosevelt Road
Westchester, IL 60153

Bobbs-Merrill Co.
4300 West 62nd Street
Indianapolis, IN 46268

Bowmar Publishing Co.
622 Rodus Drive
Glendale, CA 91201

Califone Div. Rheem Manufacturing
5922 Bowcraft
Los Angeles, CA 90016

California Test Bureau/McGraw-Hill
Del Monte Research Park
Monterey, CA 93940

Children's Press
1224 West Van Buren Street
Chicago, IL 60607

Communican
Box 541
Welton, CN 06897

Doubleday & Co.
Garden City, NY 11530

Economy Co.
1901 West Walnut Street
Oklahoma City, OK 73125

Educational Developmental Laboratories
1221 Avenue of the Americas
New York, NY 10020

Educational Testing Service
Princeton, NJ 08540

Educators Publishing Service
75 Moulton Street
Cambridge, MA 02138

Fearon Publishers
6 Daves Drive
Belmont, CA 94002

Field Educational Publications
2400 Hanover Street
Palo Alto, CA 94002

Follett Educational Corp.
1010 W. Washington Blvd.
Chicago, IL 60607

Garrard Publishing Co.
1607 North Market Street
Champaign, IL 61820

Ginn and Co.
191 Spring Street
Lexington, MA 02173

Globe Book Co.
175 Fifth Avenue
New York, NY 10010

Grune and Stratton, Inc.
111 Fifth Avenue
New York, NY 10003

Gryphon Press
  220 Montgomery Street
  Highland Park, NJ 08904

Guidance Testing Associates
  6516 Shirley Avenue
  Austin, TX 78752

Harcourt Brace Jovanovich, Inc.
  757 Third Avenue
  New York, NY 10017

Harper & Row, Inc.
  10 East 53 Street
  New York, NY 10022

Holt, Rinehart and Winston, Inc.
  383 Madison Ave.
  New York, NY 10017

Houghton Mifflin Co.
  110 Tremont Street
  Boston, MA 02107

Innovative Sciences, Inc.
  800 Broad Street
  Stamford, CN 06901

International Reading Association
  800 Barksdale Road
  Newark, DE 19711

Jamestown Publishers
  Box 6743 Providence
  RI 02904

Johns Hopkins Press
  Johns Hopkins University
  Baltimore MD 21218

Keystone View Co.
  1000 Center
  Meadville, PA 16335

Lyons and Carnahan, Inc.
  407 East 25 Street
  Chicago, IL 60615

Language Research Associates
  Box 95, 950 East 59 Street
  Chicago, IL 60637

Learning Concepts
  2501 North Lamar
  Austin, TX 78705

Marco Hearing Instruments
  7375 Bush Lake Road
  Minneapolis, MN 55435

Macmillan Publishing Co.
  866 Third Avenue
  New York, NY 10022

McGraw-Hill Book Co.
  1221 Avenue of the Americas
  New York, NY 10020

Merrill Publishing Co.
  1300 Alvin Creek Drive
  Columbus, OH 43216

Mills Center Inc.
  1512 E. Broward Boulevard
  Fort Lauderdale, Fla 33310

Northwestern University Press
  Northwestern University
  Department of Communication Disorders
  Evanston, IL 60201

Orton Socuty, Inc.
  8415 Bellona Lane
  Tawson, MD 21204

Prentice-Hall
  Englewood Cliffs, NJ 07632

Psychological Corporation
304 East 45th Street
New York, NY 10017

Psychotechnics Inc.
1900 Pickwick Ave.
Glenville, IL 60025

Random House, Inc.
201 East 50 Street
New York, NY 10022

Reader's Digest Services, Inc.
Educational Division
Pleasantville, NY 10570

RIF/Reading is Fundamental
Smithsonian Institute
Washington, DC 20560

Right to Read
400 Maryland Ave. S.W.
Washington, DC 20202

Scholastic Magazines and Book Services
50 West 44 Street
New York, NY 10036

Scholastic Testing Service, Inc.
480 Meyer Road
Bensenville, IL 60106

Science Research Associates
259 E. Erie St.
Chicago, IL 60611

Scott Foresman and Co.
1900 East Lake
Glenview, IL 60025

Slosson Educational Publications
140 Pine Street
East Aurora, NY 14052

Steck-Vaughn Co.
P.O. Box 2028
Austin, TX 78710

Teachers College Press
Teachers College
Columbia University
1234 Amsterdam Ave.
New York, NY 10027

University of Chicago Press
1130 South Langley Ave.
Chicago, IL 60628

University of Illinois Press
Urbana, IL 61801

George Wahr Publishing Co.
316 S. State Street
Ann Arbor, MI 48106

Webster Division, McGraw-Hill Book Co.
1221 Avenue of the Americas
New York, NY 10020

Weekly Reader
245 Longhill Road
Middletown, CN 06457

Zaner Bloser Co.
612 North Park St.
Columbus, OH 43215

Xerox Education Publications
Education Center
Columbus, OH 43216

Weaver-Reed Co.
2883 East Paris Ave. S.E.
Grand Rapids, MI 49508

Richard L. Zweig Assoc.
20800 Beach Blvd.
Huntington Beach, CA 92648

Appendix E

SUMMARY OF CLOZE CONSTRUCTIONS

1. Word endings:

   She _____ ed the door.

   He closed the door _____ ly.

   He has two new _____ s.

   She has two new _____ es.

2. Affixes and roots:

   They pre _____ the film.

   Please _____ graph this.

3. Syntactic-semantic signals:

   That is my _____ . (N.)

   Your new dress is _____ . (Adj.)

   The _____ is here. (N.)

   I can't _____ very fast. (V.)

   May I have more _____ ? (N.)

   That is my only _____ . (N.)

Put your pencil _____ the desk. (Prep.)

Please take your papers _____ the chairman. (Prep.)

4. Coordinate and subordinate connectors:

I was invited, _____ I didn't go.

I went shopping _____ my sister wanted me to go.

5. Anaphora:

Mother told me Mike and Linda are coming.

She is my best friend.

My best friend is _____ . (Mike, Linda, Mother)

After I saw Linda, I fell and hurt my knee. That made me decide to stay out of the race. *That* refers to _____ .

        a. seeing Linda

        b. falling

        c. hurting my knee

6. Semantic cues:

When it rains, it _____ .

The _____ soup burned my tongue.

7. Tense:

I _____ here now.

I have _____ there.

I shall _____ _____ there by this time tomorrow.

I _____ be there tomorrow.

8. Context clues:

That statue is beautiful, but this one is frumgump.

Frumgump probably means _____ .

I don't know which to choose. That statue is beautiful, but this one is gliphgum, too.

Gliphgum probably means _____ .

9. Word pattern analogies:

Right is to fight   Hate is to rate

         as   as

train is to _____ .   fade is to _____ .

   (frame, pain, light)   (raid, fate, made)

10. Relationship analogies:

Silk is to burlap

               as

soft music is to _____ .

(loud noise, tall people, cotton)

11. Connotation:

I think of myself as _____ with money.

(generous, a spendthrift, careless, stingy, careful, tight)

With regard to studying, I'm _____ .

(disciplined, carefree, lazy, compulsive, inconsistent)

12.   Varying structure:

    1.   She has one sister and one br_ th_ r.

    2.   She has one sister and one b_ _ _ _ _ r.

    3.   She has one sister and one b_____ .

    4.   She has one sister and one _____ .

    5.   She has one sister and one _____ .

        (brother, bother, boating, dusting)

13.   Omitting various parts of speech:

        (adj.)

The _____ _____ man walked slowly down the _____ street. He saw a _____ dog with ears and a _____ tail.

        (adj. and adv.)

The _____ _____ man walked _____ down the _____ street. Although he felt _____ . He tried to speak _____ to the _____ boy he met in front of the _____ store.

14.   Creative writing:

    a.   Every morning the man walks to the store to buy a paper.

    b.   *At the last minute* the *tramp hobbles* to *the dime store* to *grab the daily rag.*

    c.   _____ the _____ _____

        (when)   (who)   (does what)

    to _____ to _____ .

        (where)   (do what)

(Create a positive description.)

15.   Fun:

"Pass the sugar," she said _____ . (sweetly)

"I won't read you a fairy tale," he said _____ . (grimly)

16.   Random passage deletions range from easy to difficult depending on frequency of deletions and student familiarity with subject matter and writer's style.

Note: With all strategies, learning is enhanced by student discussion of his selections.

Appendix F

PROFESSIONAL READINGS

Austin, Mary C.; Bush, C.L.; and Huebner, Mildred N. *Reading Evaluation: Appraisal Techniques for School and Classroom.* New York: Ronald, 1961.

Bader, Lois A. *Reading Centers for Middle School, High School and Adult Learners.* Box 506 Haslett, Michigan: Geoffrey Michael, 1976.

Blair, G.M. *Diagnostic and Remedial Teaching.* New York: Macmillan, 1956.

Bond, Guy L., and Tinker, Miles A. *Reading Difficulties Their Diagnosis and Correction.* New York: Appleton-Century-Crofts, Inc., 1967.

Carter, H.L.J., and McGinnis, Dorothy. *Diagnosis and Treatment of the Disabled Reader.* New York: The Macmillan Company, 1970.

Cohn, Stella M., and Cohn, Jack. *Teaching the Retarded Reader: A Guide for Teachers, Reading Specialists, and Supervisors.* New York: The Odyssey Press, 1967.

DeBoer, Dorothy L. *Reading Diagnosis and Evaluation.* Newark, Delaware 19711: International Reading Association, 1970.

Dechant, Emerald. *Diagnosis and Remediation of Reading Disability.* West Nyack, New York: Parker Publishing Company, 1968.

———, ed. *Detection and Correction of Reading Difficulties.* New York: Appleton-Century-Crofts, Inc., 1971.

293

De Hirsch, Katrina; Jansky, J.; and Langford, William S. *Predicting Reading Failure*. New York: Harper & Row, 1966.

Della-Piana, Gabriel M. *Reading Diagnosis and Prescription: An Introduction*. New York: Holt, Rinehart and Winston, 1968.

Durr, William K., ed. *Reading Difficulties—Diagnosis, Correction and Remediation*. Newark, Delaware 1971: International Reading Association, 1970.

Ekwall, Eldon E. *Diagnosis and Remediation of the Disabled Reader*. Boston: Allyn & Bacon, Inc., 1976.

———. *Locating and Correcting Reading Difficulties*. Columbus: Charles Merrill, 1977.

———. *Teacher's Handbook on Diagnosis and Remediation in Reading*. Boston: Allyn & Bacon, Inc., 1977.

Ephron, Beulah K. *Emotional Difficulties in Reading*. New York: The Julian Press, Inc., 1953.

Fernald, Grace. *Remedial Techniques in Basic School Subjects*. New York: McGraw-Hill Book Company, 1943.

Gallant, Ruth. *Handbook in Corrective Reading, Basic Tasks*. Columbus: Charles E. Merrill Books, Inc., 1970.

Hammill, Donald D., and Bartel, Nettie R. *Teaching Children with Learning and Behavior Problems*. Boston: Allyn & Bacon, Inc., 1975.

Harris, Albert J., ed. *Casebook on Reading Disability*. New York: David McKay Company, Inc., 1970.

Harris, Albert J., and Sepay, Edward R. *How to Increase Reading Ability*. New York: David McKay, Inc., 1975.

Hermann, Knud. *Reading Disability: A Medical Study of Word Blindness and Related Handicaps*. Springfield, Illinois: C.C. Thomas, Publisher, 1959.

Herr, Selma E. *Diagnostic and Corrective Procedures in the Teaching of Reading*. Los Angeles: Educational Research Associates, 1961.

Johnson, Doris J., and Myklebust, Helmer R. *Learning Disabilities: Educational Principles and Practices*. New York: Grune and Stratton, 1967.

Johnson, Marjorie S., and Kress, Roy A. *Corrective Reading in the Elementary Classroom*. Perspectives in Reading No. 7. Newark, Delaware 19711: International Reading Association, 1967.

———. *Informal Reading Inventories, Reading Aids Series*. I.E. Aaron, ed. Newark, Delaware 19711: International Reading Association, 1965.

Kaluger, George, and Kolson, Clifford J. *Reading and Learning Disabilities*. Columbus: Charles E. Merrill Books, Inc., 1969.

Kirk, Samuel A.; Kliebhan, Sister Joanne Marie; and Learner, Janet W. *Teaching Reading to Slow and Disabled Learners*. Boston: Houghton Mifflin, 1978.

Kolson, Clifford J., and Kaluger, George. *Clinical Aspects of Remedial Reading*. Springfield, Illinois: C.C. Thomas, Publisher 1963.

Kottmeyer, William. *Teacher's Guide for Remedial Reading*. St. Louis: Webster Division, McGraw-Hill Book Co., 1959.

Mann, Lester; Goodman, Libby; and Wiederholt, J. Lee, eds. *Teaching the Learning Disabled Adolescent.* Boston: Houghton Mifflin, 1978.

Money, John, ed. *The Disabled Reader: Education of the Dyslexic Child.* Baltimore: The Johns Hopkins Press, 1966.

——. *Reading Disability Progress and Research Needs in Dyslexia.* Baltimore: The Johns Hopkins Press, 1962.

Newman, Harold, ed. *Reading Disabilities: Selections on Identification and Treatment.* New York: The Odyssey Press, 1969.

Otto, Wayne, and Koenke, Karl. *Remedial Teaching: Research and Comment.* Boston: Houghton Mifflin, 1969.

Otto, Wayne, and McMenemy, Richard A. *Corrective and Remedial Teaching.* Boston: Houghton Mifflin, 1973.

Pollack, M.F.W., and Piekarz, Josephine A. *Reading Problems and Problem Readers.* New York: McKay Co., 1963.

Robinson, Alan, and Rauch, Sidney. *Corrective Reading in the High School Classroom.* Perspectives in Reading No. 6. Newark, Delaware 19711: International Reading Association, 1966.

Roswell, Florence, and Natchez, Gladys. *Reading Disability: A Human Approach to Learning.* New York: Basic Books, Inc., 1977.

Schell, Leo M., and Burns, Paul C. *Remedial Reading: Classroom and Clinic.* Boston: Allyn & Bacon, Inc., 1972.

Spache, George Daniel. *Diagnosing and Correcting Reading Disabilities.* Boston: Allyn & Bacon, Inc., 1976.

——. *Investigating the Issues of Reading Disabilities.* Boston: Allyn & Bacon, Inc., 1976.

Spache, George D., ed. *Reading Disability and Perception.* Newark, Delaware 19711: International Reading Association, 1969.

Strang, Ruth. *Diagnostic Teaching of Reading.* 2d ed. New York: McGraw-Hill Book Company, 1969.

——. *Reading Diagnosis and Remediation.* Newark, Delaware 19711: International Reading Association Research Fund, 1968.

——. *Understanding and Helping the Retarded Reader.* Tucson: University of Arizona Press, 1965.

Wilson, Robert M. *Diagnostic and Remedial Reading for Classroom and Clinic.* Columbus, Ohio: Charles Merrill, 1972.

White, Margaret. *Treating Reading Disabilities.* San Rafael, California: Academic Therapy Publications, 1975.

Woolf, Maurice D., and Woolf, Jeanne A. *Remedial Reading: Teaching and Treatment.* New York: McGraw-Hill Book Company, 1957.

Zintz, Miles. *Corrective Reading.* Dubuque, Iowa: Brown Publishing Co., 1966, 1977.

Index